Kwajalein

From Stonehenge to Star Wars

by
Ted Burris
Island Historian

Kwajalein
From Stonehenge to Star Wars

by

Ted Burris

First Edition

Published by

Brundage Publishing
Room 203 Executive Office Building
33 West State Street
Binghamton, NY 13901

www.brundagepublishing.com

Library of Congress
Control Number: 2004111974

ISBN Number: 1-892451-30-1

Printed in the United States of America

Acknowledgments

No man is an island; nor is any writer. This narrative owes its existence to many people who, over the years, have encouraged and abetted its creation. Several of them are no longer with us.

In particular, I want to dedicate the book to my mother, Christine Burris, to whom many of the original recountings were done in letters home as the reported events occurred. Patience, dear soul. You are not forgotten.

Friends and acquaintances in the islands and at locations of my other work assignments over the years have encouraged me to collect the stories and get them into print. These requesters are too numerous to mention, but I may ease their minds by mentioning that several of their stories are included herein.

When I began to try to sort out and organize the material, I ran into a wall of complexity that had me stumped. I often couldn't remember whether I had written a topic, or just intended to; whether I had communicated it or just planned to.

My brother, Larry, helped me convert numerous computer files written on machines that wouldn't talk to each other into a common database, without which I would still be fumbling in the morass. Thanks brother. Conversations with him and my sisters helped to construct a framework of sorts which I have tried to follow. Thanks Sheila and Patricia.

Ah, Patricia. What would I have done without your aid? Komol dada (thank you), as the Marshallese say.

Thanks also to Leslie M., to Barry and Cheryl B., to Pam and John R., to Herb H., and to all of you of whom and for whom these stories have been committed to the page.

There are other stories to come. But without your help, I could never have gotten to them.

Thanks to those at Brundage Publishing, particularly Ben Serviss, Monique Bishop, Amanda Nord, Barrie Hoople, and Frank Resseguie.

Finally, I must not neglect to mention Winnie W. Her encouragement and support over the last year and a half have inspired me to keep going when the difficulties had me frustrated beyond functioning. Hsieh hsieh Winnie.

Ted Burris
Pine Valley, NY
August, 2004

Table of Contents

Disclaimer/Welcome to Kwajalein Atoll

Kwajalein is a place almost unique in the world. It is a military base with almost no military personnel present. It is a place created for research and development, though much of the development there has been researched elsewhere.

It is called the Ronald Reagan Test Site in honor of the man who gave it focus as a part of the Strategic Defense Initiative (also known as "Star Wars"). The fact is, such research was being conducted there a generation before that esteemed gentleman came on the national political scene.

It is a place where "the rubber meets the road." Careers have been made and broken as ideas are tested and found useful or unworkable. Machines made elsewhere are brought there for testing. Other machines, never seen before, have been made on-site. All of this in pursuit of a constantly evolving, yet ever-elusive goal.

This book is intended to tell part of the story of what is happening there and why.

More importantly, I hope to give you a taste of the human side of the Kwajalein experience. It is all too easy to become so immersed in the problems of the moment that many of the people who were employed there never developed a feel for the full dimensions of the community where they live or lived.

These stories are yours.

A noted world traveler made a comment that has stuck with me. He said, "The problem with traveling is that you see more than you remember, and you remember more than you see."

I stand guilty of the charge leveled by the savant in Robert Service's poem "The Man Who Knew:" "He writeth not according to the schools." I am not a particularly well-organized narrator. As I visualize a scene to present to you, details may pop up which lead me away from the topic of the moment. It's not a case of forgetfulness, but of rememberful-ness. It's a condition I call "divertitis," and I have to fight it constantly. Maybe that's what editors are for.

If I err in fact, mea culpa. Please remember that my perspective is that of one near the bottom of a totem pole looking up. It was of awe at the dimensions of the tasks being attempted there, and admiration of the people undertaking those tasks that drew me to Kwaj in the first place.

Some conditions, events, and people rubbed me the wrong way. Often, perhaps most of the time, I heard or saw only one side of the story, understood only part or none of the real circumstances, and always filtered what I heard or saw through my perception at the time, whether it be naiveté or experience.

It is not my intention to slander or belittle anyone, but to share the experience of almost thirty years in a place many called "almost paradise" and some called "almost Poland."

I change names, or abbreviate them to avoid that. If you have been there, I hope you'll recognize the Atoll and the people I encountered (maybe yourself) and the things we did as part of an adventure. I will never embarrass anyone if I can help it. If people embarrass themselves, they can hardly blame me for remembering it and mentioning it. For heaven's sake, I've embarrassed myself more times than I care to remember!

Of course I like to poke fun at arrogance and pomposity. Then again, I love a good practical joke—even when I am the butt of it!

***

I have spent most of my adult life working in some capacity of relationship to the U.S. government. Of course, with respect to taxes, we all have. What I am talking about here is working in the so-called government sector of the economy as compared to its private sector.

I've spent four years in the Air Force, time in the Peace Corps, and finally a discontinuous but extensive number of years working on government projects as a civilian contractor employee.

Most of my work has been in support of one branch or another of the U.S. military. Assignments in these positions have taken me around the world several times for periods ranging from a few days to nearly thirty years. I have worked alone, supervised teams of various sizes, and managed groups of well over 100. Acquaintances along the way have ranged from janitors to Presidents and Kings, Generals and Ambassadors, and even two Medal of Honor winners. I have found them almost universally to be people of high integrity, sincerity, and conviction. They have been competent in their specialties. Some have been brilliant, some not so. One or two of them were real political sleazes!

It's important to remember that none of them were bad in their own eyes. That doesn't make it any easier to like them, but it does make it easier to understand them. And that enables one to work with them.

I hope you find this narrative informative. It helps to understand where some of our tax dollars are going. More importantly, I hope it makes you shed a tear or two, laugh a bit, and enjoy your read.

Roi historian plans departure

By KW Hillis
Feature Writer

TRADEX lost a 37-year veteran of both Kwaj and Roi on Saturday, while Supply loses a 42-year veteran on Saturday.

"A storehouse of knowledge"

Edward "Ted" Burris' love of history brought him to Kwajalein Atoll, it is what he was known for while he was here and history will be his initial focus when he returns to western New York.

"I was doing graduate studies in cultural anthropology at the University of Hawaii when I ran out of money. I hired on with Global, liked it and stayed," he said.

Throughout his stay — "four years on Kwaj and the rest on Roi" — Burris spent his off hours involved with local history and volunteer work including setting up the first two scout troops on Ebeye.

Ted Burris

"He is a storehouse of knowledge and stories about the January 1944 battle of Roi-Namur and the history of development of Kwajalein missile range," said Kerry Young, Burris' coworker. "He volunteered as a frequent tour guide ... He has escorted uncounted numbers of veteran groups and other VIPs around the historic sites of Roi-Namur."

Although called the island historian, Burris doesn't look at it that way.

"They are wrong, most of it was current events," he laughed. "The biggest thing was the population growth [of both Kwaj and Roi] ... the population peaked in 1972 at 7,800. In 1972, there were 25 flights a day to Roi on planes with 30 to 54 seats. Right now there are six flights a day, with 19-passenger planes."

Originally hired as a Retail Office administrator on Kwaj, Burris ran the Furniture Warehouse before transferring to Roi as a billeting supervisor. He moved to Canton in the Phoenix Islands in 1974. In 1976, he returned to Roi and became the TRADEX senior logistician.

For the last 30 years, Burris said he has been gathering information for a book which he hopes will be published this June.

"It will include the war and the time shortly before the war ...and the fact that Roi-Namur was not considered part of the Marshalls, rather a territory of the U.S. ... until 1968," he said.

The book also includes a biography of Burris' experiences here.

"His memories of the early 1960s on Roi-Namur, the living conditions ... in the earliest months, he lived on-board ships moored in the lagoon ... and stories of the Old Jackeroo Club have entertained residents for years," Young said.

When Burris gets home, he has a plan.

"My first order of business is to get the book printed," he said. "My sister is doing the final edit."

When the book is published, Burris plans to send copies out here.

"Hopefully it will show up in the library and everyone can have a look at it," he said.

From *Kwajalein Hourglass*, February 28, 2003

Photo by Larry Allen, from 1999 Kwaj calendar

Two views of Kwajalein and the southern end of Kwajalein Atoll

Photo by Tom Trione, from 1987 Kwaj calendar

Annual staff photo at ALTAIR

1st Row: John Corrado, Wally Schubach, Dale Sponseller, Bill Cleland, Cy Pizette, Bevan Jacobs, Terry Girouard, Wendell Chancy, Gene Littlefield, George Talbot, Andy Frase, Brian Masumoto
2nd Row: Jon Stahl, Chris Morris, Dave Greene, Linda Schuett, June Foltz, Glen Wilcox, Steve Poirier, Robert Linstead, Scott Prince, Tiljab Aneo, Mark Swain
3rd Row: Don Mudd, Eric Stroud, Greg Langenheim, Jason Christian, Herb Schmidt II, Brian Brady, Rob White, Kim Olson, Fred Forcier, Jim Thomson, Mike Lundberg
4th Row: John Rowland, Vince Karasko, Jim Mathwig, Ted Burris, Bruce Kopp, Justin Kuuki, Scott Johnson, Dennis Weikle, Rob Corbin, Matt Hatfield, Fred McKeen, Frank Pichler, John Szczepanski

Chapter 1

An Introduction to Kwaj

Low 78, High 87, winds from the east-northeast at ten to fifteen miles per hour, slight chance of rain. How would you like to live in a place where this is the daily weather report?

Does the idea of a community where there is virtually no crime, no unemployment, and no federal income tax appeal to you?

Would living in a place where there is world-class fishing, scuba diving, and sailing intrigue you?

If you had your family there with you, could you accept housing rents of less than $200 per month, and a school system from Kindergarten to 12th grade that produced more national merit scholarship award recipients than any other school in the world? (If you were there by yourself, room and board was paid.)

How does the thought of living in a place whose only real product is information right on the cutting edge of various scientific disciplines sit with you?

In your decision to live and work there, would company-supported and subsidized training in computer programming and operations factor in?

Add annual vacations to your point of hire with travel time and expenses paid.

These things certainly all factored into my decision to go to the Marshall Islands.

Which I did in May of 1964.

***

What I wish to do is to recount an observer's tale of Roi-Namur, Kwajalein, and the rest of the Marshall Islands from a personal viewpoint. For a more studied approach I recommend to you Gene Sims' *Kwajalein Remembered.*

Background is necessary to set the scene.

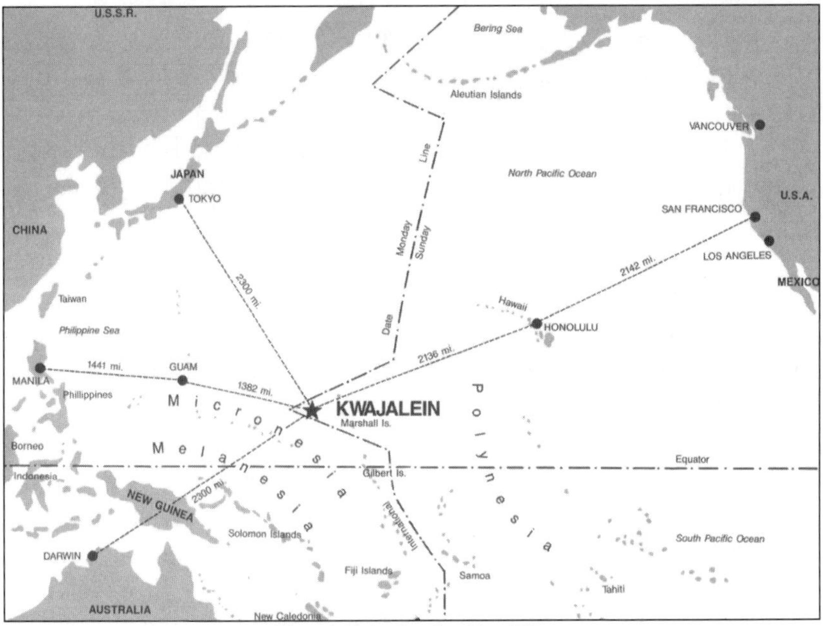

Kwajalein in the Pacific

Chapter 2

Colonial Roots in the Marshall Islands

The Marshall Islands lie just north of the equator and just west of the International Dateline. This part of the story begins with the arrival of Spanish explorers in the Marshalls some 300 years ago. Naturally, they claimed everything in sight for the Spanish crown, but they didn't actually do anything with their discovery. The islands were absolutely destitute of anything the Spaniards valued, like gold and jewels. The islands were also too far from anywhere else to be of economic interest to the Spaniards. The only thing the Spanish sailors left behind were a few cases of sexually transmitted diseases and enough babies to broaden the gene pool somewhat. The family name Pedro comes to mind.

German and Japanese presences were felt more strongly.

Germany didn't get its act together as a nation-state until the 1870s. Japan had isolated itself from the rest of the world for more than 300 years until the Meiji Restoration in 1868. Consequently, both countries were late getting into the business of establishing colonial empires. Spain, France, England, Portugal and Holland had gotten into the game earlier and grabbed most of the real plums around the world. What were left were the places no one else wanted—jungles, deserts and tiny islands in the middle of nowhere.

Germany got to the Marshalls first and set up a trading center on the island of Jaluit. One of these early colonists was Milne, the Spanish ancestor who became a major businessman in the Marshalls. They were interested primarily in three commodities: top shells, copra, and bêche-de-mer.

Top Shells are those red colored, large conic shells commonly found there. They were good for making buttons.

Copra is the white meat of the coconut, from which coconut oil can be derived.

Bêche-de-mer is a kind of sea slug that is considered to be a delicacy in some cuisines.

In return for these the Germans offered the islanders western manufactures, principally cloth and iron or steel items. And, of course, anything else they could convince the natives that they had to have.

Japan wanted the Marshalls for other reasons, mostly relating to the fact that they were in the same ocean.

But Japan had a real problem. It was one of the last seafaring nations to exit feudalism and, in consequence, found itself far behind the Western world in both war-making and maritime technology.

Being honest with themselves, they had to admit that something had to give. That something was many of their customs and traditions.

They had to bootstrap themselves into parity with the west.

Their approach was multifold.

They started by teaching their children English. That is, they taught the children of their elite families English. This program was so important to the Japanese that it resulted in a now-forgotten debate and vote in the Japanese Diet—now forgotten because it failed. The bill before the Diet may be defined thusly: that English be made the official national language of Japan! (It failed passage by one vote!)

While the bill before the Diet failed, the program of teaching English went on apace. As students gained proficiency in English, they were enrolled in American, British and some Canadian colleges to study sciences and engineering.

The scholarship of these young people was supported by their families as an investment and was heavily subsidized by the Japanese government, also as an investment.

Without this financial help those young people would not have had access to such an education. In other words, they *owed.* They were expected and demanded to return to Japan after their schooling abroad and either teach their newly acquired knowledge to others in the homeland, or to apply it to the industrialization of Japan. Their families expected them to repay the education loans, made from family coffers, with interest. In other words, they were employees of the Japanese government and of their families.

A's were the expected grade. B's were a cause for concern. C's were unacceptable. This problem still exists.

However, it is the result of it all that matters to our story. And the result was that Japan did indeed bootstrap itself into an industrial powerhouse.

The second fold of their approach to surviving in the modern world dealt with access to raw materials. After all, what good does it do to be able to produce commodities if you lack the raw materials necessary to feed and power the industrial plant?

And lack them Japan did. It had no coal, it had no iron, and it had no oil. What it did have was manpower. What it could not wrest from the sea, it had to acquire by other means.

Other means?

Well, you might be able to get what you need through trade. And Japan did a lot of that. Of course, if you're a seafaring nation, that implies that you have to protect your sealanes. So Japan built a formidable navy that needed ports. This brings our story closer to home.

Other means?

There's always diplomacy, which can result in agreements, alliances, and pacts; through any of which you could gain access to needed materials. These can be of benefit to all signatories, or not, depending on your relative strengths going into the negotiations. So, in the real world it is wise to remember that benefits are relative and that the documents that assign them may be of a transient nature.

Oh yes, I forgot to mention another "other means."

You start by asking yourself, "Where are the things I need?" This is followed by the question "Is the population there able to resist my projection of force there? If the answer to this question is "no," well, you just take over! It's called colonialism.

Colonialism is neat! It lets you tell the benighted population what to think, how to behave, what work to do (at what wage), where to live, and all that good stuff! And you own the company store!

Naturally, you need a slogan to make everything okay. Something like:

White Man's Burden – England, Holland, Spain, France
Manifest Destiny – U.S.A.
Making the World Safe for Democracy – U.S.A.
Deutschland Uber Alles – Germany
Greater East Asia Co-Prosperity Sphere – Japan

For example, Japan took over Mongolia for coal and iron. Russia was weak, China was weak, Korea was weak, and Mongolia was weak. And nobody else cared. Japan took over Taiwan in 1895. China was weak, the Philippines were weak. And nobody else cared. For allying itself with Britain against the Germans in WWI, Japan was ceded control of the German holdings in the Pacific by the League of Nations under provisions of the Treaty of Versailles in 1920. These holdings included The Marianas, The Carolines, and The Marshall Islands.

There's another step closer to home. So, let's jump now to the Marshalls and see what Japan did there in the twenty years between 1920 and the beginning of WWII.

Chapter 3

Go or Die: The Japanese Take Over

The Japanese first invited the missionaries to leave. Catholic and a variety of Protestant denominations (mostly under the auspices of the North American Missionary Alliance out of Boston) had been allowed by the Germans to establish congregations. The Japanese instruction to them all had two options: Go or die. They left.

All trade with Westerners was prohibited. Westerners were prohibited from trespassing anywhere in the Marshalls. In effect, The Marshall Islands disappeared from sight within the Greater East Asia Co-Prosperity Sphere.

This worried the U.S. Navy a bit. After all, The Marshalls were the closest of all the Japanese mandated islands to American holdings in the Pacific (i.e. Hawaii and the naval base at Pearl Harbor).

What happened was that almost immediately after the ceding, Japan began to militarize many of the atolls in the Marshalls, in direct violation of conditions of the ceding treaty, which specified that none of the islands were to be militarized. Not a problem! If we don't let anybody in to see what we're doing, who's going to know?

They brought in 600 Korean laborers. Beach bunkers, gun emplacements, command posts, trenches, and tunnels were built. Bomb shelters, storage, and headquarters buildings were placed. One of the last structures built was a radar station on Namur.

The approach seemed to be working. At first the fortifications were strictly defensive.

But with the maturing of the concept of naval aviation as a mode of force projection, the islands—whose previous assets had been limited to coconuts, top shells, and sea slugs—gained another asset of perceived value: location. What had been considered the middle-of-nowhere suddenly became the forefront of a ring of defensive installations protecting Japanese interests and communication throughout the Greater East Asia Co-Prosperity Sphere.

The Imperial Japanese Navy came to view the islands as stationary elements of the Imperial fleet that were able to nurture its mobile elements, and develop them accordingly. They built small airfields on a number of the atolls in the Marshalls and equipped them with small naval and marine contingents. Designed to be mutually supporting, they were meant to shield the centerpiece of the whole complex, the Kwajalein Atoll.

A point of interest regarding this construction is worth mentioning. Most of the construction was done with saltwater cement. It is said that one man, in the employ of the Imperial Navy, traveled throughout the Pacific, overseeing the mixing of the concrete. He was supposed to have added some "secret" ingredient to the mix to neutralize the effects of using salt water in it. Normally salt water would result in the rusting of the reinforcing bars, and the entire structure would disintegrate in a short time. Not so with the buildings he built. Look at them today. Where they weren't damaged in bombardment, or by the later ravages of tourists, it is easy to think that they might have been newly completed. American scientists tried for years to determine how he achieved what he did. No luck. It is said that the man survived the war and died in Tokyo in 1948 without ever revealing his secret.

We are able to get around the problem of using salt water in cement today by using plastic additives. No one knows what he used a half century ago and, since concrete continues to change chemical composition with time, the most sophisticated analytical methods today still can't answer the question.

Anyway, most of this fortification was done in contravention of League of Nations mandates. But no one in the western world knew it.

Beach bunker near Speedball on Roi Island. Walls are four feet thick. Cupola on top was bunker commander's observation point. Photo by Pam R.

This lack of knowledge about what was going on within Japanese-held territories was worrisome to the United States, particularly to the Navy who was responsible for defending U.S. interests wherever they might be. They tried a number of times to insert ships into the territories claimed by Japan.

But the U.S. for the most part was still exercising the neutrality and isolation policy fostered in reaction to the trauma of World War I.

The Navy wanted to find out what was going on, but they didn't want to embarrass the U.S. government by being caught in the act of doing it. After all, "Gentlemen do not spy on gentlemen."

So circumspection was the order of the day. Listening posts were set up to intercept Japanese naval and government radio traffic. Considerable effort was devoted, successfully, to breaking Japanese codes. And all of this was done in the greatest secrecy. No one would admit to doing it, but it happened.

We'll talk more about the pre-WWII Kwajalein later. For the moment, let's consider the factors that attracted Japanese interest.

Chapter 4

Kwajalein's Features and Japan's Fortifications

As atolls go, Kwajalein Atoll is big! It consists of ninety-six islands and islets, give or take a couple. An islet is any piece of land that is above water at high tide. These islands and islets sit on a reef that surrounds the world's largest lagoon. There are lots of coral heads in the lagoon, but its average depth is 168 feet, good for anchoring the largest ships of the era. Shaped roughly like a boomerang, it extends from Kwajalein island north by northwest just under fifty miles to Roi-Namur, heads west about fifty miles to the island of Ebadon, and then arcs back southeast and south to Kwajalein. The maximum width is about eighteen miles. There are a number of deep-water channels through the reef giving access to the lagoon from the open ocean.

Clockwise: (outer islands) Legan, Illeginni, Meck, Eniwetok
Photo by Nate Jackson, from 1987 Kwaj calendar.

The average sea state in the lagoon is less than half of the average sea state just outside it. This means that if the waves on the ocean were three to six feet high, one would find waves in the lagoon in the range of one to three feet. Thus the lagoon offers significant protection for shipping within its boundaries.

The reef was built by thousands of years of coral growth starting underwater on the lip of an ancient volcanic caldera (the opening of a volcano). The coral built upon itself until it reached sea level where it could go no higher. This was once, undoubtedly, one of the largest volcanoes that ever existed on Earth. Most volcanoes have calderas that measure size in acres. This one measures well over 1,000 square miles!

The Japanese were interested primarily in only four of the islands at Kwajalein Atoll: Kwajalein itself; Ebeye, three miles north of Kwajalein; Ennibur, three miles south of Roi-Namur; and Roi-Namur. The rest of the islands were left mostly to the native Marshallese.

On Kwajalein, the Imperial Navy set up a naval base.

On Ebeye they set up a seaplane base.

On Ennibur they constructed a major radio and communication station (from which they could communicate directly with Tokyo and all points nearer). They also put on Ennibur a rest and recreation center for the naval personnel assigned to the atoll. Ennibur was also said to have sited a radio intercept station from which the Japanese intercepted both military and civilian radio traffic emanating from Hawaii.

Incidentally, there is a small story relating to the rest and recreation center that was told to me in the strictest confidence by a Marshallese lady, on the condition that I never divulge her name as the source. She said that the Japanese co-opted Marshallese girls and young women to provide "comfort women" services to the naval personnel using the center. Payment was said to be a half-cup of uncooked rice per "service."

Roi-Namur was turned into the largest Japanese airbase in the Marshalls, as well as a supply and provisioning point for Imperial Navy submarines operating in that part of the Pacific.

Most of this buildup had been accomplished in almost total secrecy by the summer of 1937.

Let's fast forward now to the events leading to the Japanese attack on Pearl Harbor and the American involvement in the Second World War.

Chapter 5

Pearl Harbor Scheming

The transformation of Pearl Harbor into a major U.S. Navy base was started in earnest as early as 1907, and was immediately noted by the Japanese.

Britain had Hong Kong and Singapore, the Dutch held Jakarta, and the Americans had Subic Bay in the Philippines. Of course all of these places were potential obstacles to the realization of the evolving concept of the Greater East Asia Co-Prosperity Sphere. But all of these colonies, in the minds of the Japanese militarists, could be neutralized by force of combined arms, that is to say that working together, the Imperial Army and the Imperial Navy could get the job done.

Only Pearl Harbor really irritated the Japanese strategic military planners. Because of the base's isolated nature, neutralizing Pearl Harbor would have to be an all-Navy show.

As early as 1923, cadets in the Imperial Navy War College were presented with a theoretical, strategic, and tactical exercise designed to develop a workable plan to do just that.

It took fourteen years to develop and debug the plan. There were huge technical problems to resolve.

For example, the plan called for the use of carriers to strike the first blow. It had to be overwhelming, fast, and devastating. That meant lots of airplanes and lots of carriers, which they didn't have. So Japan built carriers, at the expense of battleships, which infuriated the big gun admirals in the Navy high command.

Another issue was that the plan called for torpedoes that would stay shallow when they hit Pearl Harbor's shallow waters.

Conventional aerial torpedoes went deep when they first hit the water and would probably bury themselves in the mud of the harbor bottom. No such torpedo existed. So they invented one.

Then it was necessary to practice. The Imperial Navy took over an island in the Inland Sea that had most of the features of Pearl Harbor. And they practiced, and practiced for two years.

There is no need to go into detail on the performance of the attack on December 7, 1941, except for one thing.

The plan called for two long-range flying boats, Kawanishis, to fly from Ebeye over Pearl Harbor.

The first unmarked Kawanishi was to go from Ebeye straight to Pearl Harbor for a target confirmation just minutes before the arrival of the attackers, then to escape to the southwest as far as French Frigate Shoals, where it was to land, refuel from a submarine, then return to Ebeye.

The second plane, also unmarked, was to go first to French Frigate Shoals, refuel, then overfly Pearl Harbor and do a photographic record of the damage inflicted and return directly to Ebeye. These photos were to be processed aboard the plane and an assessment radioed to the Japanese fleet. On the basis of that assessment, The Imperial Navy would decide whether a second strike on Pearl Harbor was warranted.

As it happened, there was a U.S. Navy buoy tender at French Frigate Shoals working on the warning and navigation buoys there. The submarine dared not surface, so the two Kawanishis were warned off and returned to Ebeye. After all, no one wanted to give the Americans any hint that there were Japanese ships or planes anywhere near Hawaii.

Consequently, the Japanese fleet commanders never got the word that their planes had largely missed the repair cranes on the piers and the fuel farms at Pearl. This was to have serious consequences for the Japanese in the years that followed, because many of the ships that were damaged (and even some of those sunk) were eventually returned to service against the Japanese.

The Imperial Navy had, nevertheless, achieved a major coup at Pearl with minimal loss to themselves. They were concerned that a second attack would be met with heavy defensive fire that would undoubtedly mean heavy losses in planes and crews. They were more concerned that they had missed the American carriers. None among them knew where the enemy carriers were. (They were, in fact returning to Pearl from a trip to Wake Island, where they had delivered some planes for that island's defense.)

So the Japanese high command on the scene decided to retire to safer waters and not make that crucial second strike. Who's to say that none of us might have made the same decision?

Tactically, the attack on Pearl Harbor was brilliant. Choreographed and executed by Admiral Yamamoto (who had been against the plan from the beginning), it succeeded beyond the fondest dreams of the Japanese high command back in Tokyo.

Strategically, it sealed the fate of Japan because it validated Yamamoto's warning to the military government that such a move would awaken the "sleeping giant." It answered Churchill's prayers, and gave President Roosevelt the leverage he needed to bring the American people into the war against the Axis powers.

Chapter 6

Facing Down the Axis Powers: America Fights Back

What happened next? It's time to get back to the Marshalls to see what happened there, because that's where America hit back first.

Before Doolittle's raid on Tokyo, before the battle of Midway, the U.S. Navy cobbled together a fleet that sortied against Japanese installations in the Marshall Islands.

A mere seven weeks after Pearl Harbor our Navy executed air strikes against all of the islands in the Marshalls that had airfields on them. I can't give you exact figures for all the damage inflicted, but I know that at Roi-Namur fifty-four Japanese aircraft were destroyed in the air and ninety-two on the ground.

The raid was ballyhooed in the stateside press to raise the morale of Americans who had heard nothing so far but news of loss and defeat in the Pacific.

But not much more happened immediately in the Marshalls. That first raid was in the nature of a hit and run operation.

Our resources had been seriously depleted at Pearl Harbor, and the need was both widespread and critical all over the Pacific.

For the first year of the war our efforts were largely spent trying to stabilize a rapidly deteriorating situation. We lost Wake Island, Guam, and the Philippines. We lost Attu and Kiska in the Aleutian chain of Alaska. The British lost most of their holdings in Southeast Asia, as did the French and Dutch. Some say these losses were a way of trading space for time—time to let American industry convert to full-scale wartime production.

It did.

But back to the Pacific.

The Pacific theater of operations was put on the backburner by events in the Atlantic and Europe. Everyone among the Allies (except China) agreed that Hitler and the Axis had to be dealt with in Europe and Africa first. Japan could wait.

In Europe, Germany and Russia had penned a secret non-aggression pact that allowed the Germans to run rampant wherever they wished in Western Europe. With the exception of Britain and British-controlled Egypt, Western Europe and Mediterranean North Africa fell.

Britain soon stood by itself and was almost totally dependent on supplies from the U.S. This meant they needed for huge numbers of ships to ply the Atlantic. American shipyards blossomed. But German U-boats decimated this cross-Atlantic shipping until convoy shipping was implemented. Large elements of the U.S. Pacific fleet were transferred to the Atlantic to protect those convoys.

Then Hitler committed one of his really big goofs. His heart hadn't really been into the idea of beating Britain. Oh, he wanted Britain out of his hair to be sure, and operation "Sea Lion" was laid on with the objective of accomplishing just that. But Goering, his air marshal, assured Hitler that the Luftwaffe (the German Air Force) could do the job by itself. So Hitler conditioned the execution of "Sea Lion" upon Goering's promise. As it turned out, that was a promise that couldn't be kept.

As the months after the Battle of Britain slipped by, Hitler's covetous gaze turned eastward. Eastward was "lebensraum" (living room), and the oil of the Caucasus. Eastward was grain from the Ukraine and the mineral wealth of Russia.

Russia?

Didn't Stalin and Hitler have a non-aggression pact in place? So what? Wasn't it true that the Ukrainian people were not really Russian? And didn't they want out from under the yoke of Communism? And weren't they "untermunchen" (less than real people) anyway? They didn't really count in the scheme of things. That's how Hitler's thinking went. And here Hitler had all those wonderful Blitzkreigers sitting around in the west with nobody to beat up. So he turned them east.

In any event, Operation Barbarosa got underway in the late spring and Russia reeled under the assault. You might say that with Barbarosa Hitler stabbed Stalin in the "pact."

So we started sending huge convoys of food and war material to Russia by way of Murmansk and Archangel. These had to be protected, and even more ships from the Pacific fleet were transferred eastward. After all, "The enemy of my enemy is my friend."

While we were busy helping Russian and Britain, the Japanese were busy in Asia and the western Pacific. One of the places they took was Singapore, which had been protected by large numbers of five inch guns, all oriented toward the Straits. These guns were transported to Japanese holdings all over the Pacific, including Kwajalein and Roi-Namur.

After the February '42 raid, things quieted down somewhat in the Marshalls. Oh, there was the occasional nuisance raid when we happened to be in the area and had a few bombs and bullets to spare. The USN conducted fairly regular reconnaissance flights to make maps and keep an eye on things. These were largely unopposed, especially until Namur got a radar station in August of '43.

But the Marshalls weren't forgotten.

The military situation for the Allies in the Pacific finally stabilized, and planners could begin to think about going on the offensive.

What were the goals of such an offensive to be?

Well, the grand goal of course was Japan's defeat.

To do that we had to destroy, or at least neutralize, the Japanese ability and will to continue fighting.

The final plan called for a three-pronged offensive. The objectives of all three thrusts were the same: to cut Japanese supply lines; to liberate occupied territories and to reach places in range of the Japanese home islands, from which we could bomb Japan properly.

* The earliest thrust was from India east and north into occupied south Asia and China.
* The second thrust was north from Australia through the western Pacific shield archipelagos to the Philippines and beyond.
* The third thrust was across the central Pacific. (This is the one we will focus on.)

The central Pacific thrust began in November of 1943 with amphibious attacks against Tarawa and Betio in the British Gilbert Islands. These lie directly south of the Marshall Islands.

Tarawa, an atoll in the Gilberts just south of the Marshalls, was a brutal introduction for U.S. Naval and Marine forces to the fighting qualities and tenacity of the Japanese defenders. Casualties were horrendous and mistakes numerous. We won, but it was a "Pyrrhic" victory in the classic sense of the term. In other words, win enough battles like that and we lose the war!

Chapter 7

Operation Flintlock – Kwajalein in Four Days

The lessons were not lost on American planners. Kwajalein was the next target for American operations, and our high command did not want a repetition of the events at Tarawa.

Their planning for the Kwajalein campaign addressed each of the problems they encountered at Tarawa and resulted in major changes in both strategy and tactics for the taking of Kwajalein.

The relevant changes are listed here because they worked and particularly because they left a legacy that the folks at Kwajalein must still contend with to this day:

> * *Tarawa*: Short preliminary bombardment by naval guns and aircraft.
> * **Kwajalein**: Extensive and intensive pre-invasion reduction of enemy defenses.
> * *Tarawa*: Invasion from the sea against the primary target islands. (Not all of the islands at Tarawa were as heavily fortified as Tarawa itself.) I should mention that the heaviest Japanese weapons on these islands were always oriented toward the sea.
> * **Kwajalein**: Invasion from the lagoon, first against the less well-fortified neighboring islands for the purpose of setting up land based artillery (more accurate than ships' guns at the time). Then the use of covering fire from these guns for a "rolling barrage" against the enemy on the main islands.

* *Tarawa*: Overall command and control was poor and resulted in confusion that contributed to the heavy casualties.
* **Kwajalein**: First use of a dedicated Command and Control ship.
* *Tarawa*: Offloading of support material directly from cargo transports to the invasion beaches while under enemy fire.
* **Kwajalein**: Offloading of support material onto secured islands nearby, but out of range of Japanese guns. This allowed the cargo ships to leave the dangerous operations area and return to the States for new loads for future invasions in the drive.

The "Flintlock" fleet was split into three parts.

Majuro Atoll got the attention of the smallest contingent, seventeen capital and troop ships. There was one Japanese soldier on the main island—a warrant officer in charge of government property. That part of "Flintlock" must have gone into the record books as the most lopsided military confrontation in the history of warfare! (Though it is not recorded that he put up any resistance.)

The balance of the rest of the fleet was split about evenly between Kwajalein and Roi-Namur at Kwajalein Atoll.

In the south, the Army's "Hourglass" Division did the honors. (That's how Kwaj's *Hourglass* newspaper got its name.) On January 31st they took the islands Little Buster, Big Buster, Ebeye, and Gugeegue on the east reef north of Kwaj, and Carlson and Carlos on the west reef (also north of Kwaj), along with smaller islands bordering the passes into the southern lagoon.

Simultaneously in the north, the Marine Corps' 4th Marines (in their first combat action) took the first three islands south of Namur and the first two west of Roi, along with deep water passes into the north end of the lagoon.

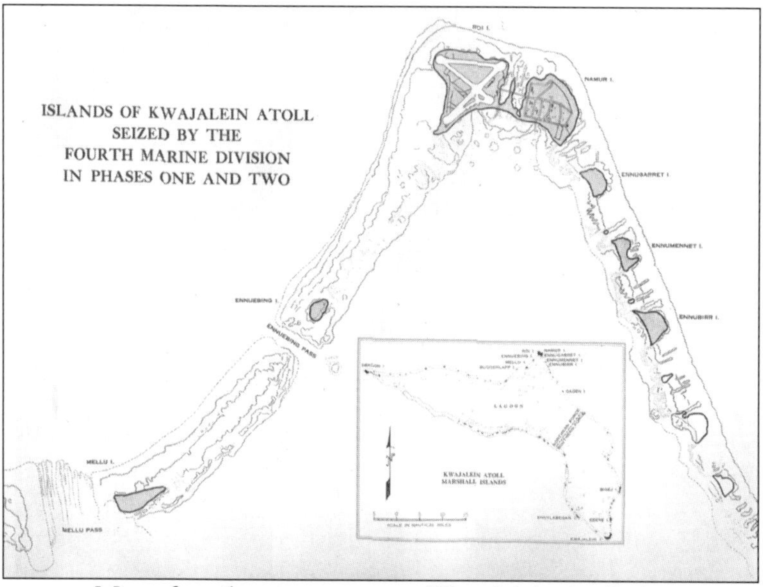

Map of northeastern corner of Kwajalein Atoll, the largest island is Roi-Namur.

As chance would have it, Ennibur, three islands south of Namur, went into the records as the first of the mandated territories of Japan to be seized by the Allies during WWII. It was the 4th Marine Division that did the job.

As soon as these islands and passes were secured, Navy cargo ships slipped into the lagoon and began offloading tanks, guns and the like. They dropped and scooted, for several reasons. For one thing, they were largely defenseless and hugely vulnerable. They didn't want to be where bombs were dropping and artillery shells were falling. Besides, they had to get back to Hawaii or the mainland to pick up another load for the attack on the next island as the Navy punched its way across the Pacific.

The Navy and U.S. planners had been largely unprepared for the violence, duration, or stiffness of resistance they encountered at Tarawa. They didn't want that problem repeated.

I can't tell you how much war material was made available for the combat forces attacking Kwajalein, but I know that the 4th Marines had at their immediate disposal twelve fire units.

A fire unit, as defined at that time, was enough to keep the entire invasion force fed, cared for, and fighting for one day. In plain terms, every Marine could be completely re-equipped from socks to shooting irons with the material available twelve times during the course of the battle!

That was what Yamamoto meant when he warned the Japanese government, before the war, not to "wake the sleeping giant."

Kwaj fell to the U.S. Army and Navy in four days.

Roi fell to the U.S. Marines and Navy in four hours. Namur was in American hands before noon on February 2nd, 1944.

By the time Japanese resistance ceased, "Operation Flintlock" was recognized as an outstanding success. And within that operation, the 4th Marines' capture of Roi-Namur was considered to be a quintessential example of a well-planned and well-conducted amphibious assault.

So good, in fact, that the Battle of Roi-Namur was immediately entered into the curricula of U.S. war colleges, and staff officers of all services studied it in detail to glean insights into the planning and execution of all future amphibious operations.

Let's look at the battle of Roi-Namur a little more closely to see why the battle went as well as it did.

LIEUTENANT COLONEL AQUILLA J. DYESS

U.S. Medal of Honor winner, 4th Marines. He also won the Carnegie Medal Award for civilian bravery. Photos from *The Fourth Marine Division in World War II.*

PRIVATE RICHARD K. SORENSON

U.S. Medal of Honor winner with the 4th Marines. He fell on an explosive device to save his buddies.

Chapter 8

Roi-Namur in One Day

When the Japanese took control of the Marshall Islands at the end of WWI, they immediately began developing the islands as an airbase. Roi was to have three runways and airfield support facilities such as hangars, repair ships, and the like. The power plant for the two islands was located on Namur. Namur also housed the entire garrison of Imperial Marines, airfield support staff and Korean laborers (about 3,600 people). The indigenous population on Roi-Namur was moved to a small island three miles south of Namur, on Ennibur, though some were utilized there by the Japanese as day menials.

All residents lived on Namur; Roi was completely devoted to being an airfield. To facilitate movement from quarters to work place, the Japanese connected Roi and Namur with a permanent causeway that crossed over most of Akadrik, a stretch of land known as "the quiet place." Across this causeway ran power and communication cables, a one-lane road, and water and fuel pipes.

The main power plant was on Namur and consisted of two large, ten foot high German Diesel engines driving generators of great capacity.

The airfield had a complement of well over 100 planes at the time of the first raid. By the start of the run up to the invasion, Japan had replaced those losses, and the complement even increased somewhat.

As the first stage of the assault began on the 31st of January '44 with bombing and the seizure of peripheral islands (to be used as artillery bases), Roi-Namur received 2,400 tons of bombs and ships' fire. This was the heaviest preliminary bombardment any target in the war, thus far, had ever been subjected to. The result was devastating!

Ninety-eight aircraft on the airfield were destroyed. Every building (save three that I know of) was penetrated or at least severely damaged in spite of many of them having walls and roofs three or four feet thick with reinforced concrete.

Japanese warehouse on Namur. Holes were blown through three feet thick, reinforced concrete walls by direct hits from fourteen and sixteen guns of the U.S. Navy invasion fleet. Photo by Pam R.

The Japanese Headquarters building, which was on Namur just south of where the ALTAIR radar sits now, was totally demolished and many of the highest-ranking officers in residence there died. This effectively left the remaining Japanese defenders without leadership.

The real wonder is that any resistance at all was possible, yet resistance there was.

By the night of the first day of the invasion, U.S. forces had occupied all of Roi and about two thirds of Namur. The Marines had the job completed by 10:00 on the morning of

February 2nd. They had faced down and defeated 3,600 Japanese defenders, 240 of whom were taken prisoner.

Marine casualties were less than 500. I don't have the exact statistics available. For those of you who are interested, I recommend Carl W. Proehl's book, *The Fourth Marine Division in World War II*.

Immediately after the cessation of hostilities the Seabees moved in and began cleanup and conversion of the Islands for our usage.

Please excuse me if I seem to slight events at Kwajalein at this time. They were certainly not insignificant, and will be addressed.

But there is little use in paralleling description of cleanup and conversion. Suffice it to say that the U.S. Navy turned Kwajalein into a major U.S. base in the Pacific.

My understanding of Roi-Namur is more personal, of longer duration, and more studied.

So we'll return there to continue the narrative.

Aerial view of Roi-Namur looking west toward Ebadon.
Photo by Nate Jackson, from 1987 Kwaj calendar.

Japanese command post, left, and fire bunker and bomb shelter that took a beating when the U.S. landed on Roi in 1944.

Southeast corner of the Japanese airfield command post on Roi, looking north. The hole in the roof (five feet of reinforced concrete) shows what a thousand pound bomb could do when delivered by a U.S. Navy Dive-bomber. Photo by Bridget Rankin, 1999 Kwaj calendar.

Japanese bunker on Namur. It suffered several direct hits from Naval rifle fire during the invasion, but parts of it look as though they had been poured last week. The bunker is made of salt water concrete with a coral aggregate base.

Memorial to the 3,400 Japanese soldiers who died in twenty-four hours defending Roi-Namur in February 1944. Photo by Pam R.

Chapter 9

The Aftermath – Years of Cleanup

Roi-Namur was a mess!

Large amounts of unexploded ordinance lay everywhere, everything from sixteen inch naval rifle rounds to 1,000-pound bombs. Explosive ordinance teams moved in to disarm and dispose of these so that the real cleanup could begin in some measure of safety (The cleanup has still not really been completed yet!).

The runways were cleared and plated with pierced steel planking (PSP). Hangars and repair shops were built. And the whole infrastructure of a major air base was re-established, under new management.

Detritus from the battle was carried or bulldozed to the eastern edge of Roi and the western edge of Namur south of the causeway and turned into landfill. It very nearly filled the entire space between the two islands, hence Roi-Namur.

Two large ammunition dumps were created in the days following the battle. Then disaster fell from the sky.

On the night of February 12th, 1944 the Japanese flew a raid against Roi-Namur from their navy base at Truk, in the Carolines. There were only six planes in the raid, but they arrived over Roi-Namur at 3:00 in the morning and caught our defenders with their guard down. The bombs they dropped hit and ignited two ammo dumps, one on Roi and the other on Namur. The planes were gone in a matter of minutes, but the fires and explosions went on for hours. All anyone could do was duck for cover. It was three days before the last of the fires was extinguished, and cleanup had to start all over again. This too, went into the record books. It was listed as the second largest loss of war material (after Pearl Harbor) suffered by the United States during WWII!

Things slowly got back to "normal" after that raid, and the battlefronts moved ever westward.

The Navy undertook an "inventory" of the islands around Kwajalein Atoll. Teams went from island to island and asked two questions: "Who lives on this island?" and "Who claims this island?" The Navy and the U.S. government wanted to know whom they had to deal with when they were making land use agreements.

The "inventory" process worked fine for every island on the atoll except one: Roi-Namur.

When the team got to Roi-Namur, and asked, "Who lives here?" no one stepped forward. When they asked, "Who claims this island?" again, no one stepped forward. A probable explanation is that the Marshallese were superstitious of soldiers' ghosts killed on the island, since the fighting had been so brutal, and declined to have anything to do with it! Consequently, the entry on the official "inventory" for Roi-Namur was worded thusly:

"Roi-Namur—no native residents, no indigenous claimants. This is United States Territory, seized from the enemy during the course of hostilities."

This "inventory" list was presented to the United Nations Trusteeship Council in due course in 1946, and was accepted by them as a *de facto* and *de jure*—legal in fact and legal in law—document. Thus, when the United States Trust Territory of the Pacific was established by the United Nations, Roi-Namur was not part of it!

Incidentally, I went to the UN on a vacation, and looked up this "inventory" to see if for myself.

What does this mean for the U.S.? That we have our own private island to do with as we see fit.

Meanwhile, back at the war.

Kwajalein and Roi-Namur were almost immediately relegated to the rear lines in the Pacific. That does not mean they weren't busy. Roi-Namur was doing a booming business putting damaged planes back together or scrapping them. Kwajalein was a much larger island, with good port facilities. It became a major way station between the western Pacific and the States.

It really needed an airfield of its own. The Japanese had started such a strip shortly before the invasion and the Navy completed it. The completed strip was twice as long as the longest at Roi-Namur.

Now Kwajalein could handle the largest of airplanes and their crews.

Roi-Namur began to slip into somnolence and was officially closed at the war's end. The Navy kept a couple of people assigned there between the end of the war and 1957 as placeholders to validate our claim to Roi-Namur as U.S. Territory. The downtime wasn't to last.

Kwajalein didn't experience the same slowdown.

Chapter 10

Operation Crossroads: Nuclear Testing

For starters, almost before the war was over the Marshall Islands came under consideration as a possible site for "Operation Crossroads."

"Operation Crossroads" was to be the United States' program for the development and testing of nuclear weapons.

They needed a place far away from anywhere else—preferably a place where no one lives, for both safety and security reasons.

The Marshall Islands fit the bill. Their total population at the time was about 7,000 people spread over thirty-seven atolls. These atolls were scattered over an area of roughly 12,000 square miles, at least 2,000 miles from any population centers. And we already established a presence with a significant naval base at Kwajalein.

Our government negotiated an agreement with the Marshallese hierarchy for the use of two of the more remote atolls, Bikini and Eniwetok, as test sites. The couple of hundred residents native to the atolls were relocated to other islands close by.

Over the next twelve years, scores of tests were conducted. Details of that program are given in the book, *Operation Crossroads* by Jonathan M. Wiesgall, which I recommend to any of you who may have an interest in such matters.

Kwajalein served as the logistical support base for all these tests.

I do, however, want to mention two of the tests conducted at Bikini: the Alpha and Bravo tests.

The goal of those tests was to assess the effect of nuclear weapons on surface fleets.

The target fleet consisted of ninety-eight ships from many sources. There were a number of cargo ships and an even larger number of warships, ranging from an aircraft carrier and battleships down to a PT boat (Patrol Torpedo boat; a fast motorboat with torpedo and machinegun capabilities) and a submarine. Most were obsolete vessels from the U.S. inventory. A few were war prizes, seized from the enemy at the end of WWII. One was the *Prinz Eugen*, a German battle cruiser.

The Alpha test was an airdrop that exploded 2,500 feet above the target fleet. Six ships were sunk and a few more damaged, but still afloat. The Navy breathed a sigh of relief and published a statement to the effect that this test proved that the Navy was not doomed to go the way of the Dodo.

The Bravo test was an underwater blast. It sank sixteen more of the target fleet ships. The Navy was somewhat quieter about this test.

The real damage to the test fleet was not immediately obvious. But it didn't take long to show itself—every ship was rendered radioactive.

The day after each test sailors were put aboard each surviving ship with brooms and mops and scrub brushes to try to decontaminate it. They were notably unsuccessful. The boffins put their heads together and concluded that the reason decontamination of the ships wasn't working was because the water in the lagoon was itself radioactive, which it was.

So seventy-six ships were towed to Kwajalein lagoon (which wasn't radioactive), and efforts to decontaminate continued for eight months. Many approaches were tried but none worked well enough to render the ships habitable again.

Question. What the heck do you do with a radioactive boat? They couldn't be used, and nobody was in the market for radioactive scrap metal!

The *Prinz Eugen* itself solved one of their seventy-six problems. It had taken unrealized damage in the tests. When it began to drift away, attempts were made to ground it on the reef. It didn't quite make it. It "turned turtle" near Carlson and is visible to this day from Kwajalein.

We finally gave up on the other seventy-five target fleet survivors. They were towed out of the lagoon and scuttled a half-mile west of Carlson in 14,500 feet of water! It was the largest collection of ships ever intentionally scuttled.

So went things at Kwajalein during the late '40s, through the mid-'50s and on. Naval activity diminished, and with it, the Naval population declined. It reached the point where the Navy wanted to shed itself of the responsibility.

From the standpoint of the Naval careerist, assignment to Kwajalein was considered to be a "sunset cruise," the last thing before retirement.

But research and development didn't stop.

Chapter 11

Government-Contractor Partnership

For decades since the beginning of WWII, the government had been experimenting with contracting civilians to take over activities that had previously been the purview of the military services. After all, they reasoned, the job of the military is to fight.

The concept that finally evolved was referred to as GOCO (Government Owned, Contractor Operated). Materials used in such a facility were referred to as GFE (Government Furnished Equipment); information needed to run the facility was titled GFI (Government Furnished Information).

There has evolved an organizational intermediary group within the Civil Service to proctor the contractors for the government. Their job is to oversee the contractor's compliance to its contract and to assure that the GFE and GFI control processes are accurate, adequate, and thorough. They are also tasked with the performance evaluation of the contractor.

It was these performance evaluations that were the basis upon which the contractor earned income from the contract. Superior performance could raise the contractual fixed fee by several percentage points for any given reporting period.

Corporations that seek such government contracts like them, not because there are huge profits to be made, but because they need not have large investments in company owned material. That's all government furnished.

The evolution of this arrangement has not been entirely smooth. As they say, the devil is in the details. But we'll get to that later.

I brought the subject up here because it illustrates the way in which what had started as a purely military base could morph into something completely different.

War is a horrible thing. But it certainly accelerates the development of technology. Look at the effect WWI had on the development of the aircraft.

WWII did the same thing for radar, rockets, and atomic science.

So did the Cold War.

By the mid-'50s advances in nuclear weapons and rocketry converged into the ICBM (Intercontinental Ballistic Missile).

The problem was that we (the U.S.) needed some kind of defense from these missiles. Our government assigned the task of missile defense to the Army. Oh, the Navy was involved in missile research of their own. They had the Polaris Submarine project underway. But their focus was more on delivering them than on stopping them. That was also the focus of the Air Force. I mentioned that the Air Force was setting up shop at Roi-Namur, at the north end of Kwajalein Atoll, even as Kwaj was being expanded on the southern tip of the atoll.

What the Air Force was working on was a program called Project PRESS. I didn't know it then but that stood for Pacific Region Electrical Signature Studies. They would fire an ICBM from Vandenberg Air Force Base on the California coast and study it throughout its trajectory with sensors and telemetry until it landed somewhere near Kwaj. (The missiles weren't very reliable or accurate in those days.) They were particularly interested in improving accuracy and in the payload re-entry characteristics.

These things went up, and they came down, albeit a long ways away. The real question was in which direction to fire them.

North, toward Alaska and the Aleutians? No can do. The Soviet Union wouldn't stand still for that! A miscalculation could lead to WWIII!

How about further west into the broad reaches of the Pacific? Same answer. Here substitute Communist China!

Where, then?

Wait a minute! How about the Marshall Islands? We're already testing stuff there. In fact Kwajalein lagoon would make a pretty good target area. It's big. Practically nobody lives there. It's shallow. We can recover the instrumentation payloads. And if we miss, no big deal. There's nothing for hundreds of miles in any direction but seriously deep water. No chance of the Ruskies snatching any of the secret stuff. And it would be a great place to test radars.

Not only that. There's an island there that belongs to us. It's called Roi-Namur; and we don't even have to negotiate with the Marshallese for it!

However, both the Army and the Air Force wanted the range.

Chapter 12

Who Controls Kwajalein?

The Air Force's argument was persuasive. "We have the east end of the Western Test Range at Vandenberg Air Force Base in California. That's where we fire the ICBMs from. We have mid-range tracking at Barking Sands in Hawaii. Kwajalein is the logical Western end for the range. That's where the ICBMs come in. And besides we already have the Kiernan Re-Entry Measurements Site (KREMS) at Roi-Namur."

The Army's argument was equally persuasive. "The DOD (Department of Defense) has charged us with developing the Ballistic Missile Defense system. The Air Force is right. Kwajalein is where the ICBMs come in. That's why we need Kwajalein."

As an ex-Air Force type, I naturally favored the Air Force. Of course, that didn't matter in the least.

We were all concerned about who got it.

My mind was eased somewhat when an MIT acquaintance of mine (working on the technical end of a mission) reasoned, "Look. It doesn't make much difference to us which one gets it. Their only reason for being here at all is to act as a conduit for moving DOD funds to the contractors here, and to move materials here to support the community."

Made sense to me.

Competition between the services has been a fact of life for all of recorded history. What the Army gets, the Navy cannot use. Or the Air Force. Personally I always felt that the Army had never forgiven the Air Force for splitting off in 1947.

Anyway, the debate raged on through the summer of 1964, and the DOD finally made a decision in October.

I had been on Kwaj about four months when the decision was announced.

The company courier bag was on the inbound plane, and I was sent to fetch it. This time the plane was Air Force. A couple of Army non-coms (as in non-commissioned officers, i.e., Sergeants) were in the crowd meeting the plane.

Some of the aircraft crew entered the terminal heading for flight operations.

"Hey, Air Force!" said a grinning Army non-com.

A sergeant from the flight crew turned around. "You called?"

"Yeah. Guess who won!"

"Guess who won? What do you mean?"

"We mean guess who Kwaj is going to belong to?"

"Who?"

"Us, flyboy! You lost!"

The Air Force flight commander, a Major, turned around. "That's nice." Then he turned to his co-pilot and said loudly, "Let's see them run it without us."

Red faced, the two non-coms left.

Minor incident? Word gets around.

For eight months after that the Air Force accumulated Kwaj bound mail at Hickam, not until they had a pallet full, but until they had a planeload. Then we'd get 30-40,000 pounds at one shot. Bills were a month or more late. Time-dependant letters were a month or more late. Perishable cargo arrived spoiled.

The Army screamed. Finally the DOD itself had to step in and order the command at Hickam to move Kwaj mail and perishables "as received."

That broke the immediate logjam.

But a couple of months into the "mail strike" I was walking behind two Army officers.

One said to the other, "What's this PRESS thing at Roi?"

"Oh, that's an Air Force project. It's funded out of Hanscom Field, in Massachusetts."

"Isn't that just peachy! Let's see them run it without us!"

When I left the islands in 1987, Roi-Namur was still getting the short end of every stick the Army could throw at them.

Chapter 13

The Time Warp

PRESS was originally intended to give us a better understanding of the physics of missiles re-entering the Earth's atmosphere.

PRESS's home was on Roi-Namur, as a part of the KREMS installation mentioned earlier. The first sensor at KREMS was TRADEX (Tracking and Discrimination Experiment).

In 1957 when the surveyors moved in, the Navy moved out. There has not been an active-duty military man posted to Roi-Namur since.

Construction on TRADEX commenced in 1959 and the radar went online in 1962.

There is a story about the early days of TRADEX that deserves to be told as it was related to me some years later.

The problem that gave rise to the story is a time warp. Literally!

Kwajalein is 5,000 miles west of California. That means that when it is noon in California, it's only 7:00 in the morning at Kwaj. No problem. We can live with that.

No problem? No! Problem!

Kwaj is also west (by a hair) of the International Date Line. That's where the world's day begins. This means that when it's 6:00 in the morning at Vandenberg, it's only 1:00 in the morning at Kwaj—but that 1:00 is the following day at Kwaj!

If your family lives on the East Coast of the U.S. and you live at Kwaj, 8,000 miles away, you can tell them that you are eight hours behind them and a day ahead at the same time!

Confusing? It sure is!

***

TRADEX from its parking lot. Photo by Pam R.

Joint nominals had been practiced over and over prior to the test; these are dry runs involving everybody connected with the "mission."

This was the first real test for TRADEX. The Air Force was going to fire an ICBM from Vandenberg, and TRADEX was going to track it from acquisition to re-entry and splashdown.

The day before the test, all of the engineers who lived at Kwaj and commuted to Roi-Namur were given the day off and told to rest.

They did. Some were out fishing. Some were out scuba diving. Some were out on the golf course playing a round or two.

Suddenly, the control console at TRADEX lit up.

"This is Vandenberg. Time to launch is T-minus 60 minutes and counting!"

PANIC!

Get the planes! Get the aircrews! Get the engineers! The planes are down for maintenance. The aircrews are scattered. The engineers are all over the place.

On Roi-Namur, the console operators and technicians (who mostly lived there) were rounded up (mostly) and rushed to their workstations.

TRADEX was brought up in time to take the mission! Roi-Namur saved the day!

Well, that's the way I heard it.

Chapter 14

Anatomy of a GOCO: The Setup

Kwajalein "morphed" again, this time into a missile range. A GOCO range.

So, here's the layout.

There are four prime contractors (primes): DOD, Research & Development/Engineering, Construction, and Logistics Support.

Each prime has its subcontractors (subs). Each sub may have specialist subs of their own. Every contractor, no matter how small, has its own hierarchy from manager on down.

Each sub answers to the next higher authority in its own chain of command. It has to get its own job done within the limits of personnel and budget allocated.

Faced with limited numbers of housing units, the matter of who gets what becomes extremely complicated. Each chain fights for the best and the most it can get. Each job slot is assigned a level of importance.

The DOD hired construction contractors, principally Martin Zachary, to do the building. Martin Zachary hired subcontractors as needed.

However, the real authority (and responsibility) rested with the organizations that did the research for the government. MIT was a power there; so was Bell Labs. Beneath them there was a second rank of companies who did the yeoman's work of R&D, companies like RCA and Raytheon, Burns and Roe, Kentron, Martin Zachary (construction), Sylvania, and many others.

Each of this second echelon of companies was subcontracted to MIT or Bell Labs. Each of them generally had at least one contractor subordinate to themselves.

Near the bottom of this pyramid of companies, at least in terms of money and prestige, was Global Associates, responsible ultimately to the Navy, but charged with the supply and housekeeping for the others. Global ran the school, the hospital, most of the base operations. They ran the marine department and the local airlines. The stores and clubs, and billeting, the newspaper and radio station, the roads and grounds and the recreation department, all were Global's responsibility. It was the company who employed the Marshallese (some 600 of them) who worked on the range.

The hierarchies of these companies made up a chain of command parallel to the Navy's. They were the real bigwigs on the atoll.

Chapter 15

The Ph.D. Advantage

A basic break point is whether a given position is authorized accompanied housing. This means that, if your position is sufficiently important, you can bring your family with you. If it's not, you can't. You'll be there on "bachelor" status. "Bachelor" in this case doesn't necessarily mean you're unmarried. Indeed, most of the "bachelors" do have families of their own "back in the world."

On the scientific side of things, there was a difference in the method of personnel selection.

You're probably familiar with the phrase "It isn't exactly rocket science." At Kwajalein, it *is* exactly rocket science!

Jobs in this arena were so technically demanding that qualified personnel could virtually name their own price. And that price was high.

For example, let's say I have an advanced degree in metallurgical engineering. You, as an employer, come to me and say, "Ted, we have a slot open at Kwaj for a good metallurgical engineer. Would you consider doing a tour (usually three years) there?"

There's a rule of thumb that says if I have a position open and there are 10,000 people I could get to fill that position, it makes little difference to me which of those 10,000 actually gets the job. On the other hand, if the job is critical and must be filled, and if there's only one person who can do it, then I must have that person—whatever the cost.

Anyway, I'm thinking to myself, would such a move affect my career negatively or positively? Would my kids suffer from such a move? After all, they're in good schools now. Would three years at Kwaj leave them behind their classmates when we return home? How's the medical care there? I'd have dozens of such questions.

You, as an employer, had better have the right answers to all of these questions.

With my education, experience, and proven ability—and with what you are trying to accomplish out there—you really do need me more than I need you.

Blunt? Yes. Egocentric? Perhaps. Realistic? Yes. It's a sellers' market; and I'm the seller.

At one time there were more than seventy PhDs working on Kwaj at the same time!

Chapter 16

The Marshallese Advantage

What other background do we need to fill out the picture of Kwajalein?

We must bring into the picture the Marshallese.

The Marshallese will be inextricably interwoven throughout the rest of this narrative, but we need a thumbnail sketch to show the framework from which their interactions with us arise.

U.S. and Republic of the Marshall Islands flags. Photo by Pam R.

What are the salient points?

To understand the relationship between them and the U.S., their history and society must be taken into account.

First of all, they are survivors. They cope!

Their ancestors were counted among some of the finest seafarers ever. Along with the Polynesians and the Melanesians, the Micronesians found and settled most of the bits of land scattered in the vast expanse of the Pacific. "Micronesian" is a Greek derivation that means small island. They invented ways of navigation that continue to astound us today.

For the Marshallese these methods included listening to the sea. Their canoes had incorporated into the hull an "earbed" upon which a navigator could rest his head and tune in to the rhythm of ocean currents and waves. Stick charts were their maps. Islands were not separated by miles and direction—they were separated by time and currents.

Total population in those pre-contact days is not known, but was unlikely to have been more than 3 or 4,000. Infant mortality was high, so high in fact that it became the custom not even to name a child until its first birthday. Until then it was just "the baby." Even today, the most important birthday a child has is when it becomes one year old. Then it becomes a real person.

Population grew slowly. By 1944 it was estimated to be on the order of 7,000. The UN took a census in 1960. Population 14,907. Today it's in the neighborhood of 61,000.

Still, as a people, the Marshallese have never been numerous. The atolls' carrying capacity for humans is low. In fact, some of the more remote atolls in the Marshalls have never had a permanent population. The most critical resource such atolls lack is a source of fresh water.

People clustered where potable water was available. Of course the empty atolls were known and claimed, but were only sporadically visited to glean whatever might be of use. It is ironic that when such places were visited, the visitors had to carry fresh water with them.

Most of the atoll didn't (and doesn't) have decent topsoil. This lack was so pronounced that when the Germans took over the islands and tried to establish a copra trade, they would ballast their ships with topsoil taken from whichever port they started from on a trip to the Marshalls.

The Marshallese call Americans (and all outsiders) “ribelli.” This translates approximately to “people who wear clothes.” They refer to themselves as “rimaj,” meaning “the people.” Cultures all over the world have some term of similar intent. It separates “us” from “them.”

When I arrived at Kwaj in 1964, the Marshallese could recite their family lineages back seventeen generations. Name a “ribelli” who can do that!

Photos of Marshallese

Photos by Pam R.

Chapter 17

The Marshallese Way of Life

Traditional Marshallese society was Matriarchal, Matrilineal, and Matrilocal.

Matriarchal means that the women ruled the roost. They made all of the important decisions.

The Leroij (woman chief or queen) controlled land distribution to the families. She allocated land usage rights to the family's heads. Every family had the right to use land somewhere. The Leroij dictated what piece of land went to which family. Lots of politics here. Wheeling and dealing was a continuous activity.

The basic land unit was called a "weito." Because islands sat atop narrow reefs, a weito is defined as a parcel stretching from the ocean side edge of the reef across the island to a man's height deep in the lagoon. The width of this strip of land was variable and depended both on a family's need and upon its relationship, both social and political, with the Leroij.

Marshallese usually congregated on the largest islands of the atoll, or, where some special resource such as fresh water was available. Fresh water was so critical that all families had access to it, regardless of whose weito it was on.

All of the land on the atoll was divided into weito, and a family could hold weito on islands that were not inhabited on one or more atolls. The wealth and status of a family was counted in how much weito they held.

Everything on a weito became the "property" of the holding family. Everything that grew there, or swam there, or floated onto its beaches became the resource of the holding family. They could consume it, or trade it, or fabricate goods from it.

Transit across weito lines was guaranteed to everyone, so no family was isolated from the rest of a community. The reef between islands, the ocean, and the lagoon outside weito were open to all to utilize and harvest as they could.

An exception to weito was the ancestors' islands. These were the cemeteries. No houses could be built on them. Nothing could be harvested from them, except in extreme emergency.

Weito vary in value. Those in the middle of an island usually have the heaviest plant and tree cover, whereas those at the ends of an island taper off and usually have more scrubby growth. Also, the ends of islands can change as tides and currents move sand around. On the other hand these same tides and currents can deposit valuable things on the beaches at the ends of islands.

Matrilineal means that people reckon their affiliation through the female line, rather than the male.

When a man marries in a matriarchal society, he takes his wife's family name.

The way it worked in traditional Marshallese society was that the man made a contract to work for the wife's family for a certain number of years. His labors are committed to her family's benefit, and if things don't work out after awhile, he is free to go his way.

He is not responsible for the raising of their biological children, but he is responsible for the raising of his sister's children! This is called the *avuncular* relationship.

The children look to their mother as mother, to their mother's sisters as mother, to their mother's sisters' children as brothers and sisters, and to their mother's brothers as "fathers" in the supportive sense. Crazy? Not necessarily.

Look at it this way. Children are prized. If you're a woman and have a baby, you know the child will be cared for because it's part of your family regardless of whom the father was. Besides, if you're normal and sexually active, you may not be sure yourself who the father was. So what?

In areas of the world where matrilineality is or was the rule, wild stories began to filter back to the home front when sailors and other explorers made first contacts. The girls there were happy to have sex with you? They may have wanted a baby with light skin, or blue eyes, or blond hair. They may have traded favors for some valued item promised them, like maybe a steel knife, or some iron nails. Or maybe just to see if you were "different" from the other males they knew.

This is hard for the average Judeo-Christian morality to swallow. And one consequence was that the first thing missionaries did when they got to such a place was try to convince the locals that such behavior was "sinful." Sex outside marriage was "sinful." Sex for the fun of it was "sinful."

See how I get carried away? We were talking about lineages.

There aren't many lineages in the Marshallese population. In the first place, everyone tries to claim as close links as possible with the first Leroij. In the second place, the gene pool is admittedly small. There has been more widening of this base in the last 100 years than in all the history these folks can remember before then.

Let's get back to the third point.

Matrilocality. This simply means that the husband moves into the wife's family home, or at least with her onto one of her family's weitos. Establishing a new household outside these parameters was simply unthinkable.

I mentioned social structure earlier, matriarchy. The Spanish weren't there in numbers enough or long enough to hardly notice it. The Germans and missionaries were, but they really didn't care who they dealt with as long as order was maintained. "Whatever worked" was their motto.

The Japanese did care. Strongly patriarchal at home, they flatly refused to deal with women. The traditional matriarchal structure of Marshallese society became endangered.

The last traditional Leroij was still alive in 1966 when I met her on Majuro Atoll. Don't take as gospel the name I assign to her. I'll call her Nerani, but my memory may be playing tricks with me on this point.

Nerani was about ninety years old and blind when I met her. She lived apart from her people on Majuro and was, shall I say, revered by them.

Anyway, in 1916 and the years just after, she was faced with a major problem: the Japanese ignored her.

She could not represent her people in dealings with the newcomers. Nerani did, however, have three sons. In traditional society, in times of conflict, sons of the Leroij were the "war chiefs." They led expeditions. They organized work parties and, in many other ways, implemented the will of their mother. In normal times their day-to-day decisions were obeyed as the decisions of Iroij (Leroij was the name of the first non-mythical "queen;" its masculine form is Iroij). When disputes arose, as they sometimes did, Nerani was there to make a binding decision. Her word overruled that of her sons, but she used it sparingly. She delegated negotiating authority to her sons. This was new to them and they liked it. She was now out of the "official" governing loop.

The men in the community took to this new authority with gusto. But it broke a centuries-long cultural norm, and was not universally accepted. It resulted in a serious rift between the largest Marshallese communities and the populations of some of the more isolated atolls. These changes have dramatically affected the Marshallese way of life.

But as recently as 1966, individuals or families who felt they had been wronged could go to her and plead their case. Her decision still overruled that of her sons.

***

I recall a statement made to me many years ago by Mom's Mom, Gramma Shanley. "Teddy," she said, "I have lived in the most exciting time in all of history. I grew up when horses were pulling trolley cars over rails set in brick cobbled streets and canal boats along towpaths."

"Lighting was from candles and kerosene lamps. Fifty cents could get you a good bedroom and an all-you-can-eat breakfast in the dining room of my father's hotel. A five-course meal, family style, would cost each diner forty cents all by itself."

"And I've seen the United States land a man on the moon and get him back safely to Earth!"

"All that in just one lifetime! Who could have experienced more?"

Who could have experienced more?

Try the Marshallese.

I was walking along an oft-driven dirt road on Namur to one of my outer warehouses when I spied a white stone newly exposed in the track. By its color it looked out of place, and it was smooth with a visible straight line on it. It had been worked. I dug it up.

It was a stone adz, fashioned from a fluke of a giant clamshell. It measured about six inches wide and sixteen inches long. The back still retained some of the shape of the shell it came from, but smooth. The sides were parallel, and the face was perfectly flat. The working end had been filed down to a sharp edge. Extensive grinding on local sandstone had obviously formed it.

During the course of its use part of the cutting edge had broken and the implement had been abandoned to the jungle.

It was clearly a pre-contact artifact. That made it at least 150 years old, because as soon as the Marshallese had contact with westerners and their metal tools, stone tools fell out of favor.

Precisely how old? Who can say? Recent work by archaeologists indicated that the Marshallese have lived there for at least 1,800 years, and that their ancestors were the first human populations on the islands. This is in consonance with the general peopling of those islands in the central Pacific, some of the most recently populated places on Earth.

There I was, in the later years of the Twentieth Century, looking at a Stone Age artifact!

So let's call it 150 years. People still living had witnessed the birth of the atomic and space ages right there.

How's that for change in a short time frame?

Social institutions arise in response to technology and contact with other cultures. There is always a gap between the development of any level of technology and a people's incorporation of that technology into their cultural asset base. This gap is referred to by social scientists as the cultural gap.

What fills the gap? Education.

What is lost? The comfort of tradition and the assurance of cultural self-worth.

People all over the world are still coming to grips with these changes.

When people try to assert traditional values, conflict arises. Traditional values don't fit.

Look at the mess in the Middle East for prima facie evidence of the result.

What can we do to assure the peace of the world? **Perhaps a balance between the new and old ways, as is on Kwaj, is the answer**.

Chapter 18

The Trust Territory

I mentioned that the U.S. found itself in control of a lot of bits and pieces of islands by war's end. The first thing they did was take inventory of their acquisitions, marking most with the phrase: "Captured from the enemy during the course of hostilities, indigenous claimants." At the war's end the United Nations, in a concession to the reality of the situation, validated the presence of the United States governors of the islands within the newly established Trust Territory of the Pacific. The announced intention of the Trust Territory was to work itself out of existence by bringing its populations into the Twentieth Century, then letting them govern themselves. What actually happened was that the United States initially practiced a policy that can only be described as "benign neglect."

Churches sent missionaries into the islands. A few businessmen traded there for copra, coconut oil, and seashells. Native handicrafts provided a small source of income for the inhabitants. A few teachers were sent in to the larger population centers. A few rather basic medical facilities were introduced. Trust Territory offices were established under the aegis of the UN Other than that, most local populations were left pretty much to fend for themselves.

The Marshall Islands were a part of the Trust Territory. But they were different. They were different because they were the most isolated, with one of the smallest native populations. And they were different because the U.S. had some problems that created a need for isolated islands to pursue development of atomic weapons, then of some sort of defense system against intercontinental ballistic missiles.

The names Bikini and Eniwetok refer to atolls in the Marshall Islands. So does Kwajalein. We had bases on all three of these atolls, and we talked the Marshallese into evacuating certain islands in these three atolls so that we could "conduct experiments aimed at insuring world peace."

Chapter 19

A Kwaj Cat Turned Roi Rat

It seems to me an intrinsic fact of human nature that people who live in a cultural center tend to consider those who don't to be "country bumpkins." You see it at every level, everywhere in the world. "They're like us, mostly. But we're a little bit better."

Of course, this sentiment is reciprocated; to the bucolics, the urban folk are "city slickers," not to be trusted.

The same thing happened in the Marshall Islands. To the rest of the people in the Trust Territory, the Marshall Islands were "the sticks." To the Marshallese at Majuro, Kwaj was almost the sticks; Bikini surely was. Of course, we overseas Americans developed this mindset as well.

Don't laugh too quickly—there are "Kwaj Cats" and "Roi Rats." I'm a Roi Rat and glad to be one.

But it didn't start that way.

***

What prompts a person to decide on working away from home? More than that, what could induce a person to opt for a job outside the U.S.?

In my case, I had had some overseas experience. I had been to the Far East while in the Air Force, and taught school in Borneo with the Peace Corps. In Taiwan I met an American civilian who worked for Philco-Ford. He was a tech-rep who maintained the crypto-gear at the base I was on. He seemed to me at that time to be leading an adventuresome life.

Anyway, there I was at the University of Hawaii, in the Masters' bypass program, going for a degree in Cultural Anthropology. I was pretty well disgusted with what I was studying. The thought of being tied to that field through a doctorate no longer appealed to me.

Besides, I was broke—again.

It was time to get a real job or starve.

I knew I wanted to work overseas. But I was under severe restrictions as to where I could go, imposed by the DOD because of what I had done while I was in the Air Force. I couldn't go to a communist country for the rest of my life. I couldn't go within 250 miles of a fighting front anywhere. I couldn't go to any country that even had a land border on a communist country for ten years from my date of discharge; that meant until September 1969. Sort of cut down on my options, didn't it?

I had already been kicked out of the Peace Corps where I had been teaching Chinese kids how to speak Chinese (I had learned in Yale) because the commies were saying the Peace Corps was a haven for CIA spies and agents. Such were the times.

The ad in the newspaper read, "Wanted: Clerk for retail office at Kwajalein."

Now that sounded interesting! The location fit the bill; no land borders. There was no sign of fighting going on within 250 miles of there.

And it seemed to fit another secret criterion I had hoped for. What was going on was research and development on the cutting edge of several sciences. That meant that there were probably lots of educated people there. Maybe some of their smarts would rub off on me!

So I applied with Global Associates, and, in due course, downrange I went.

I received my departure time: "Be at the main terminal at Hickam Air Base at 4:00 Wednesday morning. Our representative will be there to give you the papers you need. Good luck!"

The plane was a Northwest Airlines DC-6, under Navy contract.

At 7:00 we boarded the plane and by 7:20 were airborne. The adventure was o*n*!

Three hours later we made an approach to Johnson Island, and after one look out the window we were told to pull the shades down. What they were doing at Johnson was so secret that we weren't even allowed to see outside the plane once it was on the ground! I found out later that Johnson was a repository for war gases. Years later, the DOD exploded a nuclear weapon in space near the island and the electromagnetic impulse from that explosion knocked out all the lights on Oahu in Hawaii, 700 miles away!

Anyway, that was in the future. What was on my mind was Johnson Island, a sand spit! No grass, no bushes, no trees. *Oh, man*, I thought, *What am I getting into? That's* bad*! And it's only 700 miles from Hawaii! What will Kwaj be like?*

We landed on Kwaj at 5:30 Thursday afternoon after a flight of twelve and one half hours. Notice the day change? We had crossed the International Date Line.

Now, I'm going to walk you through the next couple of hours. Those of you who have been there will recognize the routine. Those who haven't probably understand that new places have an immediate impact that fades into familiarity with exposure. You see things more clearly the first time. They etch themselves into your memory. A week or a month later, you pass the same things and hardly notice them. Know what I mean?

Security people boarded the plane and asked for one or two VIPs who were aboard. They were escorted off. Then we got a lecture on security, what we could and couldn't do on Kwaj. We were read a short list of offenses that would lead to immediate termination of our contracts. First among these was fighting. No excuses. Whatever the reason for a fight, both parties went! We were also told to obey the off-limits signs.

Debarking was done in a very rigorous order (by now the plane was like an oven, sitting there on the tarmac with engines off). First were military officers and their families. Next in line were technical company personnel who were returning to site and had their families with them. Then tech company personnel on bachelor status returning to site. Then new tech company personnel. Then support contractor personnel and/or their families returning to site. You get the idea. Last on the list were support contractor personnel newly arriving on bachelor status. That was me.

There was a spectator area just outside the terminal building. People who had nothing else to do flocked there to see who was coming in. Plane arrivals in those days were often the event of the day.

In one corner of the spectator area, there was a signpost with signs pointing in every direction: Sidney 2,601; Moscow 8,004; New York 7,928; Vladivostok 5,821; Tokyo 2,920; Harold's Club (Reno) 6,012; and on and on.

Near the entrance, there was a monument of half of a giant clamshell. It stood on end and was nearly six feet tall.

Inside the terminal our company reps met us and handed out the "Welcome to Kwaj" kits. These included a check-in sheet, a mess pass, a map of the island, and a security flier. We were escorted into security for photo IDs and fingerprinting.

By the time this was completed, the baggage had been offloaded and we picked up our bags. Next, I went to the transient hotel across the street for towels and our billeting assignments.

"You've got bachelor quarters, second deck, northeast bay, cubicle 8, bed 3."

This was my home for the next three years. As private as a cattle barn, but noisier. Twelve beds (six bunks) to the cubicle. The latrine was a block away down the hall. Open toilets, open urinals, one shower room with twenty-four showerheads, twelve sinks. Air conditioning was by open window. Bunk by the window and you got what air there was. You also got wet when it rained.

Downstairs was the post office, Macy's (the retail store), and the snack bar. There was a covered walkway downstairs leading from the bachelors' quarters to the general mess. Support contractor supervisors and tech support bachelors had better quarters, usually two-man air-conditioned rooms. A few, like the orderlies at the hospital, had single rooms in a small wooden structure next door privately referred to as "placenta palace." This referred to the use of afterbirth as fertilizer for the flower garden they kept there.

The "Yuk-we-Yuk" Club (Marshallese for thank you) was off-limits to support contractor bachelors. So was the school, the commissary, Emon Beach, one of the theaters, one of the swimming pools, and the entire housing area. Oh well.

My contract said they would pay me $2.37 an hour, forty-eight hours a week. Unlimited overtime for anything over eight hours a day and over forty hours a week (overtime was time and a half with two times base for Sundays and holidays). I had a meal card (room and board were provided), and free medical and dental. Free tickets to Honolulu once a year for R & R (the hotel cost was on me). Two weeks paid vacation with free tickets to point of hire once a year. With paid travel time and weekends, we could stretch that to almost a month. And all of our paychecks were free of federal income tax!

I was in tall cotton!

We arrived on May 8th, 1964 on a Saturday. And tomorrow was a day off.

Sunday we walked around and I found the office where I was to report to work Monday.

We also found the sign.

The sign was on a four by eight piece of plywood at the corner of Lagoon and Sixth Street. It read, per Navy Regulation, thus and so: *No dogs or bachelors permitted in housing area.*

That sign had a checkered and rather short future. A week after we saw it, someone or someones pulled it down. The Navy had it put back up. Then, in a very strange and unexplained, very localized fire, it burned. The Navy ordered it replaced. The new one burned, and was never replaced.

I must tell you that many of the conditions (such as the sign) I described changed as soon as the Army took over, some immediately, others over the course of several years.

There were always restrictions, but in general conditions improved for everybody as the build-up on the base continued.

My first job assignment was clerk in the retail office. I kept inventory records, ordered supplies as needed, filed paperwork, and acted as a general factotum in the office. Not an inspiring job, nor challenging. But there was opportunity for advancement. And I could leave the office from time to time to pick up incoming mail or material for the retail activities. As I moved up in the ranks, I learned about how government funds made it down to Kwaj, and how companies were picked for specific projects.

Chapter 20

SOPS, SOWS, and Other Sacred Cows

As I have mentioned earlier, the Army had won the bid for the range, but still needed to conduct it intelligently. Now, the process of spending government money is never undertaken lightly. The accumulation and spending is a process, as political as it is economic, and is the main activity of governments everywhere. Checks and balances abound throughout. And when it's done right, everyone benefits.

GOCOs are a case in point.

The government has a facility through the use of which certain predefined goals may be accomplished. We are going to spend a bit of time looking at a small part of the end game portion of this process.

One such GOCO is Kwajalein. No matter what else is being done there, someone had to maintain the physical plant of the installation and keep it usable and habitable for the people who live there.

So the DOD, the responsible authority, decides what it wants someone or some company to do, and it generates a draft RFP (Request For Proposal).

This draft RFP is published and bids solicited. Interested parties make detailed bids based on what the RFP seems to be asking for. Perhaps twenty or thirty bidders respond to the RFP. Since RFPs themselves can run to hundreds of pages, and since bidders must respond point by point, this is time consuming and expensive—and at this stage the expense comes straight out of the bidder's pocket.

The DOD reviews the responses to its RFP, and the culling process begins. Some of the bidders obviously don't have a grasp of the RFP's breadth or implications. These are dropped and the list of candidates shrinks.

There are always questions. The DOD may have to amend, or even rewrite its RFP. The amended RFP is sent to the shorter list of bidders. More bidders drop out, or are culled.

Surviving bidders are invited to Kwajalein for a walk through to observe the incumbent's operation and the physical plant itself. Naturally, the incumbent contractor doesn't want to help the competition any more than it is obliged to. I was told, on a number of occasions, to clear my desk and cover certain information-rich charts on the walls, in preparation for such walkthroughs. The rule of thumb was "Be polite, but don't give any information away."

More bidders may drop out at this stage. The money they've spent to get them this far is still their own. More questions arise. The DOD may have to amend its amended RFP.

Surviving bidders are asked to make a "best and final" bid based on the latest version of the RFP, which constitutes a SOW or Scope of Work.

Every statement in the best and final bid must be cross-referenced to the SOW. This bid is a commitment on the part of the company to satisfactorily perform the SOW.

Lawyers on both sides scrutinize the bids to make sure all the i's are dotted and the t's crossed.

Then DOD decides, through a convoluted process, which bidder offers "best value" for the contract dollar, and makes an award.

The winner and, perhaps the first runner-up, are reimbursed their bidding expenses. All other bidders leave the field sadder and poorer. But perhaps they have learned enough in the process to do it better the next time.

Control over the contractor doesn't stop with the winning of a contract. That's when it really starts.

By the time the contract is awarded, enough hairs have been split, questions raised and addressed, and so on, that the SOW is often much larger than the original RFP was. The SOW says, “Contractor, this is what you must do to satisfy the contract;” and the contractor must reply in writing words to the effect of, “Yes. We agree to abide by every item enumerated in the SOW.”

One of the items always included in the SOW is that the contractor must write a Standard Operating Procedure (SOP) describing precisely how it will address each obligation to satisfy the SOW it has accepted.

The writing of these SOPs begins at the outset of each contract and continues, usually throughout the duration of the contract. Each SOP begins with a reference to the precise point in the SOW being addressed—by chapter, page number, paragraph, and line. Length of each SOP can vary from a couple of pages to fifty or more.

Once accepted by the contracting authority, they become the basis on which contract performance is evaluated. They also stand as job descriptions for each position on the contractor’s staff.

Most staff members working a contract never see the whole contract. Many of them never even see the SOW, but every one of them sees the SOP(s) relating to his or her particular duties. And each employee is expected to be able at least to say which SOPs govern his or her activities. This holds particularly true for anyone seeking promotion.

The contractor is responsible for nothing that is not specified in the SOW. Nor can it ignore anything that is.

This being said, it must be understood that change occurs, and disputes happen.

A new facility is constructed, or one becomes obsolete or inactive. New programs commence, or old ones are completed and funding for them is stopped. Staff levels rise or fall.

Things done far away from Kwajalein impact operations there. Congress passed a new law. Military budgets are cut or raised. Technological development has a huge impact. Kwajalein's isolated location also poses an interesting question: Since Kwajalein Atoll offers no natural resources, is it even possible to support and maintain a large military-sanctioned operation, much less support its employees?

Chapter 21

The Logistics of Kwaj: 5,000 Miles Away

Supplying Kwaj

One major thing that differentiates USAKA (U.S. Army Kwajalein Atoll) from the standard military bases in the U.S. and around the world is the nature of its supply systems. Over the years the United States government and military have developed the most complex, comprehensive, and capable supply activity the world has ever seen. Though I have spent most of my adult years dealing with various aspects of logistic operations, describing this in detail is far beyond the scope of both this narrative and my ability to do so. Entire libraries have been written defining the process and explaining its administration. Attending to the needs of a community which at one time reached a population of nearly 8,000 Americans is a daunting task.

When you consider that your resource base is mostly from 5 to 8,000 miles away, the dimensions of the problem begin to take shape. Remember, you have to bring in everything; and I mean everything. Food, fuel, clothing, retail goods, medicines, school needs, aviation and marine parts, movies, beverages of all sorts, bikes, all sorts of automotive and industrial machinery, fire and safety equipment; the list just goes on and on. Not only do you have to acquire and get it there, but you have to store, inventory and issue it. Anything you want to build, modify, maintain, or repair has to be funded, acquired, shipped, received, and processed for use. To top it off, each and every cent has to be accounted for because this is a government activity. The process for doing this is called logistic support. And because this function was so important at Kwajalein, for decades the logistic support contract was kept separate from the technical support contracts.

Logistic support probably accounts for more than half of the annual budgets at every level of government. Not only that, but it probably accounts for the largest single block of government employees at every level, either directly or indirectly.

American taxpayers have been known to grumble that their tax dollars are dumped into some black hole from which the people derive no benefit.

Au contraire! Taxes go almost instantly back into the national economy. Remember, every government employee is supporting a family that recycles that money through banks, grocery stores, and every kind of retail and manufacturing enterprise imaginable.

Marine supply, Aviation supply, Petroleum Oil Lubricants (POL), Medical supply, School supply, Compressed gases, Metal supply, Lumber, Food supply, Tool supply, Construction and Maintenance supply, and Automotive supply are some of the categories of material that are regularly bought through the government supply system. But the technical and scientific supplies, used for the cutting edge research that is being done, don't fit so comfortably into the government system. At KREMS, we stocked nearly 70,000 line items of specialized material which were so unique that the government system was unaware of them. Some of them were one-time buys, and many were developed by manufacturers to satisfy the specifications of on site engineers for use only at Kwaj.

Take TRADEX radomes for instance. These were electrically transparent Mylar bowls about a foot across with an integrated flange for bolting to the outer end of the feedhorn on the TRADEX antenna. They were used to keep certain pressurized gases in the waveguide to the feedhorn in order to prevent the slightest hint of moisture from getting in. Otherwise, short circuits could occur that would destroy the transmitter. At the center of the bowl the Mylar thickness was $1/10{,}000^{th}$ of an inch thick plus or minus a half millionth of an inch; the flange of the same piece of plastic was one eighth of an inch thick. The graduation from one eighth of an inch to $1/10{,}000^{th}$ had to be absolutely uniform or the wave form from the transmitter would be distorted and useless. Molds were made. Only about one attempt in ninety produced a dome that met specifications.

When TRADEX was designed in the late '50s, 100 spare domes were ordered. Exposure to tropical sun made these domes brittle. It was felt that 100 would be enough to last the seven-year life expectancy of the radar. Twenty-six years later we ran out of spares.

It was unbelievable luck that the original molds were found back at Moorestown, where a worker a quarter century earlier had tucked them away on the off chance they would be needed again some day. They were.

The government was not equipped to cope with this sort of long term storage problem. We were.

PLOPS

"Ted, the TWT PLOPS wants to look at what just arrived. Before we stock it, they want to get some measurements. Take the mule and trailer from furniture warehouse out to RESUP. Pick up the TWT, and deliver it to the back door of JTO. There'll be a guard to let you in. PLOPS is waiting on it." The instruction was clear and the job simple. But what the heck was PLOPS?

When I first heard the term Project PRESS (Pacific Region Electrical Signature Studies) at Roi, I wondered why on Earth the Air Force had a public relations activity going on in the middle of nowhere. I'll be blunt; my first thought on hearing the term was cow pies! What was yours?

PLOPS is the acronym for **Pl**ans and **Op**erations.

In a very real sense, most of the people at Kwaj were futurists. They were involved in planning for future needs of the site. Logistics was no exception. Just for one example, they had to know how much food would be needed by the site population six months ahead of time. That's how long the pipeline for delivery to Kwaj was at the time. They also had to know what the projected population would be in that future time.

Planning for the future is what an economy is all about. It is a huge part of the activity of industries and of governments all over the world.

Your neighborhood grocery store has to have a good handle on sales so that it can have perishable foods available for sale when the customers come looking for them. Offering stale bread, sour milk, or spoiled fruits and vegetables is a guaranteed formula for losing customers and going out of business.

Governments plan years into the future in estimating what their budgets, and hence, taxes must be. You get the picture. Such planning is so complex, it's a wonder that we can do it at all.

Roads don't just happen. Buildings don't just happen. Delivery of health services doesn't just happen. Manufactured goods don't just happen. Pyramids don't just happen. Missions don't just happen.

PLOPS looks forward years into the future, often beyond present technologies, and beyond presently available materials. Coordination of the thousands of details needed to achieve future goals is PLOPS' stock and trade.

SALUD!

By The Book

Occasionally, in cases like the radomes, we as civilians had to bend the rules to get things done. The military minds on the island didn't always operate with the same flexible logic. Trying to fathom the military mentality has eluded me for more years than I can remember. Layer that with Civil Service bureaucrats working for the military and what sometimes results can be terrifying. I suppose a boffin might refer to the condition as megalomaniacal autocratic masochism. In layman's terms that means making irrational demands based on the tentative authority of some regulation for the pleasure of hassling someone while demonstrating to your superiors that you are diligent in assuring compliance with their standards.

And there are thousands of regulations to select from. By the time I left the Marshall Islands the logistics support contractor had generated more than 3,000 standard operating procedures (SOPs) to show that they were operating in compliance with appropriate government regulations. Their performance was regularly judged against these SOP's to determine how much profit they would make on their contract.

I don't know how all of the departments of all the companies worked, but I can give you scores (or even hundreds) of examples over the years of how these regulations impacted the supply departments of companies I worked for in the Marshalls.

Take TRADEX, for instance.

TRADEX radar was designed in the late '50s. Its intended life was seven years. However, it is still in use today.

In an attempt to save money, the steering mechanism from a World War II destroyer was adapted to turn the antenna. We had only one spare in supply. It had never been needed. There were no others in existence. One day we got a call.

"This is an Army base, isn't it?"

"Yes sir."

"Okay. All Army bases are run by the same regulations, aren't they?"

"I guess so."

"They are. No exceptions!"

"If you say so."

"I say so. The Army regulation with respect to supply states that if you don't use an item within two years, it should not be in your inventory. You've been crying for more storage capacity, yet you've got a lot of things here I haven't seen move in all the time I've been assigned to watch over your operation. They're taking up space you could use for better purposes. For example, what's that big white thing over there?"

"That's the spare turning mechanism for the TRADEX antenna. It was part of the material that was bought in 1959 to support the radar."

"When was the last time you used it?"

"We haven't used it. It's there just in case."

"Just in case! *Just in case*! There's nothing in the regulations authorizing '*Just in case*!' It's painted white. I want a list of everything here that's painted white! They're taking up more than half of this entire building! Get rid of them and you won't need more warehouse space!"

"But those things are unique to this radar. This is a research and development base. They can't be used anywhere else in the world!"

"That's got nothing to do with the regulations. This is 1969. If you haven't needed them in ten years, you won't ever need them. Get rid of them!"

"NO!"

"*No*?! Good. You are officially in violation of your contract which says you will obey Army directives!"

"The contract says we are to get the job done. Our work here is on the cutting edge of the radar art. We may have to bend a regulation or two to make certain we can support this research."

"You can't 'bend' regulations! Consider yourselves on report!"

We took that one straight to the Pentagon. The word came back down to the Army: Let them keep the spares!

Only then was it okay to keep the spares.

Class Structure at Kwaj

From this incident it is clear that hierarchy played a huge part in the life of the community at Kwaj. Organization was essential to maintaining order and good relations between the various ethnic, military, technical, and social groups on the atoll. There was the Army, of course. They were in overall command. The contractors were all legally subordinate to the Army because they had the DOD mandate to come up with a defense against missiles. The Army had the money to do the job, and it was the Army who ultimately paid the bills. But Kwaj was never a typical Army base. It was and still is a research and development base. As the representative of DOD, the Army was the contractors' conduit for support and access to government resources. The Army had the organization, means, and authority to carry out this support activity.

Base support was the Army's business and they accomplished this by assigning the job to civilian contractors. The Army's position at Kwaj was simply to monitor the performance of all the contractors. This monitoring took two tracks. One was to interface with the research and development (R&D) contractors to ascertain needs and review progress toward the mandate.

Aside from this general oversight responsibility, the Army had very little input to the R&D activities. The other track was to provide and maintain the myriad of elements that go into the

Transplantion of a modern American community onto a group of islands 5,000 miles from the United States.

Schools, power plants, housing, stores, clubs, transportation, recreation, supply, messing, communication, medical services, roads and grounds, commissary, churches, newspaper, radio/TV, plumbing, telephones, everything one might expect to find "at home." These things were what base support was all about. This might all sound like plebeian stuff but it was vital to making Kwajalein a community attractive enough to entice top scientists (and their families) who were necessary to accomplish the government mandates.

This sort of elitism is something of a burr under the Army's saddle. But the fact of the matter is that the level of expertise needed to accomplish the sort of cutting edge science being done at Kwaj is not widely available. There is a truism in industry that says that if there is a job to be done and if there are 1,000 people qualified to do the job, then the company does not care which of the thousand eligible people they get. The job will get done. However, if there is a job to be done that only one person in the world can do, then the company *must* acquire the services of that one individual, or the company cannot get the job done! That individual is, so to speak, in the driver's seat. This happened a lot at Kwaj (and still does). Companies have had and still need to meet the demands of these select experts. And the demands were steep: family housing, good schools, good medical facilities, good housing, and numerous other benefits, not the least of which was good pay.

I have mentioned these things here because they translated into demands the Army had to accede to. Scientists of such high caliber did not need (or want) to take just any job that came along. Moreover, a commitment to an isolated location such as Kwaj could easily drop them out of the real cutting edge research they had been involved back in the States. If they fell behind the ever evolving state of the art research in their specialties, it could easily mean that their careers would be harmed for the future.

As a rule, they had their children in the best schools available in the States. Their children would suffer if they were obliged to spend three years away from quality education. Thus it came to pass that the Army had to authorize the staffing of a kindergarten through 12th grade school far above the norm for military base schools of the time, even though the entire student population would never exceed 800. This and many other things the Army did to make a community which would meet the criteria demanded by these specialists and the companies they worked for. All for the sake of accomplishing the mandate to advance a certain technology into dimensions never before attempted.

In comparison with the total population at Kwaj, there never were a large number of Army personnel there. As I mentioned before, their main responsibility was to access government resources and to monitor the performance of the logistic contractors who performed base support. They also tried to keep the contractors from going hog wild with government money. Their job was not an enviable one. However, they did play an essential role in forwarding the very important research effort taking place on Kwaj. They still do. Their personnel and dependents had to be counted as among the socially important people on the atoll.

Parallel and of equal importance with the Army personnel were the upper echelons of the various companies. In terms of the number of employees, the logistics support contractor was by far the largest contractor on site. At one time in the early '70s, the single contract at Kwajalein made the logistic contractor the seventeenth largest company in the U.S. in terms of defense dollar expenditures.

Population wise, the logistics contractor was the most evident of all the companies at Kwajalein. They provided the teachers, doctors, nurses, pilots, supply specialists, and all of the other people it takes to make a town functional.

Picture, if you will, an American community of 7,500 or so with all of its roads, sewers, power plants, buildings, parks, airports, medical facilities, clubs, stores, and everything else one might expect to find in such a place. Make it a coastal town with a comprehensive marine department. Add the amenities which would make it acceptable to a large contingent of highly educated scientific specialists. Take all of this, pick it up, and drop it on an island 5,000 miles away from the States.

Pack in the latest in technical facilities from radars, computer centers, rocket launch sites, telescopes, and communications facilities to link people and sensors with each other on the atoll and with other range facilities as far as 8,000 miles away. These missions required real time coordination as much as one third of the way around the world! Literally thousands of people might be simultaneously involved.

Communication and data links are so important that it's reasonable to say the test range couldn't exist without them. When technology made it possible, the range in fact warranted the services of a communications satellite. The Army had to see that these links were provided and maintained. Range communications were thus placed under a separate contract. During many of the years I was there, Kentron had that contract.

Every manmade thing that was there had to be built or installed. This called for the efforts of a construction contractor capable of both very basic and very sophisticated production. Martin Zachary got the contract early on and made a huge investment in getting construction equipment to site. This paid off on all subsequent contracts for MZ. Having all the necessary equipment on site made it possible for them to underbid all competition on future contracts.

MZ's population on the atoll fluctuated according to the building schedule. At times they had a small administrative office and a few maintenance people on site. When a contract was let through the Army Corps of Engineers, MZ could quickly bring in hundreds of the needed personnel. As soon as a particular project was completed, these workers were released until the next requirement arose. It may sound strange, but there are a lot of workers who liked this mode of employment.

Some of these workers became semi-permanent residents of Kwaj. They'd come to site, work long hours at good pay for a month or two or three, then take time off at home with their families until the call went out from MZ again. Some of them worked for no one else, and made careers out of that mode of work. Most of MZ's personnel hired on from Hawaii.

And that was the case with many of the contractors who hired general laborers and non-specialists for work on Kwaj.

Thus, Hawaii has been a major source of laborers for Kwajalein Atoll.

Hawaii has limited variety of labor opportunity for its people. Agriculture, the military, and tourism have been the mainstays of the Hawaiian economy. Its population is culturally diverse. Unemployment has always been somewhat ahead of national averages. The climate is semi-tropical to tropical (the same as that at Kwaj). And most of the Hawaiians who sought employment at Kwaj would find the living conditions there not unlike what they left behind.

They were American citizens. And in a working situation where some level of security clearance was required just to be there, this was a considerable asset to all concerned.

Hawaii benefited in major ways from having its people work on the atoll. Most of the workers had families in the state and their paychecks largely went into the state's economy.

Overall, amongst the more professionally and scientifically orientated segments of the work force at KMR (or Kwajalein Missile Range), one cannot say that all states were evenly represented. If you took a hi-liter and marked on a map the states represented at Kwaj, you would find the East, Gulf, and West coast states more often than those states in the interior of the country. Why that is is hard to pin down. It has a great deal to do with the home offices of the companies that employed people at Kwaj. It also has to do with the location of the educational institutions which provided these folks with their training. It may even have to do with the fact that the government was willing to defray moving expenses only from and to the "home of record," or an equivalent distance. Travel times allowed were also adjusted according to distance from "home of record" to Kwajalein. Employees traveling from Hawaii were allowed one day's travel each way. Those traveling from the mainland were allowed two days each way.

Personnel employed by the prime contractors were a notch higher in the island pecking order than the sub-contractors. Mainlanders somehow felt themselves a bit more bitter than "island hires" (meaning mainly Hawaiians). All of the above felt themselves superior to the Marshallese. So everyone there had somone to look up to and down upon.

Which was really ironic, because the Marshallese didn't give a hoot! To them we were all foreigners! Get their dander up as "host nation" citizens, and they could force individuals or single families to be removed from the range, and even the country! This didn't happen often, but it wasn't unheard of either. In those few instances the Marshallese could go through the Trust Territory office all the way to the UN to get their grievances heard.

The order of the day was "Don't rock the boat." However, Kwajalein wasn't segregated to the point of hostilities. On many occasions all the different cliques and groups got together to put work aside have a good time, and the largest event of this kind was Kwaj Karnival.

Chapter 22

Having Fun in the Middle of Nowhere

Kwaj Karnival

One of the most anticipated annual events for years was the Kwaj Karnival. It was held once a year during the dry season. The carnival was set up in the athletic area north of the chapel and south of the tennis courts along Ocean Road. Some years there was even a little riding railroad, complete with track. Set up on the shore side of Ocean Road north of the Kwaj Lodge and south of the bachelors' pool.

I don't know how long the Navy had allowed it, but it was already a well-organized operation by the time I got to Kwaj in '64. The Army permitted it to continue well into the '70s. I think the major sponsor was the Kwajalein Women's Club. Its stated aim was to generate money for Marshallese education programs and scholarships.

The Army required that the whole event had to be handled at no cost to the government. And it did cost. I recall seeing the final report on one year's Karnival. A special account was set up in Finance for it. Labor for installing electrical service to more than forty concessions ran to near $80,000! Total costs that year were $127,000!

Tents and booths had to be set up and taken down. Lighting and equipment had to be brought out of storage and installed. Supplies had to be procured. The list went on. Every major department in Global was involved. The Recreation Dept. supervised it all.

Beyond that every other company on the range was invited to participate as a concession sponsor along with every ethnic group, recognized club, and organization.

Staffing and operation of the concessions was mostly voluntary, except for security, safety, fire, medical and finance specialists, who were paid from the Karnival fund to maintain control of the event.

Aviation laid on extra flights to Roi. Marine transport laid on extra trips to Ebeye, since it was the one time of the year when folks from Ebeye could come to Kwaj whether they worked there or not. (I suspect that, over the five days of Karnival, the entire population of Ebeye came to it at least once!) Automotive ran buses and cabs. Food service and the bakery went into overdrive for the five days of Karnival. Hundreds of thousands of dollars in change were brought in by the Bank of Hawaii to support the money booth.

Tee shirts and baseball caps, beer and cold soda, cotton candy and shaved ice, ice cream and pronto pups (Kwaj corn dogs), hamburgers and full meals of many ethnic flavors could all be had from one concession or another. Rides included the train, a merry-go-round, even, for a few years, a small Ferris wheel!

There were games aplenty. Ring toss, darts at balloons, knock down the pins with a baseball, football through the tire, coin toss, and more. Prizes for these were kewpie dolls and stuffed toys.

And there were games of chance: high/low, over and under, and Bingo. They all paid cash!

Which brings us to Jimmy P.

Jimmy lived on Gugeegue. He worked in the power plant there. He never came to Kwaj except for two things: to leave on and return from vacation; and to attend every day of Karnival. Jim would be there the hour Karnival opened, first in line at the money booth.

With a pocket full of quarters he'd go to high/low and start betting; and win, win, win! When his pockets got so full that he couldn't carry any more, he'd put $50 aside and take all the rest to a concession stand.

"How much are your pronto pups?"

"Fifty cents."

"Good." He'd count out $30 in quarters. "Give the next sixty kids who come up a free one."

On to another booth.

"How much for an ice cream cone?"

"Thirty-five cents."

"Good. Give the next sixty kids a free ice cream cone until this is gone." He'd hand the clerk a double handful of quarters and leave.

So it went until he was left with nothing but his starter money. Then it was over to the over/under booth. Where he'd win, win, win!

Then he'd start visiting booths again. "How much?" "Good. Give them free to kids until this is gone."

Jim did this five hours a night every night of Karnival. No one knew how he did it. He didn't know how he did it! He just did it.

He used to stop by the Bingo tent to get out of the sun for a bit. We talked between games.

"How long have you been out here Jim?"

"Twelve years."

"How long have you been doing this at Karnival?"

"Twelve years."

"Wow! It must have cost you a bundle!"

"Ted, I swear it hasn't cost me a dime! I'd be amazed if I'm down ten dollars for the whole twelve years!"

"Wow! With your luck you could make a living gambling!"

"Naw. It doesn't work anywhere but here, doing this. If I try to bet on anything else, I'm likely to lose my shirt."

"How long do you plan to stay out here?" He was no spring chicken.

"I don't know. I'm waiting."

"Waiting? Waiting for what?"

"Well, my home is in Hawaii and I've got a piece of land I want to sell. Guy wants to buy it. But he hasn't seen prices my way yet. He will."

"How much do you have?"

"Two acres."

"What are you asking?"

"A million per."

"Wow! Where is it, in Waikiki?"

"Naw. It's in the middle of his golf course. He'll come around."

A year or so after that conversation Jimmy called me.

"He met it! See ya around!"

I haven't heard from Jimmy since.

Anyway, back to the Karnival.

Volunteers from the Global staff on Roi-Namur ran Bingo. Most of them acted as card sellers in shifts. As soon as sales were stopped for any game, the sellers came to the cashier's table and dumped their aprons. The take was quickly counted, a chart referred, and the cash award for that game announced.

We gave back 80% of everything we took in each game. It added up! In 1972 the Bingo concession alone generated more than $20,000 for the Education Fund! One game each day was an exception to that rule. The last game each night was a cover all blackout with winner takes all. Cards for that game sold for $1 each, versus 25¢ for regular cards during the day.

Prizes usually started small at opening time and grew quickly after working hours were over. By 5:00 each evening winners were getting $100 or more. And they were doing that eight or nine times an hour! The biggest cover all blackout I recall was over $3,000!

There were some people on the island who only came out for that last game! Bingo was a favorite among the Marshallese ladies, particularly the grannies. Few of them spoke English, but they sure knew the letters B-I-N-G-O and the numbers associated with the game!

There were a couple of dozen regulars each year that got off the boat each day and headed straight to the Bingo tent to settle in for the day. They'd buy as many as a dozen cards per game. The feats of concentration and endurance those ladies demonstrated were phenomenal!

Their granddaughters would continually ply them with food and drink from the concessions. The only time they left their seats was for a quick dash to the Porta-potty, from which they'd return before the next game began. A couple of them never moved at all! I thought, *they must have hollow legs*.

The coins and bills they turned in to buy cards were amazing. The U.S. went off the silver standard in 1964. Each year at Karnival hundreds of dollars in pre '64 coins and bills came out of the Marshallese woodwork. I even started carrying some spare money with me to trade for the silver that passed through the Bingo tent. It didn't hurt that I had learned enough Marshallese to repeat the Bingo numbers in their language. They liked that.

What they liked most about Bingo was that they could win just as often as anyone else! Those winnings were very important to the families the grannies' club represented. Sometimes they made up a significant percentage of the family's annual income.

On the two or three occasions over the years when one of the grannies won the cover all blackout, it was equivalent to as much as two or more years' wages to a Marshallese laborer! I'm glad to have been a part of the Karnival.

I wasn't at the range when it was discontinued, so I can't tell you exactly when or why.

It may have been the result of a change of attitude on the part of the Defense Department concerning gambling of any sort at military installations. I know that by the time I returned there in the later '70s all varieties of gambling so prevalent in the '60s had vanished.

A just as likely excuse is the effect of population decline among the American workers there after the Test Ban Treaty of 1972. The remaining residents could not generate enough economic activity to keep the Karnival operating at "no cost to the government."

How To Lose Ten Tons in One Night

Karnival was great, but it only came around once a year, so we working types had to find other ways to cut loose every so often. This story is of a particular prank someone pulled that we found out about the next day.

The paper read, "Will the person or persons who took the 20,000-pound test block please return it?" It appeared on the last page of the *Hourglass*, the Kwajalein newspaper, where many interesting items of both civilian and military interest were committed to print.

The item in question was a concrete cube with a heavy lifting ring centered in its top. It had sat there on the sand inland from Emon Beach for more than two years. It was a rigging test weight used by heavy equipment riggers to test their gear.

Its disappearance was noted by one of the Martin Zachary employees shortly after dawn of the night it "got lost." Evidently he asked his co-workers if they had moved the block. Then Security was notified.

My friend, the investigator, told me that part of the story.

The police report was interesting. They cordoned off the area for 100 feet in all directions. Inside the ribbons were no footprints, no tread marks, no wheel tracks, no ten ton test block. None of the patrols (running every half hour) had noticed unusual activity in the area the previous night. None of the area residents had seen or heard anything out of the ordinary.

A fire department team had been in that end of the island checking hydrants that night. This wasn't unusual. The fire department always ran these tests at night because that was the time of least demand on the island's water system.

But the nearest hydrant to the cordoned area was more than 100 yards away. And the team members swore that there was no heavy equipment at all in the area while they were running their checks.

The island was searched. There were several rigging test blocks found, some lighter, one or two heavier. The lagoon waters were searched, and the ocean shore. But the specific block they were seeking never surfaced.

The last official act in the search for the block was the request in the *Hourglass*.

So much for the police report.

Did I say the block never surfaced?

Well, I suppose in the strict sense of the term that was true.

The truth is that it never moved anywhere else on the island or in the surrounding waters of the lagoon or ocean.

But it did sink.

How could a ten-ton block sink at a place where it had sat for two years without moving?

It's amazing how much sand you can flush out from under a test block with nothing more than a fire department pumper truck, 300 feet of hose, and five minutes. Block sinks. Sand is flushed back over it. Prints are flushed away. And the fire crew is off to test the next hydrant!

So, if you folks are still looking for the 20,000-pound test block out there, look down!

A Whale of a Tale

Sometimes a joke, no matter how innocuous it may seem to you, can backfire in a big way. When dealing with the military, discretion is always the safer bet. However, sometimes common sense is hard to come by.

On Kwaj, the radio station, library, and newspaper were parts of community service. There was no television available in the early days on Kwaj, but we did have a radio station, AFRS Kwajalein. And therein lies a story.

Ken M. was the station manager and announcer. He broadcast live eight hours a day. Ken was a tall man, about 6'10", and his shoe size was fourteen!

I know this story is true because Ken and I almost got fired over it. I had taken a part time job as an evening and weekend DJ.

Part of my job was to help Ken develop "the morning skit." This was a short wake up type of program that came on right after the 6:30 news. Its purpose was to get people up with a smile.

An example: "This is Ted, your roving traffic reporter. I'm standing here on top of the water tower." (There was no way anyone could possibly have got up that tower without prior permission, a key, and safety equipment. And everybody knew it.) "There seems to be a traffic jam on Ocean Road. But, if you cross to Lagoon Road at Sixth Street, you can get around it." (Traffic jam? Ha! The main means of transportation then, and now, was bike.) So it went.

Coming up with ideas for these skits was sometimes easy, sometimes not.

I don't remember which of us came up with the idea of an interview with a transient whale. But I went to the marine department one morning to tape appropriate ambient sounds. This is how the skit went on the air. (Some of you may remember it.)

Cut news feed.

Cue music, twenty seconds.

Break music.

"This is Ken M. I just received a call about a whale at Echo Pier. I'm taking our remote there. Stand by." (Remote? Heck! We barely had a microphone!)

Cue music, twenty seconds.

Segue to background.

"This is Ken again. I'm here at Echo Pier. The caller was right. There's a whale of a whale here! It must be about *ninety feet long*! But don't worry. There're two Security guys here with their pistols ready. Everything's under control."

Whale:	Ahem.
Ken:	Who said that?
W:	Ah did.
K:	But, but, you can't talk! Whales can't talk!
W:	Suh, as a southern gentlewhale, Ah resent that remark!
K:	I don't understand. How did you learn to talk?
W:	Well, suh, Ah was cruising around McMurdo Sound down south in Antarctica, when Ah came across some of those hydro phones your scientist types were dropping into the water to listen to us. What they didn't realize was that Ah could hear them back! That's how Ah learned your talk.
K:	This is astounding! But what brings you here?
W:	It's like this. Ah caught a cold. And with me that's an epidemic! My doctor, Dr. Whalebone, told me to go north to the warm climes for a rest cure. He suggested Kwajalein because it's the world's biggest swimming pool.
K:	I'm sorry to hear about your cold. But that's not what I meant. What brings you here?
W:	Here?

K: (*shouting*) Here! To the Pier—here!

W: Ah kin hear you! Y'all don't have to shout!

K: (*calming down*) Let me rephrase that. To what do we owe the honor of this visit?

W: That's better. Ah'm here because ah got a complaint, and a request.

K: What's the complaint?

W: Ah was cruisin round the pool last night and one of your underwater boats went right across ma bow without so much as a by-your-leave! It had a red star on top.

K: A red star? My God! It must have been Russian!

W: Ah'll say it was rushin'! It dang near ran me down!

K: I'll have to report this immediately! It must have been spying on our mission last night! (*Starts running down the pier*)

W: Wait a minute! Haven't you forgot something?

K: (*comes back*) Oh, yeah. The request. What's the request?

W: Ah wanna see the boss. Ah got something o' his Ah wanna swap.

K: The boss? My boss?

W: No. The BOSS boss. The main man.

K: Oh. You must mean the Colonel. Well, he's a busy man. And besides, he might not be up yet.

W: He's the only one Ah'll swap with!

K: Swap? Swap what?

W: This here thing! (Lifts fluke and lays object on pier.)

K: My God! That's a re-entry package! Where'd you get that!?

W: It hit me!

K: Hit you?

W: Like Ah said, Ah was cruising around the pool. Then Ah saw this bright light in the sky. Next thing Ah know, this thing drops into the water and whumps me up beside ma head! Ah wanna swap it for ten gallons o' liniment!

At this point the broadcast was interrupted by a phone call.

"This is Captain so-and-so! We demand an immediate, on-the-air retraction and apology for impugning the diligence and alertness of the United States Army!"

As soon as Ken and I could stop laughing long enough to get ourselves under control, we got back on the air with a sober retraction and profuse apology for impugning the diligence and alertness of the United States Army.

The phone rang.

"This is Major so-and-so. That's better!"

I can't conclude this recounting without mentioning that Colonel so-and-so came to the station later that day. He had been sleeping when the broadcast aired. He apologized to Ken for the "ill considered" statements of his subordinates. Nothing more would come of it.

"By the way, was that skit recorded?"

It was.

Could he please get a copy?

He could.

For the next week Ken got grins and high-fives from everyone he saw, including most of the other Army people on Kwaj. Sadly, the whale never made a second appearance on the show. The change of scenery must've done him good.

Chapter 23

The Spirit of Investment

Mining for Gold

Because of the nature of the contracts between companies and their employees at Kwajalein, and because of the inducements offered by the government for overseas work there, we figured that our disposable income amounted to some three times what would have been available to us holding similar jobs in the States.

Indeed, a person living there on bachelor status, one who didn't smoke or drink, could literally get by not spending any money at all on maintenance while there. Families at home were supported better than was possible had their breadwinners been stateside. And there was still money left over.

This induced many to experiment with investments that would never have entered their minds. Savings levels were high. And there was always temptation to put funds into schemes that might pay off big. Many of these were pie-in-the-sky or WBY (Wild Blue Yonder) in nature. Many didn't pan out. Some did. Those whose schemes worked out found themselves with financial assets beyond their dreams.

Jim H. served as the spark for one of these such schemes.

Jim was one of the Global pilots there at Kwaj in the late '60s. His hobby was spelunking, or cave exploration.

One day in '68, just after I had moved to Roi, he walked into my office and dropped a magazine on my desk. If my memory serves me right, it was the August 1967 issue of either

Argosy or *Atlantic* magazine. It was open to an article titled "California's Lost River of Gold." "Read this," he said. "I'm going there."

And he did. He and his son went to Las Vegas where they rented a plane and flew to the site, just over the California border on the main road to Los Angeles.

They saw signs of a lot of activity there, so they returned to Vegas and rented a car. Exiting the highway at Mountain pass, they crossed the overpass and drove some three miles south to Kokoweef Mountain where they were stopped by armed guards.

Once they identified themselves, they were welcomed in for a look-see. Jim and his son were hugely impressed. On the spot they wanted to join the enterprise.

For starters, everyone working there were volunteers, working for shares of what they might find. To say they were working on a shoestring was no exaggeration of the situation. They often didn't have enough money to buy food for the workers or fuel for the equipment they had cobbled together.

Jim made a donation of cash and explained to the leaders that he was sure he could convince others at Kwaj to chip in as well.

Here, in summary, is the story Jim H. left me to read.

In 1928 an old desert rat prospector by the name of Earl Dorr was clambering around the top of Kokoweef Peak when he came upon a hole which proved to be the top of a chimney in the mountain some 2,000 feet deep. Dorr called it Crystal Cave because of the large amount of quartz crystal in it. The entrance was at an elevation of 6,022 feet above sea level.

At the bottom of this chimney, Dorr said, he found three laterals (small natural tunnels leading away from the chimney). Two of the three petered out into holes too small to navigate. The third, he said, eventually opened into the top of a gigantic cavern at the bottom of which was a river running in a channel about ten feet wide. Bordering this river were a series of symmetric steps each a few feet higher than its neighbor. They rose, stairwise, to the sides of the cavern, which was at that point about 100 yards wide. Each step was covered with layers of basalt sand.

Upon extricating himself from Crystal Cave, Dorr went immediately to the California State Assay Office in Fresno and filed thirteen claims. These thirteen claims encompassed the whole of Kokoweef peak. As I mentioned, the mountain sits like a pimple, completely surrounded by lower lands of the northwest Mojave. The nearest mountains are at a distance of several miles from Kokoweef in every direction. The mountain is less than a mile long and less than half a mile wide. I don't recall the standard dimensions of a mining claim, but thirteen of them adjacently placed did the job.

Dorr's next move was to talk a licensed geologist acquaintance into accompanying him on an exploration of the cavern.

In short, they spent four days in the cavern and walked eight miles upstream from their entrance point, taking small core samples of the basalt sand as they went upstream and back. By the time they exited the chimney again they had a total of forty pounds of samples. Dorr had these assayed in Fresno and the results were stunning!

Dorr and the geologist wrote independent reports of their trip which corroborated each other in every pertinent detail:

The river rose and fell as if affected by tides.

Average width of the cavern for the eight miles they walked—100 yards.

Average depth of the basalt sand deposits on the shelves—three feet.

In 1928 the forty pounds of assay samples Dorr delivered to Fresno assayed out over $2,000 of gold per cubic yard!

Dorr even sent samples of the basalt sand alone to U.S. Steel Pittsburgh. He was told that it was perfect for casting sand and that U.S. Steel would pay him a handsome price per barrel for all that he could deliver.

Dorr was giddy!

Then he got paranoid. For whatever reasons, he convinced himself that other people were out to steal his claims.

That drove him to the stupidest thing he ever did.

Dorr took six cases of dynamite down into crystal cave and collapsed the only opening he was aware of to the cavern! He even signed his name at the explosion sight with the soot from his carbide lantern.

I've seen it.

Anyway, for the next ten years Dorr tried to promote financing to get back into the cavern. People thought he was crazy for what he had done. Besides, at the same time he was seeking major financial backing, he was demanding 90% of the gross income from whatever a successful venture yielded!

"Dorr's Blown Down" is massive. There are several boulders larger than freight cars tumbled precariously at the bottom of crystal cave. But Dorr claimed that he knew a way to drive an entrance at the base of Kokoweef that would get around his blown-down.

It took him about ten years to get going again. He got a few speculators who provided enough money to at least get the job started. And he eased his demands somewhat.

Then world events played a role. By 1938, when Crystal Cave Mining was incorporated, Europe was edging closer to war. And the U.S. Government began offering premiums for certain strategic metals, among them zinc.

Now it happened that when the miners had driven a tunnel in just a couple of hundred feet they hit a zinc lode. Not really huge, but under the circumstances, profitable. Dorr wanted to go right past it, but the investors said a bird in the hand was worth two in the bush. Besides, they might very well find other laterals in the course of excavating the zinc ore.

Zinc ore production and government premiums lasted about the same amount of time. Eventually the government had as much as it deemed necessary and dropped the subsidy. The lode petered out at about the same time. No other laterals or chimneys had been encountered.

Dorr died toward the end of the war, and the company sort of imploded. Various individuals and small groups bought up the claims and tried their hands. Several died in mining accidents.

Time passed until the early '60s, when Richard Hernandez and his Los Angeles cronies started their effort. They acquired the claims. They undertook what was, evidently, the first really systematic survey of the entire surface of Kokoweef mountain. It paid off.

On the other side of the mountain, but still only a couple of hundred yards from Crystal Cave, they found another opening about half way down the mountain. Very small, the opening led to a ledge at the top of another chimney.

The ledge itself was intriguing. It had been home for a fair sized family of humans several thousands of years earlier. When the remains of their fire pits was discovered, archaeologists from the San Bernadino County museum were invited to survey the site. Their findings, including the fossilized skeleton of an early horse (Eohippus) are on display at a museum to this day.

A drop of several feet led to the top of breccia which plugged the chimney. It consisted of fallen stalactites, large quartz crystals, and assorted other debris which had almost completely plugged the chimney properly over the eons.

Richard's team decided to put an adit through the side of the hill at the level of this breccia plug. They did this because of a fascinating characteristic of this "floor." If you sat on the floor and smoked a cigarette, the smoke went down through the floor, not up.

They started to clear this rubble and noticed that the diameter of the chimney was increasing. By the time I first went there and was shown the smoke phenomenon, they had dug more than 200 feet into the breccia plug. And the chimney diameter was still increasing.

They had discovered a number of laterals, all of which petered out. Moreover, when they used quarter sticks of dynamite to break up larger rocks for removal by bucket and pulley, the echo reverberated for many minutes. Even a noisemaker firecracker, used for demonstration, would echo for more than four minutes!

Enthusiasm ran high. It was what kept them going, working weekends for shares.

When Jim H. and his son came back to Kwaj, their enthusiasm infected nearly twenty of us and we were determined to support them financially, also for shares. We became known at Kwaj and at Kokoweef as "The Kwaj Connection."

Our support lasted for a number of years. I have no idea what others contributed. I probably invested as much as anyone. All I have to show for it as yet is a number of promissory notes in my safety deposit box at the bank. But, if it ever does come in, everyone connected in any way with the project will be so wealthy we'll have to hire accountants just to count the money! Personally, the investment has been worth it just for the speculative enjoyment.

The company tried to sell shares directly to the workers and the members of "The Kwaj Connection." However the State of California said it was illegal to sell shares in a treasure hunt.

One of our members heard of a guy in Santee, California who had developed an instrument that could indicate voids underground. I was due for vacation and was nominated by "The Connection" to go to Santee to check it out. I was authorized to spend as much as $2,500 for it if I thought it worked. We knew that the Cavern ran out from under Kokoweef at some point, and the hope was to use such an instrument to determine where and how far. The demonstration at Santee was convincing and I bought it. Back at Kwaj some of the engineers in "The Connection" tested it on one of the taller buildings there. The needles fluctuated at the proper points to indicate the roof and each floor of the building. So we sent it to Kokoweef. None of us could get it to work in any understandable way there. It became known as the "do-nothing machine." Oh well, it was worth a shot.

I stopped having anything to do with the project when the people at Kokoweef got taken for several tens of thousands of dollars by a con artist who convinced them that he knew "secret Chinese methods" for finding underground voids. When they gave him the money up front so he could buy some equipment, he disappeared, leaving a note saying he had to go find Solomon's mines.

I have no idea what's happening at Kokoweef these days.

***

I've told you this story to illustrate what people spent money on besides the stock market. Morey K. and Paul C. went in together on a franchise called "Little Pigs of America" (It was a fast food operation featuring hot dogs). One of them quit at Kwaj and went back home to run the franchise while the other stayed at Kwaj to help finance the startup. Eventually, the one who went back first almost ran it into the ground. He finally swapped places and jobs, while the other went back and completed the internment. Shit happens! They both wound up back at Kwaj paying bills.

***

John C. bragged all the time about how many condos he owned. I thought, *I've been here as long as he has. How come I don't own as many properties?* Then I discovered that what he really had was a bunch of mortgages. If he couldn't make the payments, he stood to lose everything. So he hung on to a job he despised at Kwaj. Over a number of years he got all of the mortgages paid and now he's doing very well, thank you.

***

A friend stopped by my desk one day with a cigar box (a big one) in his hand. He had recently returned from a trip to Australia where he had visited Coober's Peddy to see the opal mines there. The box was totally filled with polished 5/16th inch thick slabs of black fire opal!

"I need $1,400 right now," he said. I didn't have it. I wished I had it. Someone else did. He's on easy street now.

People didn't go to Kwaj for the money alone. Some really liked it there. Those who did best there went with a specific goal in mind. When that goal was achieved, they left. Financial wizardry wasn't necessary all the time—sometimes luck had a part to play. One close encounter almost bankrupted my partners and me!

The Four Winds

Two friends of mine were experts on sea vessels. Lee W. was licensed to pilot ships up to 5,000 tons, and Sid K. worked for Kentron as a professional diver. He was licensed to do marine survey. That means assessing the sea worthiness of boats. He knew his stuff.

One night, we were all sitting around reading a Trust Territory newsletter when we came across an interesting advertisement.

The ad read: "For sale, as is, where is (Saipan), the motor vessel *Four Winds*. Bids must be received no later than [such and such a date], when the winner will be announced."

We knew the boat. It was one of the tramp steamers that plied our part of the Pacific. The boat had about a 500-ton cargo capacity.

Sid said, "I know that boat. It's been tramping around these islands since WWII. Last time I saw it here was about six months ago. I wonder what shape it's in."

"It was floating six months ago," I said, stating the obvious.

"Hell. I've piloted bigger ships than that," said Lee. "I wonder if we could make some money with it."

"Me too," I said. "Let's think this over. Maybe it'd be worth making a bid on." We thought about it for three days, and then got together again.

Sid spoke first. "Look, before we can make any kind of decision, we've got to know what shape it's in. Tell you what. I've got some time coming for vacation. And I want to use it before my contract's up. I called a friend in San Diego who told me he'd give us 80,000 if we could deliver the ship to him there! If you guys will chip in for airfare to Saipan and back, I'll look it over."

We did. He did.

Lee and I were at the airport when Sid got off the plane from Saipan.

"Let's go get a beer," Sid said, "and I'll tell you about it!" He was very enthusiastic. We went to the Ocean View club.

"First of all, it looks like a wreck! I spent four days looking it over from keel to masthead. It's got two holds with a total capacity of 650 tons. There's an eighty-ton crane on board and working. Bilges are dry and their pumps are working. No 'rust-throughs' in the hull. The owner told me it's been fifteen years since it was hauled."

"The bridge looks like shit, but that's mostly cosmetic. All the instruments work. Engine room is filthy, but the engines work. Hell, it's even got an ancient radar on it that works most of the time."

"I'm inclined to say let's GO FOR IT!"

"I've got some news too," said Lee. "While you were gone I talked with a friend in Japan who told me he'd have a high dollar cargo ready in six months to go to Portland, Oregon. If we have a boat there when the cargo's ready, it's ours to deliver."

"Here's my two cents," I said. "I may be able to get cargo for us to take to Japan from here. You know the Japanese are always looking for scrap metal. Well, there's a lulu right here in the lagoon over by Carlson."

***

I was referring to the *Prinz Eugen*, the German battle cruiser that ran with the *Bismarck*. It was taken as a war prize in Brest, France at the end of WWII and eventually became part of the target fleet at Bikini during Operation Crossroads, which I mentioned earlier. A survivor of the test, it was moved to Kwajalein along with the other target fleet survivors in an attempt to decontaminate them in non-radioactive surroundings. It had suffered unrecognized damage during the tests and began to sink at anchor in the lagoon at Kwaj. An attempt was made to beach it on Carlson, but they didn't quite make it. It "turned turtle" there with its props and aft end out of the water.

If we could get those three props off intact, the Japanese would have paid a premium for them! (One of the three has since gone to the Kreigsmarine Museum in Germany.) Be that as it may, in 1967 they were still there "for the taking." Well, almost.

The problem was that the *Prinz Eugen*, like everything else on the bottom of Kwajalein lagoon, was claimed by Lejelan K., the last King of the Marshalls, as property of his and the Marshallese people!

The U.S. Navy had never objected to his claim even though the ship had been U.S. property. It was sunk, after all, as a result of nuclear testing, and had been written off. Beyond that the U.S. government wanted nothing to do with it, nor any responsibility relating to it. In their bureaucratic hearts I think they even approved of his claim because it got them off the hook.

Nor had the Army disputed his claim. I'm not sure whether they even knew his claim existed.

Whatever the case, suddenly, there was a chance for Lejelan to exercise his claim and maybe make some money in the doing.

So I made an appointment to see him.

"King Lejelan," said I, "the *Prinz Eugen* belongs to you, doesn't it?"

"Yes!"

"Would you like to make some money, perhaps quite a lot, from it?"

"Yes! But I haven't figured out how."

"Some friends and I are considering bidding on a cargo boat that's up for auction. Let's see if we can work a deal here. We'd like to bring our boat in and salvage the propellers and whatever else we can from the ship and take the stuff to Japan, where we think there's a good market. If we can get the props off intact, the Japanese would pay thousands for them. Even if we have to cut them up there's still a good market for them as scrap. The metal they're made of can be recast. Maybe we could even get parts of the drive shafts. They are high molybdenum steel, much in demand."

"You can sell that stuff?"

"We think so. We would like to act as your agent in this business. And we need your help."

"I like it. What do you need from me?"

"We need three letters from you. One is a contract for us to act as your agent in the matter of salvage of parts of your ship, the *Prinz Eugen*. The second is authorization for us to bring our boat into Kwajalein Lagoon to pursue this project and to dock it at the Ebeye pier. The third is a letter of permission for us to sell the materials we collect and split the proceeds with you."

"When you say split the proceeds, what sort of split?"

"Fifty / fifty."

"Make it sixty / forty in my favor and you've got a deal!"

"I'll talk to my partners about the split. You do understand that this whole thing is contingent upon our winning the bid."

"Of course."

Lee and Sid agreed to the split. We got our letters and the contract from Lejelan. So we sent in a bid on the *Four Winds* five weeks before the deadline. Then we waited. Waiting was the hardest part.

We were on tenterhooks. As the days passed our dreams of profit inflated. We were going to change careers! Just the leg of the trip from Kwaj to Japan might double our annual total income. Selling the boat in San Diego would double it again!

Our three contracts at Kwaj came up within a month of one another.

Sid would go to Saipan first and get started on the cleanup.

Two weeks later Lee would be there to work with him.

Finally my contract would be complete and I would join the other two. (*There couldn't be too much difficulty in being a deckhand*, I thought, *not when you were a one third owner of the boat.*) Time grew short and tension grew high. In our minds we were already wallowing in our well-gotten gains.

At long last the fateful day arrived.

We clustered around a radio waiting for the evening news. The denouement was sudden and bitter.

Someone had outbid us by a mere $1,000!

Gone were new adventures! Gone were houses or cars, or stock market portfolios! Gone were dreams!

We were left sitting in the Crossroads Club nursing beers and whining about shattered tomorrows.

Three hours later we were still there feeling sorry for ourselves, when another newscast came on.

"This is Radio Saipan. The expected typhoon has arrived with high winds, heavy rains, and strong tidal surges. It's high tide here and the storm couldn't have hit at a worse time. Damage is extensive here and on Tinian with several planes on the airfield there being destroyed.

"We have a report that the MV *Four Winds* has sunk at its pier here on Saipan!"

"As is. Where is!"

There was no possibility that the new owner could have gotten insurance on his prize in that short a time!

I'm here to tell you that while I'm not sure what to think about God, I have a profound respect for whoever assigned that guardian angel to keep us three men out of that tub!

Jaklik Telmong: Native Businessman

Not all of us had traumatic experiences with investing in sea vessels. Jaklik Telmong's fortunes went quite the opposite in that field.

Jaklik was a friend of mine from the furniture warehouse days, the most reliable Rimaj (Marshallese) in my crew. He showed up every day and was thoroughly familiar with the routines of warehouse activity. He was tall and carried himself with a bearing that elicited respect from his co-workers, both Marshallese and Phillipino. His English was adequate to understanding both instructions and requests. I had him as one of my team leaders.

He came to me one day and said, "Ted, I need help."

"I'll do anything I can, Jaklik. What's your problem?"

"I build boat." he said. "I like go fish. Boat almost done. Now I need engine. But no more money for buy engine. Can help?"

Jaklik was an older man in his late fifties, honest and reliable. I was making $4.50 an hour at the time. He was making 60¢ an hour.

"You want to fish for fun?"

"No, not for fun. For make money."

"How will you make money?"

"I sell fish on Ebeye pier. Many women want buy fish. They give forty cents for one pound!"

"What kind of fish?"

"Every kind. They like buy all fish I can catch."

I suspected this was true. One of the ironies of the impact of Americans on the Marshallese was that the Marshallese changed to a "tin can culture." They preferred buying manufactured goods, including food, to procuring their own.

"Tell me about your boat. How big is it?"

"Is big enough. Is twenty-eight feet."

"That's a good size. It must have taken a long time to build."

"Yes. I save money five years. Then build two years."

Jaklik obviously was very committed to his project.

"Will you be quitting work here?"

"No. I start fish 4:00. Bring boat back 7:00. Wife sell fish. I come work."

"That's good, Jaklik. You do good work with me."

I had a couple of thousand dollars in a savings account at the Kwaj office of the Bank of Hawaii. And my needs were small.

Jaklik's project seemed to me a good way to use some of the money to help a friend bootstrap himself to a better life. Jaklik had already invested a huge percent of his assets and efforts in his dream. And he convinced me he would make it click.

"Yes, Jaklik, I can help you. What do you need?"

Jaklik flashed a smile that showed both relief and concern.

"I need two engines, but one is enough. Too much money for two."

"Have you decided what kind you want?"

"Yes. Johnson Seahorse forty horsepower."

"How much for one?"

"One is six hundred dollar."

"Jaklik, that amounts to six months wages!"

"I know. But can make big money selling fish!"

He was right, of course.

"Okay, Jaklik. You are right. But you are right too in saying you need two motors. You need the second one for insurance. You want to fish outside the lagoon. If one motor stops the next land is the Phillipines, 3,000 miles down current. I can loan you $1,200. Can you get two motors delivered to Ebeye for that?"

"Yes! But it take maybe three months. Can?"

"Okay." I wrote him a check and we went together to the bank to cash it.

The motors took slightly over three months to arrive. By that time the boat was finished and ready for them.

Within thirty days of the motors' arrival, Jaklik returned the loan! Two months later he gave me another $600!

Jaklik was very successful. He'd leave Ebeye at first light each morning. Usually he was back before noon. Ebeye pier would be lined with ladies anxious to buy anything he had caught. The work was very strenuous. Jaklik took on a hired hand with whom he shared the profits. He sent at least a couple of his children to college in the States. They all did well.

One of Jaklik's sons and two of his grandchildren are named after me.

And he named his boat *MyFriendTed.*

Chapter 24

Brand-X – Russian Eyes

Jaklik used his boat to better his lifestyle. Other vessels were used for less noble reasons, such as, international espionage. Well, here we were, doing research that might help us to defend ourselves against the rockets of the Soviet Union, and there was a Cold War going on.

If you were the Russians, wouldn't you do the same thing? That is, park a spy ship offshore to watch what was going on here.

Do you remember stories about a ship called the *Pueblo*? (For those born after 1970, the *Pueblo* was a U.S. spy ship that was captured during the Cold War.)

For decades the Russians deemed the installations and activities here sufficiently important to warrant constant observation. They still do, but now it's done with satellites, while in the early years it was with spy ships.

We were of two minds about having them here. On the one hand, what was going on here was really secret and we didn't want the Russians to know about it. On the other hand there were occasions when it was to our advantage to have them confirm, by their own first-hand observation what we really could do.

On the whole we tolerated their presence.

We were not willing to become involved in an international incident by trying to force them away from these shores. Their claim to freedom of the seas was as valid as ours. And it could very well have been that such a move on our part would have resulted in reciprocal action against our "assets" doing the same thing around their borders.

I won't grace it with the term "gentlemen's agreement." Let's just call it a mutually acceptable stand-off.

The Russians claimed they were merely fishing boats. Of course they never really specified what they were fishing for. We could have noted (but didn't) that it was strange that all of their "nets" looked strangely like antennae of various ilks and all were above board. I suppose they might have had a passion for flying fish.

The ship was nicknamed *Brand-X*, as in we were "#1" and they were the competitor. Actually, *Brand-X* was probably two boats that relieved each other about every six months. As for the crew and technical staff aboard *Brand-X*, their six month cruises must have been largely dull, boring and lonely as well as crowded. There was probably very little privacy. Of course, if you had a thing for deep sea fishing, you might have thought this was like going to heaven. And assignment to *Brand-X* surely beat the mukluks and parkas off a tour at a northern Siberian radar station!

On the whole, *Brand-X* (ship and crew) was circumspect. They didn't want confrontation any more than we did. Usually they stayed well offshore, out of sight or hull down on the horizon. When something interesting was happening, they would come in close for a look-see.

When we launched sounding rockets from Speedball, *Brand-X* would surge in virtually to the edge of the reef to watch the liftoff from closer than most of us on the island were permitted. For the most part there was no attempt to interfere with the goings on. But not always. See the section on Speedball to see what happened when *Brand-X* got too close!

There was plenty of evidence on the uninhabited islands around the atoll of occasional visits by crew members of *Brand-X*. Empty vodka bottles and wooden crates stamped with Cyrillic writing were common finds. Maybe those folks just wanted to get the feel of solid land under their feet for a couple of hours, maybe they took turns having picnics. It's certainly possible.

In the earlier days of the research and development effort here, the accuracy of incoming payloads was never warrantable. So, for safety's sake, we demarcated large areas of the ocean up vector of the atoll and within the lagoon itself as hazard areas during missions. These areas were swept by plane and boat to alert trespassers of the danger they might be in. We urged boaters to vacate these areas for the duration of the mission.

Naturally, the Russians didn't feel themselves constrained by the U.S. attempts to clear the mission area of ships before a mission occurred. Planes flying between Kwaj and Roi were directed to "sweep" as far as fifty miles out to sea to warn ships to evacuate the area. Consequently, many of us riding as passengers on these flights got to see *Brand-X* up close and personal. We would overfly the ship, sometimes only 100 feet above their mastheads, taking pictures all the while. During such times, the ship's crew would usually stay out of sight under their awnings. These overflights were not confrontational in any respect; they were more in the way of letting them know we knew they were there.

I must tell you about one such flight.

***

Getting the crew members to show themselves became something of a challenge to us.

Someone came up with a brilliant idea.

Picture, if you will, a pallet.

Nailed to the pallet is a battery-powered color wheel.

This is a wire circle with several "spokes." Between each spoke was a different color of cellophane. The wheel was turned by a small electric motor. A bright light source was fastened on the pallet to one side of the wheel so that it shone through each cellophane segment as the wheel turned.

On the other side of the color wheel is a coil of Lucite plastic. The Lucite had a diameter of about an inch. There was close to 100 feet of Lucite in this coil. It was fastened to the pallet with one end pointed directly at the light source (picture a coiled snake with its head rising from the center of the coil). The end of the Lucite in the center was raised on a dowel and supported by large rubber bands so that it could move randomly (within limits). The last six inches (the snake's head) was straightened so that it pointed directly away from the light source at the other end of the coil. The dowel held this "head" about two feet above the pallet. The color wheel was shrouded so that it could not be seen from the "head" of the "snake" (except where the light source shone onto the other end of the coil).

The light shone into one end of the coil, ricocheted its entire length and exited the other end as a brilliant spot.

We were flying a DeHaviland C-7 "Caribou" at the time. That was the plane with the drop down ramp at the rear for cargo loading.

There was a mission coming up. There were reef and ocean sweeps to be made.

We strapped the pallet to the lowered ramp so that the "head" pointed out the rear of the plane. And we went *Brand-Xing*.

We found them and did our usual low pass flyover. Only this time we pulled up so that the "head" was pointed directly at the ship.

Now, shift your mind's eye to the perspective from the trawler. What do you see?

An "enemy" plane is "buzzing" you. From the darkened interior of the rear of the plane there is a brilliant light bouncing erratically in constantly changing color pointing right at you!

"What the hell is *that*?"

People came boiling out from under the awnings! They had cameras with three foot lenses! They had huge binoculars! There were even a couple of guns!

The pictures we took (between bouts of laughter), I was told, were clear enough that people back at CIA (or somewhere) could put names on more than half of the trawler's crew. That was probably the most exciting thing that happened to them on their whole cruise!

Barring that incident, life with *Brand-X* was never really confrontational. We were, in our way, as isolated as the folks aboard the ship. They were locked for six months at a time to the vicinity of Kwajalein atoll. There were even the occasional (very occasional) instances when we directly contacted them—one way or another.

The FM station on Roi (KVZI) served this purpose one night. The station has always been staffed by volunteers, so the DJs play pretty much what they want to listen to. For about three years I had my own program on KVZI (from 1968 through the early '70s).

I should tell you that we didn't really broadcast in those early days. The station had a power output of two watts. And that was dumped into the power lines. The result of this was that you could hear it on the island and almost nowhere else. The problem was that we didn't have much in the way of frequency control. Our motto at the time was "KVZI, the station with a smile—all the way across your dial." The station was located in a trailer on the north shore of Roi. My room was in a wooden barrack on the lagoon shore near the terminal.

I like different kinds of music: choral, classical, country, and folk. I also like "muzak." It's usually instrumental, selected to blend in with the background and meant to fill the spaces in our aural environment without being intrusive. Good music to read by.

The human voice is my favorite instrument. But not when it is shouting, screaming or ranting, nor when it is smothered by 200 watts of pain per channel by instrumental "accompaniment." So, I can't say I'm particularly fond of vocal assault, or "rock."

That being said, there's still a world of music I enjoy. I understand that I'm in a minority in my musical taste, not that

I'm alone. In fact, music served as the common ground between myself and *Brand-X*.

Now, my show on KVZI ran two (sometimes three) nights a week from 9:00 to midnight, or something similar.

As I said, I have a great liking for classical music.

And some of the best of it has been composed by Russian or Slavic composers.

Over the years I had accumulated a number of good recordings, both tape and vinyl. I decided to try a complete evening of their music. I even had a tape of the Red Army Chorus.

I wrote to a cousin who was an historian at the State Department and asked him to send me a Russian dictionary. Over about a month's time I dug out the words I would need for a one minute speech. Then I ran the program of all Russian music. At the end of the program I said, in Russian (though I know it had to be the world's most botched grammar), "We have dedicated this program to you folks on the boat watching us watching you watching us. When it comes down to it, we are all in the same boat. Hope you enjoyed the music."

Then I shut the station down and started walking along the beach toward my room.

It was probably just as well that no one on Kwaj could hear KVZI.

But out on the horizon a small light began flashing: "Thank You," in morse code.

***

Brand-X was tolerated because its presence suited our purposes from time to time. There were also issues of international law to be considered if we had attempted to oust *Brand-X* from these waters.

With the break-up of the Soviet Union came the end of the Cold War, leaps in the progress of space technology (spy satellites and all), and the collapse of the Russian economy. *Brand-X* was finally deemed too expensive to maintain and keep on station here. But we had our share of fun before she left.

Chapter 25

Adventures in the Air

The Stories of Bob C: Fearless Pilot

Sure, lots of stories were centered around seafaring vessels; after all, Kwajalein was in the middle of the ocean. But plenty of stories took place in the air as well. Here's a sample of the tales told to me by my friend, Bob C.

Bob spent some years at Kwaj as a pilot in the aviation department for Global. I got to know him when he flew the mission flights to Roi and had to wait there until the mission was over. We'd sit around the office at the terminal and jaw.

The stories he told didn't happen at Kwaj. In fact, they happened over the Atlantic, in Europe, the Mideast, and in Africa. Nor were they typical of the experiences most Americans who spend their lives in the U.S. go through. But they illustrate the history Bob brought with him to Kwaj, and shared with his friends and neighbors there. For Americans who work overseas, these stories had the ring of truth.

Besides, they're just good stories.

Bob was in the U.S. Army Air Force during the later years of WWII and for a couple of years afterwards. He left the service and became a commercial pilot flying freight and ferrying planes around the world. In due course he met, courted, and married a German girl named Ilse. (She, incidentally, was one of the most beautiful women it has ever been my pleasure to meet.)

Right after the war, he took any kind of aeronautical job to keep his hand in the flying business. He flew all around the world, wherever the work was.

***

On Kwaj, Bob was authorized family housing, albeit a trailer, where he and Ilse lived with their three small children during the years I knew them. The trailer was situated on the lagoon shore of Kwaj, and the view out the living room windows was beautiful. They entertained a lot.

Bob approached the Army and asked permission to build a fence around their small yard.

It was granted, and he did.

Then he asked permission to build a small tool shed to hold his gardening tools.

It was granted, and he did.

Now Bob had an exquisite collection of finely detailed N-gauge model trains, mostly of machined brass, and mostly of German origin. They were all working models, and his layout of tracks for them took up more space than was available in the trailer. So he asked the Army for permission to construct another small shed adjacent to the tool shed to hold his collection.

Permission was granted, and he did.

As I mentioned, Bob and Ilse entertained a lot. So his next request didn't seem too out of line. He asked permission to build a patio from the living room door to the west end of the trailer and completely across the west end thereof. It took a while, but the Army finally said okay.

He did.

But the Army balked at his next request.

He submitted a formal application to have the trailer removed so that he could complete his house!

That's the kind of guy Bob was.

Here are some of the stories Bob regaled us with.

***

"I was co-pilot once, taking a replacement engine to Baghdad for a Pan Am jet that was grounded there. The pilot, Jim, and I had teamed for about six months and he had been into Iraq several times prior to our teaming. I hadn't.

"The word came down that there was a 707 on the ground at Baghdad in need of a replacement engine ASAP! The engine was to be our only cargo. It was strapped down in the middle of the cargo bay. I should tell you that our plane opened in the front and rear for cargo handling.

"We caught a good tailwind and brought our C-97 into Baghdad about 10:00 in the morning local. We parked the plane, opened the cargo doors and waited for the Iraqis to offload the pallet.

"'Come on,' said Jim. 'Let's get a hotel room.'

"'What!?'

"'Let's get a hotel room.'

"'What do we need a hotel room for? They'll have this unloaded in a few minutes! We can be back in Brussels by suppertime!'

"'Do what you want,' Jim said. 'I'm going over to the airport hotel to get us a room. When you get tired, come on over.' And Jim left.

"Thoroughly confused, I sat there and watched him go. Then I watched six Iraqis board the plane—three through the front end, and three through the rear. They unstrapped the pallet. Then three got in front of the pallet and three got behind it. And they pushed against each other. Four hours later I met Jim at the hotel bar.

"Next morning Jim and I were at the plane at ten minutes to ten. Six strangers were there, pushing against one another! At 10:00 three of them left and the other three pushed the pallet off the plane. And we took off.

“I learned later that Pan Am had been charged 144 man hours by the Iraqi Government for offloading the cargo. Six man teams had worked three shifts around the clock pushing against each other!”

Bob continued, “Another time Jim and I went into Baghdad with a full load on a C-54. We both went straight to the hotel. The next day we preflighted and taxied out to take off. Jim had the radio tuned to the tower frequency. We turned on to the run-up strip (the short connector strip between the taxiway and the runway) and were just ready to take off when Jim said, ‘Quick! Back it up! As far as you can!’

“‘I can’t. The props on a C-54 don’t reverse!’

“‘Lemme have it!’ Jim said. He turned the nose wheel left, locked the right main gear and revved the right outboard engine while feathering the other three. This made the right wing rotate counterclockwise around the right gear and pulled the left main gear backward! Then he reversed the procedure. He locked the left main gear, turned the nose wheel to the right, and revved the left outboard engine while feathering the other three. This made the left wing rotate clockwise around the left gear. And everything to the right of the left gear moved backward!

“It was beautiful to watch! He crabbed the plane back and forth this way and the plane backed up until the runway was well clear.

“Then we waited and Jim explained why he had done it.’

“‘Listen to the tower channel,’ he said. ‘There are Iraqi planes flying near here. They just asked permission to land. I saw them a few minutes ago. They were flying in the curve abreast formation (like the fingertips of a spread hand).’

“The problem is that no one gave them the order to change formation to land!

“I looked off the end of the runway and there they were, coming in to land curve abreast! Their formation was wider than the runway!

"The middle finger plane touched down on the runway's centerline. The ring finger plane managed to stay on the edge of the runway. The other three missed it and crashed!"

***

Bob told the story about the time he and Ilse were living in Brussels, Belgium. As it happened, her mother lived just across the border in Germany. It also happened that the German customs men didn't much like German women marrying foreigners like Bob. They were always courteous to Bob, but they took delight in hassling her at every opportunity. They would scrutinize her luggage with a fine-toothed comb. If she had even one cigarette too many, they'd tear the lining of her suitcases looking for contraband. This made her so mad that she couldn't do anything but swear for the next hour.

"I was flying for the Belgium government at that time," Bob said, "flying cargo into the Belgium Congo. This was during the Mao Mao uprising and civil war there.

"We never knew, when we left Brussels, who might be in control of the airport at Leopoldville. So I bought myself a small machine pistol of German manufacture—a Schmeiser 9mm. I got three clips for it and carried the works in a slim attaché case. This I kept in my locker at the Brussels airport office of my company. When I flew to the Congo, it went with me. I developed a ritual with it—as soon as I debarked the aircraft, I would lock the Schmeiser in the locker. I never took it home."

Returning from such a flight one day, Bob got off the plane and there on the tarmac were Ilse and the two children.

"Come on, Bob. We're going to visit Mama!"

"Hold on," Bob told her. "I've got to stash my flight suit and this thing."

"There's no time, Bob. Today is Mama's birthday and we've got to get over there!"

"Well, I don't know…"

"Hurry up! There's no time to lose!"

They went to the usual border crossing and the routine went as usual. The children passed through, then Ilse. She was hassled as usual, but she took it with good graces because she knew what Bob had in his attaché case. Automatic weapons were outlawed in Germany! This time Bob would get his!

"I stepped up to the customs counter. The agent looked at my attaché case."

"Ah, Capitan, do you have anything to declare?"

"Well, yes. I guess I do."

"What is it?"

"Well, I just got back from Leopoldville and I didn't have time to put it away."

"What is it?"

Bob smiled.

"A machine pistol."

"Oh! That's bad! May I see it sir?"

"Of course." Bob laid the case on the counter and unlocked it.

"Open it, please."

Bob did.

"Hmm. A Schmeiser." The customs man picked up the gun, looked it over, put it back, looked at Ilse, then turned back to Bob and smiled. "You have good taste in weapons, Capitan. Go."

"*Men*!" Ilse screamed! She wouldn't speak to Bob for a week!

***

Bob finally made aircraft commander. That is, he was the pilot instead of the co-pilot.

In his new job he was ferrying aircraft across the Atlantic, mostly from the States to varying places in Europe. It was the custom in his company for pilots to team up. There was value in knowing the qualities and habits of the man you were flying with.

Long hours together in the isolation of a cockpit tested the compatibility and tolerance of both pilots. When you got on well with your teammate, you were safer. It was that simple.

Pilots and co-pilots teamed when they could. Sometimes the partnerships lasted for years.

Then there were navigators. Navigators came from a company pool. They were usually assigned on a flight-by-flight basis. It was rare for a navigator to team up with a pilot and co-pilot, but not unheard of.

"We had just finished our pre-flight walk around the plane," Bob said, "When we looked up and saw a guy walking our way from flight operations. He was wearing cowboy boots. Under one arm was a tube that we assumed carried navigation charts for the flight. In one hand he had a thermos bottle, in the other, salami! On his head he wore a beanie—with a propeller on it!

"Our first reaction was to wonder what the heck we had drawn this time!

"'Oh brother! What kind of a ding-a-ling did we get stuck with now?'" Bob muttered to his co-pilot.

"'Hi, you Bob? I'm Paul.'

"'You navigating this flight?'

"'Yeah. Weather's clear to Greenland. There's a front moving in on Reykjavik, but if we get lucky with the jet stream, we'll beat it. If not, we can divert to Shannon. Should be a piece of cake.'

"'Got our comm frequencies?'

"'Right here.' Paul patted his map case.

"*Well*," Bob thought. "*He's got confidence. And he seems to be prepared. We'll see. But that beanie*!

"We introduced ourselves and began the flight. We made St. John's, Newfoundland within thirty seconds of Paul's estimated time of arrival (ETA), and our concern diminished some. We made Greenland within one minute of his ETA and were feeling a lot better about Paul. But the report from Iceland wasn't encouraging. An hour out of Greenland they were flying over undercast. And it was evident that the front was going to arrive at Reykjavik before they did. Another two hours and they had overcast as well. Then the word came: Reykjavik was closed!

"'Pilot to navigator. Paul, lay us a course for Shannon.'

"'Got it right here,' said Paul. 'Course (such and such), ETA four hours and twenty-three minutes. Piece o' cake.'

"'Thanks. We've got about five hours of fuel.'" Bob started to worry again.

Time passed. They had been flying now between under and overcast skies for more than three hours. No stars visible; they couldn't see the sea.

"'Pilot to navigator, how we doin'?'

"'Right on the mark, chief.'

"Four hours had passed.

"'Pilot to navigator. When do you figure landfall, Paul?'

"'Eleven minutes, boss.'"

Eight minutes later Bob saw the first break in the undercast he had seen in hours. Three more minutes and they were over it. And there was the coast of Ireland with a recognizable checkpoint in sight. They made Shannon within three minutes of Paul's ETA.

"Paul, let me shake your hand. That was beautiful! You can navigate for us anytime! But how the heck did you do it?"

"'It's like this,' he said. 'I eat this here salami at a predetermined rate. And when it gets down to here, we're over the coast of Ireland!'"

Paul certainly was strange, but he knew what he was doing. Soon after, Bob offered to team up with Paul based on his expertise.

***

Paul, in an uncommon move for navigators in those days, took Bob up on his offer and joined the team. The three of them worked as a team for several years.

On another trip, same route:

"Navigator to pilot. Change course to one-eighty degrees and hold it for one minute."

They were in mid-Atlantic at the time, heading for Iceland. This change of course would send them straight south down the middle of the ocean.

Bob didn't understand it, but he had come to trust Paul, so he turned south.

One minute passed.

"Navigator to pilot. Change course to ninety degrees and hold it for one minute."

Bob did it. "What gives?"

"I'll tell you later."

Another minute passed.

"Navigator to pilot. Change course to zero degrees and hold it for one minute." (Zero degrees is straight north.)

One minute later.

"Navigator to pilot. Resume original course."

Their course looked like this:

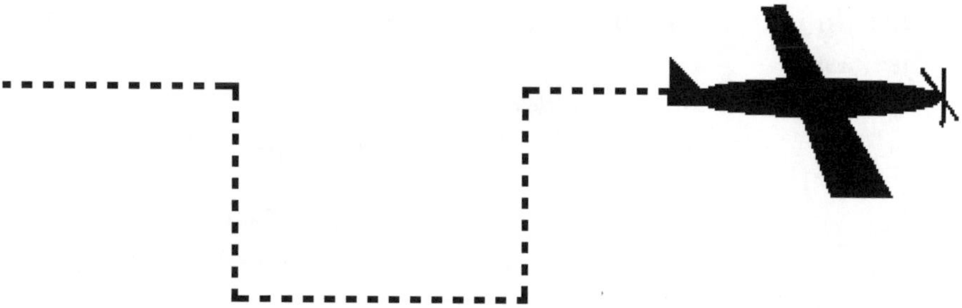

"Joe," Bob said to his co-pilot, "take over here for a minute, will you? I've got to see what that idiot behind us has done this time."

Bob unstrapped and walked back to the navigator's station.

"Why the hell did we do that?"

"I'm sorry," said Paul. "I was eating spaghetti from my thermos here and I dropped some right ahead of us in our flight path." He pointed to a small blob of spaghetti on the map in front of him. "I didn't want us to have an accident. So I flew us around it!"

***

The three of them landed in Algiers one time with a load of cargo from the States. They were going to be "deadheading" (flying with no cargo) back to the States.

"How long are we going to be on the ground here?" asked Paul.

"About four hours," Bob said. "Better get some rest."

"That's all right," Paul replied. "I've got something to do."

Paul started off. "Where you going?" Joe asked.

"To the Casbah!"

Three hours later a truck pulled up to the plane. Paul got out. In the back of the truck were two bales of hay and a small jackass!

"What the hell is *that*?"

"Mary (Paul's wife) asked me to get her a pet here," said Paul. "This is it!"

"We can't take a jackass on the plane!" shouted Bob.

"Sure we can." said Paul. "We're going back light, ain't we? Don't worry. I'll clean up the mess, if it makes any."

Paul was driving an old MG. When they got back to New York, Paul somehow stuffed the little jackass into the passenger seat of the MG. He gathered six tickets on the drive across New York City to his rural home in New Jersey. But he always claimed the look on Mary's face made the whole effort worthwhile.

***

Sometimes when Bob was up at Roi, sitting out a mission, control would ask him to fly a small boat sweep of the area, or check on what *Brand-X* was doing.

Anyway, I occasionally got the chance to ride along on these sweeps. Though nothing extraordinary happened on these flights, I always found them pleasurable and relaxing. For all he's been though, I think Bob did too.

Range Rats

Now, having just recounted Bob C's stories, some people may think they don't belong in a book on Kwajalein because they didn't happen there.

They belong all right. Let me tell you why.

Those of us who wear the title "range rat" do so willingly and with some measure of pride. In the grand tapestry of the United States we are not many, but still a significant part of the interface between the U.S. and the rest of the world. To understand this, you have to understand that natives of other countries around the world seldom see Americans.

The largest single group of Americans abroad is military. Their presence is usually temporary. They reside on bases, isolated from the indigenous peoples they are among. To the natives, they are all aliens, and many perceive them as enemies.

The second largest group of Americans is tourists. There are both good and bad things about American tourists.

The bad thing is that they are transient and just passing through. Everthing else are positive points: they grease their way with American dollars, they create jobs and they are naïve (read: suckers). Most of them don't haggle over prices. This may be their trip of a lifetime and they don't want to spend it arguing. This has resulted in the establishment of a two tier pricing system—one for "us," and a higher one for the tourists. After all, few of them understand the exchange rates anyway.

In many countries there is a thriving cottage industry in instant antiques. American tourists will buy anything they can carry or mail "to show the folks back home." In many countries, tourism is the biggest industry there is.

Next come businessmen and industrialists. Per capita they are probably the people of most economic importance around the world. Their intention is to exploit the least expensive labor markets to produce the goods they sell. These people will build a \$1 million plant in an area where \$1 or \$2 an hour is the best wage the locals can hope for. Missionaries, medical people and "range rats" make up the final major group of "Overseas American." Each of these groups has their own agendas. The thing that's different about them is that they all plan to stay for awhile. Most of them learn the local languages because they interact with the locals more closely than any other Americans.

I remember Elton and Alice B. He ran a Protestant church on Ebeye. She wrote the first Marshallese-English dictionary and her magnum opus was the translation of the King James Bible into Marshallese.

Father H. had a brass band down at Majuro that was straight out of "The Music Man." He had a tin ear and couldn't play any instruments himself. But his band traveled all over the Pacific and the U.S. These folks did the work of God as their various denominations interpreted it.

Some Americans with medical training choose to quit the rat race in the States and work in parts of the world where the need is greatest.

Range rats take their skills and experience wherever there is work to be done. Local living conditions matter little to them as long as the pay is right.

An Uninvited Guest

Bob's stories may not have happened on Kwaj, but that doesn't mean strange airplane-related events were foreign to the atoll.

One time, someone paid a visit.

To quote Snoopy, "It was a dark and stormy night."

About 1:30 in the morning John S. walked out of the old power plant. His destination was the terminal building kitty-corner across the intersection, not 100 yards away. He was headed there to get a candy bar out of the vending machine in the hall.

It was raining and he was in a hurry to get across the street onto the porch at the security end of the building when something caught his attention.

It was an airplane. An old one. A man was tying it down between the north end of the terminal and the fire department. No one else was in the area.

John ran to the Security office where Pete LH was on duty. Pete didn't know anything about the plane.

Nor did the roving patrol. Nor did the fire department that handled aircraft communications for the island.

Pete spread the alarm, and folks came streaming out to see what was going on.

It was an astounding sight!

There was an antique twin engine Lockheed Electra, vintage 1935, cloth covered!

The pilot was an elderly Japanese man who spoke no English.

Fortunately, we had several Japanese-speaking Americans from Hawaii who could translate for him. One of them was roused and came to our rescue.

The pilot said he was seventy-eight years old.

He said he was ferrying the aircraft to Hawaii and got lost in the storm. He said he was running out of gas, and had just about given up hope when he spotted our beacon, and then the runway lights at Roi. So he landed.

I was awakened to bring a folding bed to Security so they could keep an eye on him until morning.

The next morning the plane was thoroughly inspected by everyone who could dream up an excuse to do so. No bombs. No spy cameras.

The conclusion was finally reached that the pilot was no threat to national security. And it was decided to move the plane to Kwaj where the aviation department could more adequately check it out.

The pilot had told the truth. He didn't have enough gas left to fly from Roi to Kwaj. We had to fly several drums of AV-gas from Kwaj just to refuel him for that flight. I never heard anything more about him after he left Roi.

I'm just glad we were there for him that dark and stormy night.

Lindy R's Close Call

Here's a story about another close call in the air, involving a retired Air Force pilot named Lindy R. I can't say when Lindy and his wife Gladys got to Kwaj, since they were there before I arrived. I do know that about one year before he retired (again), he celebrated his 17,000th takeoff and landing, just at Kwajalein Atoll! He was good!

Which reminds me of a conversation I had one day on a flight to Kwaj from Roi. Lindy had been flying an old C-47, and had a landing gear problem on his approach to Kwaj. The light that confirmed the landing gear was down and locked indicated that it wasn't. So the Kwaj Fire Department foamed the runway, just in case.

In the event, the landing went smoothly. It turned out that the switch that turned the indicator light green had broken.

Because the incident included the precautionary foaming of the runway, it was defined as a "near accident" that required an Air Force investigation.

The time was a few days after Lindy's "near accident."

Sitting next to me was an Air Force Major. He was muttering to himself.

"Why me? Why the hell did they send me? What am I supposed to say?"

"Excuse me?"

"Oh. Pardon me. I'm from Hickam. I've been sent down here to investigate the 'near accident' at Kwaj the other day. Now I'm supposed to go tell Mr. R. what he did wrong. And he didn't do anything wrong! Look. I've got just over 600 hours flying—mostly in jets. Mr. R. has over 28,000 hours flying recips (or airplanes with propellers)! And I'm supposed to dress him down? Why *me*?"

I certainly didn't envy that Major!

Amelia Earhart's Map Case

As strange as those last two stories are, an even more curious thing related to planes happened on Kwaj. But first, I must explain the situation.

By the time of the *Four Winds* debacle I'd been at Kwaj one year and had a pretty good handle on my job, so I was casting around for something else to get into.

I heard that the Aloha Council of the Boy Scouts was looking for a neighborhood commissioner for Kwaj. I volunteered.

There already was a scout troop on Kwaj.

What the Council really wanted, they said, was someone to see about introducing the Scouting program amongst the Marshallese. In summary, we started two troops on Ebeye and one on Majuro.

Let me illustrate some of the problems we ran into.

To accelerate interest in the program, the Council let us know that they had reserved ten places for Marshallese Scouts at camp Pupukea on Oahu. They sent us ten applications.

Competition for the ten places was lively, to say the least. But, in due course, ten kids were selected to go to Hawaii. They had to get the applications filled out.

Now those applications were long and required that the applicant sign his name in three different places on the form. In the end, we got a total of twenty-seven different names!

What this really reflected was problems the Marshallese were having in changing from a matriarchal system to a patriarchal one, and how that affected the Marshalleses' family names.

But the Council didn't know that.

"What! We can't take twenty-seven kids!"

That misunderstanding was resolved and ten kids went to Pupukea for two weeks.

Then they tried to get back to Ebeye.

There were no regular commercial flights into Kwaj in those years. It was MAC (Military Airlift Command) or nothing. In the event, several of the boys wound up spending as much as a month in Hawaii waiting for a seat on a MAC flight back to the islands. During their waiting they were hosted by a retired Coast Guard Admiral, to whom great kudos!

Organizational meeting for the program on Ebeye took place after work and often lasted until just after 9:00 at night. That meant I had to wait for the 11:00 boat back to Kwaj.

And therein lies the genesis of a very remarkable conversation I had with an old man in 1965. Onisimus C., my co-worker and translator, was always trying to find things for me to do to fill the intervening hours.

One night he said to me, "There's an old man here you might like to talk to. He was born on Likiep, but he's lived most of his life here on Ebeye. He knows a lot of the history here." Onisimus took me to him and introduced me.

During the course of our conversation I asked him, "When was the first time you saw Americans?"

"Before the war."

Before the war? I wondered. *That's strange. Americans weren't allowed out here before the war.*

"How long before the war?"

"Five years."

Five years? Let's see. That would make it 1936.

"What happened?"

"A big airplane came down on the ocean side."

"A big plane. You mean four engines?"

"No. Two."

"What happened?"

"Two people got out. A man and a woman. They stood on the wing."

"Then what happened?"

"The captain made me take my boat and go get them."

"The captain?"

"The Japanese officer."

"Did you talk to them?"

"No. The captain told me not to. He said they were spies."

"What happened then?"

"The captain took them away. They got in a boat and went north."

"Can you show me where the plane came down?"

"Sure."

The old man took Onisimus and me to the southeast corner of Ebeye, right where the perimeter road turns north. On the island side of that corner were two A-frame houses sitting parallel to one another. Midway between them were four coconut palms in an east-west row.

"The airplane was exactly in line with those trees."

"How far out?"

"About a hundred yards from the edge."

About that time we heard the last boat from Kwaj approaching, and had to run back to the pier. Nothing about the conversation rang any bells with me, and I soon forgot it.

Until 1968 when I transferred to Roi.

Frank S. was the island manager at the time. He had retired as a light colonel from the Army Corps of Engineers. I must tell you that his seventeen-year stay in the position of island manager is probably the only thing that kept the Army from posting some active duty person to Roi.

Frank and his wife Mabel lived on Kwaj that whole time, but he spent several nights a week on Roi. He was so much a part of the island that he seemed to many like some force of nature there.

We were talking one day, and the subject drifted into the history of the place. And that brought back to my mind my conversation with the old man on Ebeye. I told Frank the story.

"Well! That explains it!"

"Explains what?"

"Where the plane came down!"

"You lost me."

"Come here. I want to show you something."

He reached into his desk drawer and brought out a letter.

"I've been corresponding with this man for years. Most of the letter wouldn't interest you, but you should read this part, starting here."

I read.

The letter was from a retired Navy commander.

It read, "During the war I was with Naval Intelligence. During Operation Flintlock I was assigned to come ashore there at Roi and look for any sign of the transit of Amelia Earhart or Fred Noonan. In the back corner of the burned out main hangar, under a pile of trash, I found a blue leatherette map case. It was empty. All the maps had been removed. But the cover of the map case was embossed, in gold, with the letters AE! In accordance with instructions, I turned it over to my superiors."

Burned-out hangar where the map case was found. Photo from *The Marshalls: Increasing the Tempo*.

Frank said that the commander and he were both satisfied that the map case had indeed belonged to Amelia. But neither of them, he said, could figure out where the airplane was.

I don't know whether she did have a blue leatherette map case, but his word was good enough for me. I was galvanized!

As soon as I could, I went back over to Ebeye. I had to get more details and the answers to a couple of crucial questions.

The old man had said that the plane had landed "about 100 yards off the edge." I didn't know whether he meant off the edge of the island, or off the edge of the reef. It made a difference.

If the 100 yards were from the edge of the island, it would have put the plane right at the edge of the reef. Where it might still be.

On the other hand, if the 100 yards were from the edge of the reef, the plane could have pancaked on the ocean with 1,000 feet of water under it.

In either event, the ocean currents, which are strong there, may have swept the plane some distance south along the reef toward Kwaj.

I had to find out what edge the old man was referring to.

I went back to Ebeye to find out.

"Is the old man here?"

"No. He went back to Likiep to die."

There was only one thing left that I could think of to try.

I went to the Army and told them my story. "Would it be possible," I asked, "to get the recovery barge, or even the little yellow recovery sub to check out the edge of the reef from the south end of Ebeye toward Kwaj?"

"We wouldn't touch that with a ten foot pole!" I was told. "And, if you want to keep working here, quit asking questions about that subject! Just forget it."

I stopped asking questions, at least where they might be heard by Army ears.

That is not the end of the story.

During my years at Roi, I became acquainted with a number of the Marshallese who lived on Ennibur. Several of the older ones recounted a story that averaged out to this:

"When I was a child I sometimes went with my mother, or father, to Roi. This was during Japanese times, and we weren't permitted to live there. But my mother worked in the officer's mess washing dishes and cleaning. So I got to go along once in awhile. It was a great adventure.

"One day in 1937 we were walking past the jail, and I saw a white woman with short, light brown hair. She was wearing a working suit. She was holding on to the bars of the jail window, looking out at us. The next time I went there she was gone. Somebody told me the Japanese put her on a plane and took her to Saipan."

The building is still there, next to the Japanese radar station on Namur. I dubbed the building the "Amelia Arms."

As of April 2003 I can say that at least three of those Marshallese, two old ladies and an old man, were still alive on Ennibur.

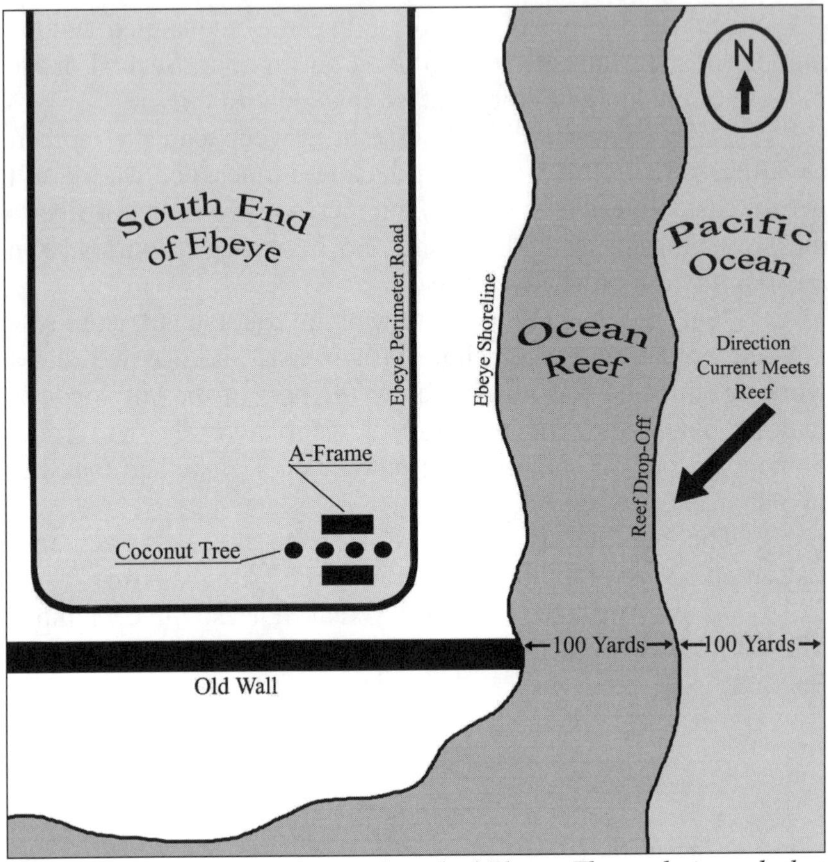

A sketch map depicting the south end of Ebeye. The scale is such that from 'Echo' Pier on Kwaj to the Ebeye Pier, the distance is approximately three miles.

37mm gun bunker bulldozed to the shore for use as riprap.
Photos by Pam R.

Beach bunker on northeast corner of Roi

Chapter 26

Kwaj's Dangers and Realities

EOD

Even if I did manage to locate Amelia's plane, it would have been too damaged to notice with the naked eye on the ocean floor. Yet some relics from WWII stayed as vital as the day they were produced. Sadly, this mostly concerns explosive ordinance, hidden deep (and not so deep) all along the atoll.

From the site orientation required of all newcomers to Kwajalein: "Watch where you step. If you see anything that looks like a bomb or a bullet or an artillery shell, *Leave it alone. Report it.*"

That admonition applied and applies to everyone on Kwajalein Atoll: Marshallese, Americans, visitors, adults, children—everyone!

Looking at the islands today, you see sun-drenched vistas of a golf course and tropical vegetation, paved roads, homes and white domes covering technical installations, tall antennas sprouting all over the place, and much more.

It's easy to forget that there's hardly a square foot of the islands we live and work on that wasn't battered, gouged, and churned by devices meant to kill and maim.

Navy planes dropped 2,400 tons of bombs on Roi-Namur alone in the run up to invasion. Hundreds more tons of rockets, napalm and machine gun ammunition were directed at the enemy by strafing aircraft. Navy warships delivered tens of thousands of rounds of artillery—everything from twenty millimeter to fourteen inch or larger weighing up to a ton apiece at Roi-Namur. And that was before the first Marine landed!

Enemy ammunition bunkers exploded spewing more tons of explosives out to sea and all over the islands. As the battle progressed, land based artillery struck in rolling barrages ahead of our advancing troops.

After the immediate fighting stopped we quickly built up huge ammunition dumps of our own on Roi-Namur.

On the night of the 12th of February, 1944, six Japanese bombers flew on a token raid from Truk. Quite by chance they struck two of those dumps. The planes were over Roi for less than three minutes. The fires and explosions continued for more than five hours! The result was counted in war annals as the second largest loss of war material suffered from enemy action by the United States during World War II, surpassed only by the devastation at Pearl Harbor. American casualties totaled more than from the invasion itself. Few were killed, many were injured.

Cleanup began on the 1st of February, even as the fighting continued. It was led by EOD (Explosive Ordinance Disposal) teams and the Seabees (Construction Battalions).

Today, sixty years later, the cleanup continues under the auspices of EOD. Two tracks are followed by EOD for disposing of unexploded ordinance there.

The most usual one is disposal off shore. On this track the unexploded material is collected in some safe area until there is enough to warrant a boat trip. When the seas are calm and the load sufficient, it is taken by boat a mile or so offshore and dropped into several thousand feet of water, one piece at a time.

The second track is taken when an item is deemed too dangerous to process in the method described above.

When an item is too heavy, too sensitive, or too bulky to be safely handled aboard a boat, it is destroyed with explosives. This requires the construction of a three-sided berm made of beach sand. It may be as high as twenty feet. At Roi-Namur it is situated on the beach at the farthest point of the island with the opening of the berm facing the ocean. The item is carefully placed within this berm so that any blast would be directed away from the island. It is wrapped with primacord or C4 plastic explosive which is detonated by remote control. The object of this exercise is to cut the item apart and burn its contents. This burn can go two ways.

In a low order burn the explosive catches fire and burns furiously for a few seconds until it is consumed. In a high order burn there is an actual explosion which can shake windows for several miles. When this happens the island is protected by the berm.

Dangerous work. EOD is up to it.

Let me recount some events which I took part in, witnessed, or heard about over the years.

***

An acquaintance at Roi was playing with a very small bullet, not the whole cartridge. It was a Japanese .27 caliber. It went off in his hand and he lost about one quarter of an inch of the tip of his left index finger.

***

Ray B. was running a bulldozer on Namur one day. He hit an unexploded mortar round that detonated with burning white phosphorous. Fortunately for Ray, the blade of the dozer protected him completely from the explosion.

***

As billeting supervisor on Roi during the '70s, I had oversight of seventeen custodians who had to clean buildings in the administrative, billeting, retail and recreation areas. One of these was the gymnasium which was located in the row of FOM buildings across the street from the Roi terminal. It's not there today. In its place are a pavilion and a plant nursery.

What happened to the gym?

When it was constructed, excavation was deep enough to put in footers and to pour a concrete floor. They should have dug deeper.

No one can be sure whether it was a bomb, an artillery shell, or a mine. Something exploded. For years it had lain buried and undetected just below the excavation level below the building's floor. One noon it went off, taking out about half of the building. Fortunately, everyone was at lunch and there were no casualties.

***

I walked into Ajax BQ one day and knocked on a door. Terry, the occupant, had asked me to come over. He invited me in.

On his desk was the fuse to a Japanese five inch artillery round. Bright and shiny, it looked brand new. It even had its two safety pins in it. He had dug it up out by the five inch guns which are such a tourist attraction these days.

He'd covered it with vinegar for about three weeks. Now it looked like a new penny.

I was scared out of my wits.

He sat there with a hammer and chisel, tapping on the nose of the fuse, trying to loosen the threads so he could unscrew it!

"*Stop*!"

"Huh? Why?"

"*Back away! Don't touch it!*"

He backed away.

"What the hell are you doing?"

"What's it look like? I'm taking it apart so's I can clean the shit out of it and send it home. It'll make a cool paper weight for my desk."

"Don't you know what that is?"

"Sure. It's a Japanese thingamajig! See the writing on it? That's why I asked you to come over. Can you read that stuff?"

"Terry, go over to the couch. Lay your tools on the coffee table. Sit down. And listen to me."

He did.

"Weren't you ever in the Army?"

"No. I got a deferment as an engineering student so I wouldn't have to go to Nam."

"Okay. Listen. I'm going to tell you what you've been pounding on. It's the nose fuse to a Japanese five inch artillery round. It's live. There's enough explosive in there to blow the roof and all four walls out of this room!"

He turned a little pale. "Yeah?"

"Yeah. Besides that it's an initiator. It's very sensitive to shock. When it goes off it sends fire down a diffuser tube to set off the main charge and explode the whole shell. Not only that, but the "shit" you wanted to clean out is Picric Acid. It's nasty stuff, much nastier than we used. One of the problems with it is that as it sits it starts to break down and fluid from it leaches into the threads of that thing and crystallizes. Any friction will set it off. And it's been sitting for almost thirty years!"

"Oh." Terry was even paler now. "I never was very good in Chemistry."

"We've got to get this thing out of here. *Now!* Wait here."

I went down the hall to the janitor's closet and got a roll of bubble wrap. When I got back to Terry's room he was still on the couch, shaking. We wrapped the fuse in bubble wrap about a foot thick.

Then I did one of the dumbest things I've ever done. I put the package in my truck and we took it to Security.

Pete LH was at the desk.

He looked up. “What dat?”

“It’s a fuse.”

“Get Dat Outta Here!”

I carried the package across the street to an empty spot and gingerly laid it down. Pete brought out a Danger sign which we placed over the package. He called EOD.

The next morning the EOD team came up from Kwaj to prepare it for deep sixing.

Terry was there. “Can you guys fix that thing so I can send it home?”

“*Hell no*!”

***

One time, one of the heavy equipment operators was trenching with a backhoe near the Outrigger Club (once known as Atlas BQ) when his bucket hit something metallic. It was a “Long Lance” torpedo warhead. We had to evacuate most of the housing area until EOD took it away for disposal. Two more Long Lance torpedoes were uncovered on Roi right next to the third tee on the golf course. Grounds keepers had been mowing within half an inch over them for decades. EOD extracted them and play resumed.

TRADEX radar had been up and running about six years when some guys trenched right against the foundation to lay in some conduit. Within a foot of the foundation they uncovered an unexploded 1,000-pound bomb! If that had gone off TRADEX would have been history.

***

During one of my absences from Roi a Marshallese family was picnicking on their land on second island. They had a cooking fire going on the lagoon beach. Two kids were killed and an adult was severely injured when two 75mm shells buried in the sand under the fire went off due to the heat of the fire.

***

World War II has not yet claimed its last victim. Sadly, at Roi, its fatal history continues.

Speedball, Olympus, Illeginni, and Meck: Island Launch Sites

It's ironic how a place that's built for the designing of deadly weapons is plagued by them. But the difference between the leftover WWII explosives and the rockets we produced and tested was that our missiles weren't intended to kill, just to collect data. Over the years, Kwajalein Atoll has built up an extensive library all about rocket science, but this information wouldn't have come so readily if we had only one or two launch sites instead of the four on the atoll—Speedball on Roi, Mount Olympus on Kwaj, Illeginni on Illeginni, and nearly the whole of Meck Island.

I left Kwajalein in November of 1973 to take the position of Base Support Services Manager on an Air Force contract at Canton, in the Phoenix Islands. I had a staff of 120 plus personnel and was responsible for supporting all operations except administration, finance, supply, and engineering. I had four division supervisors in billeting, retail services, recreation, food services, and laundry. We ran a twenty-four hour a day radio station, published a daily newspaper, ran the hospital and fire station, the club and numerous recreational facilities such as the gym, golf course, movies, post office (one of my hats was postmaster), marina and marine department, etc. We also supported, as necessary, Air Force installations on Hull and Enderberry Islands in the Phoenix group.

At the end of 1974 the Air Force decided to close Canton and move its major radar to Kwajalein.

Canton had been used extensively during WWII and later as a tracking station during the Mercury and Gemini phases of the Apollo Moon Landing Program. However, major tracking there ended with the conclusion of the Gemini program, and during the year plus that I was there, only one mission was tracked. It was too expensive to keep the installation open for only one mission a year. Hence the Air Force decision.

I took a break of a year and some, then returned to Kwajalein.

By the time I returned to Kwaj, Illeginni had been built up on a major program. Only four major launches had occurred there, and then the island was closed. By the time I first saw it in 1977, Illeginni's facilities were already returning to the jungle cover the island had been when I left in 1974.

The project conducted at Illeginni was considered important at the time, but once concluded, funding was dropped. If nothing else, this illustrates the U.S. response to developments in the Soviet missile program during the Cold War.

***

Speedball sits on a dump. It's the closed, fenced-in area on the northwest corner of Roi. All of that part of the island consists of landfill left over from WWII. Between the ocean-facing part of the fence around Speedball and the shoreline is a strip just wide enough for a one-lane perimeter road. Oceanside of that road used to be one of my favorite scavenger-hunting places on all of Roi.

This was because of the way the Navy disposed of stuff there. Their practice seems to have been to dump trash on the reef all day, and burn it once a day. I suspect that they used gasoline to get the fire going each time, and that the dump burned until the next incoming tide put the fire out. Evidence for that scenario was in the form of some railroad tie size timbers sticking up at random angles. Around each were a series of char rings where burning had occurred, separated by rings of unburned wood.

When I returned to Roi in 1997 all of "the happy hunting ground" was riprapped over to prevent beach erosion. That's progress, I guess.

But back to Speedball. Speedball is a launch site. One 15-K launch rail remains of the two originally in use in the early days.

Speedball itself was a sort of poor man's ICBM. Based on the Nike Hydac rocket, it was designed to power out of the atmosphere and plow back in, simulating a re-entering ICBM payload. This gave the PRESS sensors a way to approximate, at much lower cost, the electrical signatures of the real thing fired from Vandenberg. You could fire several Hydacs for what one Atlas cost.

The Speedball launchings had concluded by the time I became aware of them. However, other programs came in from time to time to use the launch facilities. "Have Jeep" came out there repeatedly over the years. I never was sure what the objectives of their program were. Even though my clearance was sufficient, my "need to know" wasn't. The Army did not encourage curiosity about such matters.

DOT was another program there. I did know something about that because I had to supply old mattresses.

I can't put an exact time frame on the DOT program, but it had to be after the summer of 1968. That's when I moved to Roi.

DOT, as I recall, stood for Designating Optical Tracker.

The thinking behind the program went something like this.

Rockets, like bullets, spend most of their time coasting. Once the bullet leaves the barrel of a gun, the gases pushing it no longer count. All the aiming has to be done while the bullet is being accelerated down the gun's barrel. A bullet never travels faster than it is going at the instant it leaves the muzzle of the gun. Its speed at that point is called its "muzzle velocity." From that point on it's coasting. There are only two forces acting on the bullet for the rest of its flight: the friction of the air it is pushing through and gravity.

Air friction heats up the bullet as it plows by, exactly as much as the bullet heats the air. All this heating up of things bleeds kinetic energy and changes it to thermal energy. And the bullet slows down, even as it gets warmer.

All the while gravity is trying to pull the bullet down.

The combination of these forces acting on the bullet turns its flight path from an absolutely straight line into a complex, but absolutely predictable curve. This is called the bullet's "ballistic trajectory." That's where the "ballistic" in ballistic missile comes from.

Sir Isaac Newton, early in the Eighteenth Century, formulated the Law of Gravity and invented a whole new form of mathematics called differential calculus to make such curves predictable.

This was of immense interest to armies all over the world. For the first time they could be sure that their shells hit what they aimed at. Of course, each range required its own calculations—sometimes hundreds of them. Fortunately, soldiers at the guns didn't have to make these calculations. Mathematicians were hired to make charts summarizing the calculations. Once these charts had been made, all the artilleryman had to do was read the bottom line—so to speak.

But humans, mathematicians included, are vulnerable to error. So people began to build mechanical devices to make these calculations. They were called "difference engines" and were, in fact, some of the earliest computers ever made.

I, as always, digress.

DOT was an optical tracking device all right, but not the "you and I see" optics. It detected and tracked in the infrared part of the spectrum. These are frequencies on the spectrum just below what we humans call light. Many insects can sense those frequencies, as can some larger animals.

They are essentially heat signatures. Heat signatures stand out in the near absolute zero cold outside the Earth's atmosphere. The hotter they are, the more they stand out.

And rockets are hot! Their skins, and particularly their front ends, have been heated by air friction as they accelerated through the atmosphere toward space. But their exhaust plumes are even hotter! While their motors are burning to accelerate the rocket, prodigious quantities of extremely hot gasses are being blasted out the rear, making the heat visible from thousands of miles away.

This was the plan.

They built a sensor that could detect heat sources in space and track them with great accuracy, recording everything it "saw." To see anything at all the sensor had to have a window to look through.

Aluminum, as in rocket nose cone, doesn't make a very good "window." Neither does clear plastic. It can't take the shock of launch or the heat. It melts.

Nor does glass. It filters out the radiation frequencies being sought.

What might work?

A diamond!

But it had to be big! And flat!

Somehow, somewhere, they acquired the world's largest industrial diamond. It wasn't gem quality, quite. But it was good enough. They put just two facets on it, absolutely parallel and, voila! A "window."

It was put into the nose cone and the sensor inside was oriented to "look" through it. Now the whole package had to be sent over 200 miles straight up.

To do this, they assembled a two-stage rocket. Actually, they built three of those rockets. They were only going to have one chance with the diamond windowed sensor, and they wanted to be sure everything went perfectly before they chanced the real McCoy. The second stage was connected to the booster with explosive bolts that would be triggered by a signal from the second stage just before it ignited. This signal was sent through a thin wire just long enough to cross the junction between the two stages. It lay on the rocket's surface.

Two of the rockets had dummy payloads. And these payloads were the lightest that had ever been launched atop that particular combination of rocket motors.

When the first practice rocket was shot, acceleration was much higher than had been anticipated, and something went very wrong. The booster failed to separate from the second stage.

Our recovery boat was standing by just offshore. So was *Brand-X*, the Russian trawler. We got to splash down first.

Analysis showed that wind shear had ripped off the signal wire right where it came out of the second stage. Everyone figured that a small aluminum wind deflector would solve the problem.

The engineers went to the Global welder, Clarence P. to see if he could do the job. He could.

The second practice round was already on the second launcher. Time was of the essence. Would Clarence be willing to weld this little piece on the rocket where it was? He would be.

Speedball was cleared of all personnel except Mr. P. It was a two-minute job. Number two worked perfectly.

But the Russians had a ship in the splash down area.

Knowing that they were particularly interested in the DOT program made us on the good guys' side antsy. (My personal opinion is that they had that diamond on loan, and had promised to return it, if they could.)

What to do?

Call in the Navy! Call in the Marines! Call in the helicopter gunships!

They all came to the party!

The helicopters were based on Roi. They were fitted with long-range tanks. Two of them had a special attachment. Each held one end of a long cable, in the center of which was a special cargo net. The plan was to secure the re-entry vehicle in the net so that it could be carried horizontally (I don't know why) back to Roi.

I was told to get a dozen old mattresses and stack them two by two, six high, to make a resting place for the payload while it was flushed with fresh water.

Timing for the operation was complex. The DOT shot had to be approaching apogee (high point) and properly oriented just as the ICBM was launched from Vandenberg. It was to observe the powered portion of the ICBM launch and as much of the rest of the flight as possible before it re-entered the atmosphere itself.

There were Russians in the landing area. Someone told me that they had scuba teams with inflatable rubber boats in the water.

So did we.

The landing area was in international waters. So we couldn't really force them away. On the other hand, we had no intention of letting them snag the prize.

Launch day came. The helicopters left. The rockets flew.

Luckily for us, our boats snagged the prize first. In due course the helicopters returned, gunships escorting the tethered pair. The payload was very gently laid atop the pile of mattresses. Marines formed a guard perimeter around the payload. And they guarded it for forty-eight hours. For two days straight the techs flushed it with fresh water from the lens well. It had taken on some salt water when it splashed down, and they wanted to be certain there was no trace of that left before they took it away.

I never heard anyone say whether it did what they wanted. But there were a lot of TDY types smiling for the next couple of days.

***

Launching rockets is always a dangerous business. In the early days of the range it was even more so. Remember, we were dealing with research and development then. Early rockets ran on toxic, explosive fuels, which is why the assembly and launch facilities had to be situated as far from island residential populations as possible—and downwind as well. Assembly buildings were very close to launchers and oriented so that, if an explosion occurred, blast effects and debris would be directed out over open water or straight up.

Safety was always the first order of business. Everything in the launch buildings was electrically grounded, including the personnel (they were wired to the grounding system to prevent any chance of an errant static buildup or spark)! Area evacuation and taking cover were typical on launch days. Even so, occasionally a rocket would go bananas at launch. Its altitude control or navigation system could fail and it became instantly necessary to abort a mission. This usually involved the detonation of the rocket. Debris would rain down everywhere, hence the requirement that all personnel be under a sheltering roof at liftoff or re-entry time.

Ideally, assembly buildings and launch cells would have been built underground. On these coral islands that was not practical, since to be underground was to be underwater. So the buildings were built on the surface and covered with dredged sand from the lagoon. This process created "launch hills" on the islands.

There have been many launch facilities built at Kwajalein Missile Range, used for several purposes. The first were probably at Kwaj and Roi and were used for firing weather-sounding rockets.

Roi has Speedball launch site; Kwaj has Mount Olympus. I can't say which was operational first. Both were active by the time I arrived to the atoll in May of 1964. That was while the Navy was still in charge of Kwaj.

Speedball launch site was, I believe, built under Air Force auspices in conjunction with the TRADEX radar. Since TRADEX went online in 1962, perhaps Speedball did as well. Its original purpose was to provide simulated ICBM targets for TRADEX.

The first rockets I was aware of being fired from Mount Olympus were Spartan and Sprint. These two rockets were a complementary pair evolving out of the Army's Nike missile family of anti-aircraft interceptor rockets. Spartan was a large, long-range interceptor able to reach out some 450 miles to intercept ICBMs while they were still in space. Sprint was a short-range, but very fast interceptor, referred to as a "point defense" weapon. It was hoped that it could intercept anything that got past Spartan. Together, they would form a two-layer shield. Sprint's shortcoming was its short range. It could only reach some 80,000 feet, well into the re-entry phase of an ICBM's trip to its target. Offsetting this was its extreme speed. It could get up there in a matter of a few seconds from launch. Both were said to be capable of carrying nuclear warheads, though any fired from Kwajalein had only instrumentation packages on board.

The very limited range of Sprint prompted the development of another launch site north of Kwaj and south of Roi, one that was in the very middle of the re-entry corridor. Meck Island fit the bill.

Meck Island is about twenty miles north of Kwaj, and it is the island where most of the major rocket launching facilities for the range wound up.

During intercept missions and preparation times for those missions, things could get very busy on Meck. It even had its own runway.

That runway was a problem. In the first place it took up about half of the island's width and almost all of its length. Yet it was only 1,700 feet long (about five and one half football fields)! In the second place the runway ran north/south and the trade winds crossed it at almost right angles all the time. Getting in and out of Meck in a plane was, to say the least, an adventure.

To land, you had to approach the runway from the lagoon side and at the last second crab sharply to line up with the runway. Then you had better plant the plane firmly on the runway in the first 100 feet or so, or you'd have a real problem stopping in time.

Taking off was almost as tricky. You had to go to the same end of the runway as you landed and turn so that the landing gear was on the first few feet of the runway, with the tail of the plane sticking out over the end of the island. Then you'd lock your brakes and rev the engines to absolute maximum power. The instant your wheels left the ground, you had to veer sharply right to avoid being blown into the launch hill. That could spoil your whole day! Nevertheless, our pilots flew twenty-seven flights a day into Meck, day and night, for years. That kind of flying is very tough on planes, flight crews, and passengers.

The only plane that could handle it was the thirty passenger/cargo Army C-7. Tough, tough plane!

Meck was one of the main reasons helicopters were introduced at Kwaj. They solved the problem of getting people to and from the outer islands. But they only became available out there as the Vietnam War wound down.

Before that the only planes we had were recips. Of course the jet aircraft were faster, but sometimes speed is hard to come by, even when dealing with rockets.

***

The announcement didn't pull any punches: "Attention, all personnel. What we do here is classified. Many of you have been observed taking private pictures and films of the firings from Mount Olympus!" (These were the days of the "Spartan" long range interceptor shots from Kwajalein—before the metals technology was advanced enough to build the "Sprint" terminal defense interceptor.) "In the future any unauthorized films will be confiscated, and the persons taking them will be severely reprimanded!"

This, of course, didn't deter *Brand-X* from getting full camera coverage.

But that was beside the point.

There were several camera towers scattered around Kwajalein to do the authorized filming, and like the ad said, discretion was encouraged.

One of these was right next to my furniture warehouse. We could hear the speakers in the towers, though we couldn't see the cameras themselves.

It was the practice in those days to turn the cameras on to high speed at T-20 in the countdown to a firing. On high speed the cameras ran through film at a great rate.

The announcement had come out two days before the next scheduled firing. Launch day arrived.

The countdown commenced.

At T-20 the cameras went to high speed.

At T-15 the speakers said, "Hold! We are at T-15 and holding. Duration of the hold is expected to be fifteen."

All the camera crews took that to mean they had fifteen minutes.

The film in the cameras had been severely reduced.

Replacement spools were immediately at hand, and the operators decided to quickly swap out the used reels for full ones. This would only take a minute or two.

Fifteen seconds later the speakers said "On my mark, countdown will resume at T-15. Mark!"

In fifteen seconds the rocket launched.

None of the authorized cameras got it!

That evening the *Hourglass* printed the following:

"We know what we told you the other day. But we experienced a technical glitch. If there were anyone out there who did get pictures, would you please bring the film to the Joint Technical Operations building? No questions will be asked."

It was said that they got some very usable film of the shot.

Security

Despite the occasional lapse (such as with the pictures), security was strictly enforced. After all, there are many unique aspects to maintaining security at a place like Kwaj.

What goes on in the technical areas is always classified. Some things are so highly classified that even the general population is not aware of it.

Even access to Kwajalein is restricted. For most of the years I was there, people didn't just "drop in." There was no commercial aviation there, nor was there commercial shipping.

Access control began with the stateside companies who sent personnel to Kwajalein to work on the many projects that were always underway. In the case of the scientific research companies, many of their personnel already carried security clearances. All others underwent at least cursory checks to confirm citizenship, etc. In the event that their jobs might require them to enter secure areas, their background investigations were more comprehensive, detailed, and time consuming.

This meant that their departure to the job site was not delayed overmuch, only that they were denied access to closed areas on the range. Access was controlled by a badging system. A red bordered badge meant that if you were required to go into a secure area you must be signed in and accompanied by a cleared badge holder while you were doing the business that brought you there. Closed buildings could not be declared secure until all such red badge holders were out of them. Even within such buildings or areas there were varying access requirements. Depending on the sensitivity of the work being done, these ranged from Confidential to Top Secret or even higher.

I have been speaking of the sundry technical operations areas. In the community at large most areas were open to all residents and the occasional visitor who was on official business. It seemed there was always a stream of official visitors ranging from technical specialists to veterans who had served at Kwaj during WWII. U.S. Congressmen and their staff, foreign dignitaries, and even members of the Japanese War Memorial Commission came every couple of years to rededicate the graves of fallen family members or comrades.

Security and the Army were intimately involved in managing the flow and care of such persons and groups for the entire duration of their stay on the range.

As the "official unofficial" historian for Roi I was often called upon to escort such persons and groups for the "history tour" of the island. The tours were choreographed to the minute, my portion of it being the most malleable. Depending on the time some of them spent in technical briefings, and the dovetailing of scheduled and unscheduled aircraft to Roi, I might have them for anything from ten minutes to four hours or more. Sometimes my part of the tour was canceled completely due to time constraints. I'd never know until the last minute. This made it sort of tricky in balancing my presentation in order to give them all a sense of the history of the islands. But I guess I must have done all right with it. The Army kept calling on me, and when they did I was exempted from my regular assignment.

Security was the police force for the range. In addition to controlling access to the technical assets and to the islands themselves, another resonsibility was to insure that all personnel were in appropriate shelters when the range sensors went on high power.

All Security personnel had to be proficient with firearms, first aid, and emergency procedures for fire, crowd control, and the like. They were the ones who swept the islands to make sure no one was in areas where hazardous levels of RF radiation might exist when the radars were operating at high power.

Security was in constant contact with the fire department, range safety and all the other organizations that saw to the safety and welfare of island residents.

When Security personnel were on duty they had unusual levels of authority. If a guard told a general, or senator, or visiting congressional bigwig to wait for clearance, that individual had better respond as requested. Or else.

At the same time they had to be courteous and tactful.

Not that there was a great deal of crime on the range. After all, everyone who lived and worked there had undergone a background investigation before they were permitted to come on site.

The very first thing you were told after entry/exit control personnel greeted you on your arrival on site was that fighting was not allowed. According to regulations, any violation of this dictum would get you removed from the site at once. I've seen it happen, though not often. Such an event usually meant receiving a banning letter and the loss of your job, no matter who you were. And everyone there knew it.

Thievery had the same outcome. So did drug use.

Sound draconian? Perhaps by some standards today it would. But on the whole it made the community one of the most comfortable places to live that I have ever known.

***

Due to the high levels of radio frequency radiation in the neighborhood of sensors and the inherent dangers involved in firing rockets, all outside activity in the proximity of such facilities had to cease. The people engaged in any activity had to evacuate to safe places; in the case of Roi-Namur, the entire island of Namur was off limits to outside workers.

Joint nominals were run several times in detail before proceeding with the real thing.

Such practice and training was essential to assure that every man knew his part in the mission and conducted it precisely. For the Western Test Range as a whole each mission could cost $100 million or more. It was important that nobody goofed anything up and caused a sensor to go offline. When you ran three missions a week, as happened just prior to the Strategic Arms Limitation Treaty in 1972, Security was busier than almost anyone else. Whenever an RF Hazard was declared (during both joint nominals and the real mission) danger zones had to be cleared, roadblocks established, reef and ocean areas swept (by aviation) and so on. Sensor operators could not leave their consoles, sometimes for hours on end.

Meals had to be brought in.

Holds were often called due to problems somewhere on the range. These might last ten minutes or several hours, you never knew. Security had to cope with it all.

The higher frequency radars, such as MMW, could provide almost optical images due to their wavelengths (in MMW's case, 95 gigahertz). Once the signals began transmitting in these frequencies, optical instruments took over. These included telescopes, video cameras, and other visual recording equipment. If optics were involved during night missions, it was important that all outside lights anywhere on the islands were turned off so they wouldn't interfere. Security saw to that.

Impact areas had to be cleared when an ICBM was due in. These rockets were not armed, but the mere kinetic energy of their re-entry was equivalent to about 175 pounds of TNT. People could get hurt. For years Security had a marine contingent to see that such zones were cleared of boats and people.

When the radars were operating, even at low power, no vehicles with gasoline engines were allowed in the area. They used diesel engines. The sensors were so sensitive that spark plug coils in vehicles with gas engines could give unwanted interference. Security personnel addressed that too.

Of course there was regular patrol duty, checking locked buildings at night to be sure they were locked, vehicular traffic control, and the host of other duties regularly expected of police.

Security folks worked irregular hours and a lot of them. Consequently they were given less crowded quarters when they were available. This relative privacy was a part of the benefits package they were offered to work on the range. While not paid as much per hour as some other personnel, their annual incomes were very respectable for their profession.

For almost twenty years Security was one of the branches of the logistic support contractor. In time, the Army came to believe that this might be a source of conflict. So it separated out security and set up different contractors to handle it. These contractors were responsible only to the Army.

This seems to be a trend with services on the island, but hopefully it doesn't denote a general decline in quality.

Selective Medical Services

Take a look at my right arm here, just about an inch above the inside of the elbow. Do you see that very fine line? It's almost completely disappeared now. The scar is all that remains of an incision more than two inches long that intersected a major vein leading directly to the vena cava of my heart. This was done to remove a broken medical device that had previously been inserted just below the elbow for intravenous medication. I had worn it almost a month when the decision was made to remove it from its original insertion point. Being made of a very strong, flexible plastic, these things were not known to break. Something around 1 in 10,000 was defective in manufacture. That one was. And the piece closest to the heart was being pushed along even nearer to the heart by blood flow. It had to be removed.

Ultrasound was used to define the exact position of the broken end and guide Dr. P. to its precise location for the removal.

The operation went off without a hitch. The offending item was removed, the vein sutured, and the incision closed in a procedure done so well it would have drawn praise from the most expert of Dr. P's surgical confreres.

Here I was, fifty miles north of the west end of nowhere, with a medical emergency that required immediate attention. There, in place and operating smoothly, was a medical support system that could do the job.

The hospital at Kwaj and the dispensary at Roi were constructed by the Navy during WWII. Wherever Americans served around the world the U.S. government undertook to provide them with medical services up to par with what they might have expected to find in the States.

Wherever construction commences, there is the chance of injury. Wherever maintenance goes on there is the chance of injury. Wherever human activity occurs there is a chance of injury or illness.

In tropical areas sunburn can be a problem, and the tropical seawater itself is rife with living organisms. The slightest abrasion on coral or coral sand can blossom into horrific infection. Any puncture wounds will certainly do so. Immediate medical attention is not just advisable, it is absolutely essential.

Keeping people healthy and fit anywhere is a costly, complicated business. Doing it in extremely isolated situations is even more so.

Suffice it for our purposes to say that the provision for access to medical services is recognized at all levels of government in the United States and wherever the U.S. has people pursuing its objectives.

At Kwajalein the job is accomplished by the complex integration of activities by Safety, Security, the Fire Department, Recreation, Food Services, Transportation, Supply, Water Department, Sewage Treatment, to name a few, as well as the extensive Medical staff itself. Even Human Relations has its part to play.

When a prospective employee is being vetted for assignment to the range, one of the basic requirements is a thorough physical. The subject must be in general good health. There are conditions that may be considered as medically disqualifying.

One such condition is an untreated hernia of any sort. Another is addiction to any restricted or illegal substance.

The filtering for these conditions takes place as part of the employment process itself. And persons so afflicted are generally not permitted to relocate to the range.

All of this medical information is considered in the decision to employ. If the subject passes this screening, the information is forwarded to the hospital at Kwaj and often arrives before the employee does.

So, arriving employees are in acceptably good health. It is up to the Medical Services department on the island to see to it that he or she remains so.

Accidents happen, and when they do an impressive range of people become instantly involved in the investigation and treatment of the victim.

His supervisor must write a detailed report of the incident. Safety receives these reports and analyzes them for passage to management.

The Army requires management to consider every accident and demonstrate that it has taken appropriate measures to prevent the repetition of such an accident. Their response enters into the contractor’s performance evaluation, which determines the amount the contractor earns for that reporting quarter of its contract.

As for the treatment of the patient, it was long ago recognized that the facilities at Kwajalein were not to be expected to be adequate for the most serious cases. In such cases agreements have been made with major medical institutions in the States to forward the patient to them for the proper care.

In the meantime, back at the ranch life goes on. Patients come in with cuts or scrapes or sniffles, even with fevers or broken bones. The hospital there is prepared to handle the majority of such traumas.

I have mentioned treatment of the Americans via the medical facilities on the range. A rather more complex problem is the treatment of the Marshallese.

Marshallese are foreign nationals who play host to their land that we use. Full time workers on the range are treated like all other employees. As such they are eligible for treatment at the range's medical facilities. The same cannot be said for their family members or other Marshallese who are not so employed.

But that has posed problems in a class of their own.

When I arrived at Kwajalein in 1964, Ebeye had no hospital. It did not even have electricity or water or sewage facilities. Ennibur, forty years later still does not. Oh, they have personal generators that help some, but there are no island-wide systems in place. Without such infrastructure systems, the operation of a hospital, or even a decent clinic, is out of the question.

The problem has always been one of jurisdiction. In the early years the Marshall Islands were part of the United States Trust Territory of the Pacific. Now they are independent as the Republic of the Marshall Islands. As such, the Department of Defense expected the United Nations and now their own government at Majuro to see to the medical care of their charges.

It looks good on paper. But the money just isn't there to undertake such infrastructure development. Not, at least, on Ennibur.

The U.S. has no jurisdiction and, hence no responsibility on any of the islands we have not leased from the RMI.

But what about the human side of the equation?

There we are at Roi with a good clinic, competently staffed to handle the day-to-day traumas of people. Next door is a community totally lacking such facilities.

Do we turn away the guy from Ennibur who comes in with a nasty gash from a slipped machete? How about the pregnant girl who has gone into labor and is faced with a breech birth that could kill both mother and child? What about the old man who has lost seven toes and half of his left foot due to diabetes related gangrene? Or the child who has contracted Typhoid? (That's dangerous to the entire population of the island! Even to the Marshallese on our own work force.)

Where do you draw the line?

I have said that for decades the population of Roi was exclusively male. Yet, during those years there were many Marshallese babies born in the clinic there. And many more non-staff Marshallese treated there. Even now the problem has not gone away.

In the early years at Roi we had a resident medical specialist. I remember one who stayed for several years. His name was Wayne D. Ex-Marine. Veteran of Vietnam. Good medic. Good friend.

In more recent times the hospital at Kwaj began rotating their staff members through the clinic at Roi, two weeks at a time. While they were on island, they were on call day and night.

If you've been to Kwaj, you undoubtedly know Dr. Eric L. Our paths crossed both professionally, as doctor/patient, and avocationally because we were both interested in the history of the area and its people.

Ray W. was already an old hand at the hospital when I arrived on site in '64. He never left. The last I heard he was still there.

It is clear that the Army wants to decrease its costs for operating and maintaining the Kwaj end of the Western Test Range. I once heard that the range was the largest item in the Army's annual budget. How true that is I cannot say.

My instincts tell me that cutting medical services is not the way to do it.

Quenching Kwaj's Thirst

While medical services surely makes the Army groan cost-wise, until recently it was freshwater that caused the biggest headache.

Walk with me for a couple of minutes. We'll start at the mess hall and walk south across the parking lot, past the west end of the store and the swimming pool about 300 yards. See the low structure on the right there, just off the road? That's the main access to the lens well here on Roi.

Most of our water comes from rain captured by catchments at the airports during rainy seasons, but in the dry parts of the year we depended on lens wells.

What's a lens well?

It's a porous area in the rock just beneath the surface of the island. It's shaped like the lens of a magnifying glass double convex.

In the bottom (below sea-level) sea water seeps in continuously. And that's undrinkable. But saltwater is heavier than freshwater. When freshwater creeps slowly into the lens, it rises, layering itself over the saltwater. Then it can be drawn off (carefully) and used like freshwater anywhere.

How important is it? Without freshwater the island would be uninhabitable.

The location of this lens well was so important to the Marshallese that they used it as a landmark and an azimuth guide to other atolls around this part of the Marshall Islands.

They did this by clearing straight paths from the well head to the beach on an exact line toward Rongelap, Bikini, Eniwetok, and the other atolls in the neighborhood. At the well head they erected a very tall pole, brightly colored for clear visibility from sea.

This sighting line was used to give mariners an accurate start on their journeys to these other islands.

The lanes are gone now, effaced by more recent demands on the land. But when I first saw Roi, in 1965, the faintest traces of a couple of the lanes still remained, marked by a lower level of vegetation from the well to the beach.

It doesn't take the greenery here long to infiltrate any area not maintained and kept clear. From the road we have just walked to the Speedball fence and the shore, everything was covered in 1965 to a depth of eight to ten feet. Only the muzzles of the "Singapore Guns" showed above the growth.

As usual, I digress.

The swales you see along the roads, runways, and around the golf course were placed to gather rain runoff and let it filter through the upper coral into the lens.

At Kwajalein lenses were not discovered until the early '70s. All freshwater there was distilled (at high cost) from seawater. Until they were discovered, a water barge came to Roi three times a week to draw from our lens well. Each week two loads were delivered to Kwaj and one to Ebeye.

There's a problem with lens wells. If you get too greedy and draw off water too fast, you can "break" the lens. When this happens, salt water flows in to replace fresh. It can take years to re-establish. This happened at least twice on Kwaj, and we even had a near miss here at Roi. The result at Kwaj was the installation of the reverse osmosis equipment they use now.

Osmosis is the process by which materials pass through membranes. Osmotic membranes block passage of certain molecules from one side to the other and allow the passage of others. What matters is the size of the molecule in question. Membranes can be constructed to block salt water molecules while allowing freshwater molecules to pass through. The result is a concentration of saltwater on one side of the membrane, and freshwater on the other.

Another adaptation to the perennial water problems here is the use of a dual water system.

Sinks and showers are supplied with freshwater; toilets, urinals, and heat exchangers are operated with saltwater.

There's plenty of saltwater available, oceans of it. All you have to do is stick a pipe into it and pump. Yes, there's a strainer on the intake to filter out the bigger stuff as it comes along. But there's a lot of stuff growing in that water, everything trying to get sunlight or to feed on anything smaller than it is and to avoid becoming food for anything that isn't. And most of that stuff is really small!

Take, for instance, tiny seashells. They are so small that they pass right through the strainer and get into the saltwater plumbing. They like it there. As long as there's saltwater running in the pipes, there's food available.

In the normal course of events most of these tiny shells are swept right through the system and, eventually wind up right back out in the ocean.

But a few of them get stuck. Wherever the pipe diameter decreases there are little eddy currents. If a seashell gets caught in one of these eddies, it can get lodged in the joint. From the shell's perspective, that's okay too. There's still food going by, and they're relatively safe. So they feed—and grow.

And, of course, there's always the problem of sedimentation in saltwater systems.

One thing that has proven effective in clearing clogged pipes is back flushing. Get the water flowing in the other direction, even for a short time, and much of the gunk in the pipes will dislodge and flush away. Notices in the *Hourglass* announce the times and areas where this is going to happen. Folks in affected areas are advised to have water set aside to function normally while this process is going on.

When you see a printed announcement that the "FOM" (Facilities Operation and Maintenance) department plans to "backflush" parts or all of the water system, this is what it's all about.

At Kwaj, the water supply and distribution, electric generation and distribution, storm and sewer systems, data, tv and telephone cables are all underground. Because of this, these modern infrastructures are out of sight and, therefore, often out of mind. We seldom think of them until something goes wrong.

Water covers almost 70% of the Earth's surface. Only about 10% of water on Earth is fresh. This is produced by distillation of the water at sea by the heat of the sun striking the Earth.

Water is the "sine qua non" of life as we understand it. Water may exist on Earth and Earth-like planets without life taking hold, but nowhere do we find life without water.

The finding of water is a primary objective of our space programs. Much of the work of modern astronomers is dedicated to the detection of the water molecule everywhere we look.

A Salty Atmosphere

Salt in the water wasn't the only natural obstacle to overcome in daily life on Kwaj. Salt air was a real problem. It still is. Kwajalein Atoll has one of the most corrosive atmospheres I ever heard of. Everything rusts.

When I first got to Kwaj there were several racks set up just north of the Kwaj Lodge, along the beach. On these hung hundreds of squares of material, mostly different kinds of metal, mostly coated with varying kinds of paint. Each painted square had a big X scratched through to bare metal. The metal squares were all one quarter inch thick. Many of the panels corroded through in just a couple of months. Some lasted longer. I have no idea who ran that experiment, but the racks were up and in use for several more years. They were finally torn down when the termites got too bad.

A friend once advised me "A ten speed bike? Don't waste your money on it. In six months it'll be a one speed, just like all the rest!" He was right. On average I had to replace my bike once a year. By that time it was in what everyone called "Kwaj condition." The rule of thumb is, if it's metal, paint it. When the paint gets too thick, chip it off and paint it again. When you're doing that on an antenna that weighs 465 tons and stands 212 feet in the air, that's no small job.

Strangely enough, the corrosion begins to taper off above about sixty-five feet. That's because the trade winds can support salt spray only about that high. Above that what damages the paint most is the intense tropical sunlight.

Painting at Kwaj is a tedious job. But it must be done. Painting high metal is, in addition, dangerous. Full body safety harness must be worn and used at all times!

Painting goes on all the time (well, most of the time). However, painting at Kwaj is different than it is most places back stateside. At Kwaj Missile Range, painting and any other maintenance that must be done more than about twelve feet off the ground must be coordinated with the use of the radars.

When the radars are working, the painters can't. At least not above twelve feet. In this respect, the problems are compounded even further on Namur.

Some of the most powerful radars in the world are located on Roi-Namur. During mission run-throughs and during actual missions all outside activity on the island must cease. No one is allowed outside shielded buildings on Namur at such times.

That's because of RF Hazards. The entire island is so saturated with radiation from the radars that it's unsafe even to walk around on the island.

When an RF Hazard goes into effect, the roads are blocked, the island is swept by security patrols (who must themselves leave afterwards), monitors are stationed at every exit of every building to assure no one exits, and other such precautions are taken. In some places, even the inadvertent opening of a door during an RF Hazard can cause radars to shut down! Costly error? Enough said.

During the late '60s and early '70s missions were so frequent that RF Hazards occurred almost daily. Each could last from one hour to many hours. Try factoring that into your work schedule!

Chapter 27

Fun and Games, Dogs and Pigs

The Recreation Department

Of course work was the main focus in being on Kwaj; everyone there had a job to do. But that doesn't mean we worked all the time.

We all interacted on the job, at church, and in the various facilities and activities operated by the Recreation Department.

I suspect most of the people who were ever at Kwaj never really paid much attention to the Recreation Department as an organization. But it was really critical to the morale and welfare of all the island's personnel.

The Recreation Department, which I will henceforth refer to as REC, was mandated as part of the Logistic Support Contractor responsibility by the Department of Defense (DOD). DOD specified that REC was to be operated and maintained by the logistics contractor at no cost to the government. Therefore, funding was a real problem.

To achieve this funding, DOD further specified that all proceeds from commercial activities on the range would be transferred to REC. To assure continuity of funding, DOD further specified that all retail activity on the range was to be a monopoly of the logistic contractor (LC). What that meant was that no person or group could engage in any activity which competed with the activity of the logistics contractor.

This was no license to steal for the LC. DOD dictated what percentage over cost the LC could charge for goods and services within its monopoly on retail services. These followed the standards the military charged for retail activities on its bases all over the world.

Hence, the LC had (and has) no latitude at all in determining the retail prices it charges. In any event our topic is REC.

With the population large and growing, as it was when I first arrived at Kwaj, funding was never a real problem for REC.

How that income was utilized cannot be understood without mention of Andy D. and the Cleveland Mafia.

Andy D. was from Cleveland, Ohio. His interest in athletics there and his further education qualified him for the post of athletic director and then recreation manager. By the time he came to Kwaj he was thoroughly in tune with what was needed there. He found a home at Kwaj and stayed there for more than twenty years.

To see what was needed, take a look at the personnel at Kwaj.

They don't work twenty-four hours a day. Their spare time is largely spent thinking of home and their families. They need diversion, a break in the routine of daily labor.

That's recreation.

At Kwajalein that breaks down into three divisions: Team sports, sports activities supported by the recreation department, and other group or personal hobbies or activities only peripherally supported by REC.

Let's make it clear at the outset that all of the physical plants to support such activities, like everything else on the range, were installed by the government. The Recreation services building, for example, contained many facilities such as the photo lab, bowling alley, gear locker, library, radio station, hobby shop (ceramics and such), offices for recreation administration, and more.

There were six theaters—three on Kwaj, one on Gugeegue, one on Roi, and, for a couple of years, one on Illeginni. Each showed seven different movies a week. A couple of them had two showings once or twice each week. Movies were REC-funded. They came on island once a week, if we were lucky, and circulated around the atoll theaters by plane, helicopter and boat—strictly on a space available basis. Projectionists were part time hires (through REC) and often unavailable in times of heavy mission activity (missions *always* came first). Just getting the scheduled movie to the right theater at the right time, with a projectionist sober enough to run it was often something of a small miracle.

Theater equipment breakdown was an ongoing, if only occasional, problem, especially in the outer islands. They got the castoffs from Kwaj. Sound systems were exposed to the weather and the salt air.

I have dwelt on the subject of movies for a couple of reasons. Although movies were a small part of the responsibilities of the REC department, running the theaters smoothly was no small thing. It was estimated that one third of the range's American population went to the movies every day of the week. When good movies were on the menu, that number could rise to half or more.

***

Virtually any sport in which there was any interest at all was available on the range. REC staff organized teams, leagues, and tournaments. They hired and trained officiating personnel, and did all the scheduling.

REC, through its gear lockers, supplied the sports equipment for all sports from fishing to lacrosse and softball and bowling, though they encouraged participants to bring their own equipment. They also provided uniforms (mostly caps and tee-shirts).

And trophies! If you participated, you got a trophy. Winners got engraved team trophies. It seemed to me that Range REC must have made some trophy venders in the States very happy.

***

REC ran the marinas at Kwaj and Roi. Boats (mostly Boston Whalers) could be scheduled for fishing trips, scuba dives, day trips to certain outer islands, and the like. Gear was provided. Licensed crew was provided. Classes in water safety and boat handling were mandatory.

In the early days there was no charge for the use of those boats. I think it may have been necessary for users to buy gas (at 10¢ per gallon), but I am not certain about that requirement. There were a certain number of sail boats provided for use by sailors who didn't like "stink pots" (motorized boats). Again, safety courses were mandatory, and the responsible party on each craft had to be licensed.

All scuba divers had to be certified and checked out before they were allowed to pursue that pastime.

It was scuba divers who found the wreckage of a Kingfisher Observation plane in the lagoon at the west end of Kwaj in 1966. They removed two dogtags from the plane. The plane had been shot down during the invasion in 1944, when the pilot inadvertently dropped below the trajectory of our own artillery firing at Kwaj from Carlson.

Esther and Louie S. were friends of my parents in Horseheads, New York. They had one son, David (nicknamed Buddy) who was lost at Kwajalein during the war. He had been an observer on a Kingfisher. One of the dogtags was his. I had the privilege of returning it to his mother in 1967!

***

I worked at the radio station on Kwaj as a DJ, hired by REC. The amateur radio station (KX6DC) on Kwaj was operated by the ham radio club. Its equipment was subsidized by REC. REC staffed the swimming pools on Kwaj and Roi and the swimming area at Emon Beach, as they did the golf courses, the gyms, the weight training rooms, and all the other community services facilities on site. There were even sports reporters on the REC staff who kept the public informed about all sporting activities in the *Hourglass* newspaper.

There were two flying clubs (the one at Roi at one time had as many as five planes), two gun clubs, two archery ranges. This list seems endless.

And Andy D. administered it all (with a little secret help).

His secret was that he had made an arrangement with the athletic department at his old high school in Cleveland for them to set up a training program to train staff specifically to work at Kwajalein Missile Range! The arrangement worked very well. For more than twenty years the vast majority of the full time staff at REC came from that one high school! They came qualified and trained to fit into REC at Kwaj. Many of them became professionals in the recreation business and found good jobs in their fields back in the States when they finally left the island. Collectively they became known as "Andy D. and the Cleveland Mafia."

This was by no means meant to belittle them. Their contribution to the morale and welfare of the personnel at the range was one of the factors that resulted in the then logistic support contractor (Global) holding its contract as long as it did.

***

I suppose you could say that while all sports are hobbies, not all hobbies are sports. The definitions are not exclusively precise. Both are diversions from one's work-a-day tasks. Sports usually involve, or at least infer competition; hobbies usually don't. Sports usually do not result in the production of things; hobbies often do.

REC supported the vast majority of these activities to one degree or another. Here are just a few examples of that support.

For years Mamu O. ran the hobby shop. His special expertise was in ceramics and carpentry. He was REC staff. REC provided the potters' wheels, molds, clay, glazes and working tools for ceramics. Power and hand tools for carpentry, along with the necessary accessories were supplied by REC. Mamu taught interested parties the safe and proper use of the machines and tools needed to engage their hobbies. Mamu was always there to guide and assist.

Bob F. was skilled in silver smithing and jewelry making. He was part time REC. His special interest was lost wax casting. REC provided the special slings, investment, plenishing tools and the like that Bob needed to train us would-be Paul Reveres and Fabreges.

You could request just about any hobby training you wanted and REC would scour the range's personnel for the expertise to train you. They would also advertise to drum up sufficient numbers to make a class possible. (The minimum was usually five or more students.)

REC also sponsored and scheduled fishing trips (though, if you were qualified and licensed, you could take a REC boat out by yourself). REC staff maintained the marina's boats, engines, and fishing gear along with emergency equipment such as first aid kits, radios, and the like. In the early years there the cost to the user was nominal, mostly compliance with the rules and regulations covering safe boat usage and practices.

***

So it went. REC was there to support just about any activity individuals or groups requested their help with. Did you want to have a party? REC supplied tables, chairs, pavilion tents grills and ice chests. REC could even arrange catering. (You had to pay for the food.)

REC maintained the golf courses on Kwaj and Roi, though it didn't build them. If you and a buddy wanted to play a game of golf, REC could schedule you for an open time slot. REC did not deal with the flying clubs or the gun clubs on the range, but it provided compressors for refilling scuba tanks for both scuba clubs.

As mentioned before, REC was the driving force behind the annual Kwaj Karnival. On the other hand there were scores of activities that REC had nothing to do with at all, especially on the outer islands.

Unless you were Marshallese, you had to be an American citizen to work on Kwaj. Filipino men came mostly from Hawaii, where they were born and raised. DOD had an agreement with the State of Hawaii that a certain percentage of the logistics contractor's staff be employed from the Hawaiian labor pool. Incidentally, all of the employees who came from Hawaii were required to pay Hawaii State income tax, no matter whether they worked overseas or not.

This did not mean they were culturally American. Many of them, in the early years, could barely speak English. They filled some of the more menial jobs on the range. They worked in the mess halls, on roads and grounds as custodial staff, and so forth. The better educated among them were often general helpers in the various trades needed by the logistics contractor.

When they were not working at their assigned jobs, they pretty much kept to themselves. On Roi the preferred quarters was the cubicled, non-air conditioned 8037, which they preferred because the ambient temperature range there was in their comfort zone. In quarters and around it one never heard English. But, if your language was Tagalog, Vasayan, or Ilokano, you would have felt at home.

Being from mostly agricultural and fishing backgrounds, their leisure activities fell into four categories: gardening, fishing, animal husbandry, and gambling.

Gardening had its peculiar challenges and rewards on Roi-Namur. There was no room on Kwaj for much such activity. But there was plenty of room on Roi-Namur, particularly Namur. Aside from the cleared areas immediately around the numerous sensors there, Namur was mostly overgrown with the vegetation typical of all such coral islands when rainfall is adequate. Indigenous flora consisted primarily of coconuts, pandanus, and the ubiquitous beach morning glory. Beach Heliotrope also grew along both the lagoon and ocean shores of the island. Noni fruit shrubs grew in a sort of symbiosis with the coconut trees.

Beach morning glory. Ubiquitous ground cover growing wherever saltwater and groundskeepers neglected it. Photo by Pam R.

Gardeners, mostly Filipino, would select a space just out of sight of traffic on the numerous dirt roads that cris-crossed Namur and begin site preparation.

Ideally, this was how it went.

They started with a visit to Frank S., the decades long island manager at Roi, and described to him their wishes. He would go with them to their desired site. If he knew of some planned future use of that spot, he would advise them of it. Otherwise, he never said no.

They were allowed to clear off the overgrowth in the proposed area, leaving the topsoil intact, and not bothering the native coconuts and pandanus. Frank often even arranged the quiet after an hours' use of a bulldozer or road grader to clear the area. This saved our gardeners huge amounts of time and effort.

Brush piles thus generated were allowed to dry, and then burned under the watchful eyes of the fire department who used the event as a training exercise. The ashes were eventually spread over the cleared area to enhance the soil.

Incidently, a number of "lost" Japanese structures dating back to WWII and before were brought to light in these clearing operations.

***

At one time Namur had the richest topsoil on the atoll. I have related elsewhere how this came to be.

Unfortunately for Namur, and fortunately for Kwaj, the Army mandated that the topsoil be removed from Namur and barged to Kwaj to establish lawns in the housing area there.

Consequently, the remaining soil on large parts of Namur was not very nutrient rich. Our gardeners could not afford to import fertilizer, but they used their ingenuity to fix the soil. They developed a complex system of recycling long before that term came into common use in the States.

They took fish guts and parts from their fishing activities. They took pig droppings and pig parts from Frank's pig farm operation. They took chicken droppings and parts from their chicken farm activities. They mulched up all of last season's garden plants. They raked up fallen pandanus fruits in their gardens. Everything organic that was chopped down, mowed down, swept up, or raked up in the process of keeping Roi-Namur looking good found its way to their fertilizer factory. The factory stank to high heaven, but it worked!

The icing on the cake was carbon paper!

KREMS (Kiernan Re-entry Measurements Site) alone at one time consumed nearly 400 cases of four-ply printer paper a month in conducting its business. Each case had 2,500 pages of four ply paper. Each page had three sheets of carbon paper. We had to decollate all of this paper to separate the print from the carbons. Classified carbons were burned. Non-classified carbons (more than half the monthly total) went to the gardens! It dissolved in the first rain, and its carbon went into the soil.

Do the numbers. Over the years tons of usable carbon was put into the soil on Namur. And its gardens flourished.

The gardeners grew bananas and papayas. They grew okra and onions, and beans and tomatoes. They grew squash (and pumpkins for show). They grew herbs. And they grew peppers, lots of peppers. The hotter the better. One of them even found a way to grow excellent corn. His secret was a small fish in each hill of corn seed. (Just like the American indians of the northeast.) They even grew breadfruit. Many of the things they grew I can't even name. All of it was either edible or ornamental, or both.

A lot of cooking went on in the Filipino barracks or behind it. That's not the only activity there.

Every daylight hour two or more residents could be seen repairing fish nets, both the circular throw kind and the very long surround nets which made possible their favorite method of fishing. They also spent a lot of time making new ones.

In form and function netmaking was akin to knitting or crocheting back in the States. It was light work involving a shuttle, the width of which determined the size of the openings in the weave of the net. There were only three or four basic moves used, but they were repetitive. Once those moves had been learned and practiced to the point of becoming reflexes, it was best not to give too much thought to the process. Some little corner of the brain kept count and track.

In consequence, these activities turned into social gatherings where the guys talked about everything except what they were doing.

Mostly the guys worked on their own gear, but they'd sometimes make nets for their families and friends back home. A few of the more adept ones even made nets on commission for others who lacked the skills or patience to produce their own. One acquaintance claimed that he doubled his annual income making nets. He also had the distinction of having made the largest surround net I saw in use there at Roi. It was four feet wide and nearly 1,000 feet long!

Nets such as these were only used in season when immense schools of a small, but much prized fish were shoaling on the atoll's reefs. Capturing them required the coordinated efforts of dozens of men. But the effort was worth it.

These little fish were much in demand as holiday treats in Hawaii and the Philippines. Butterflied and dried in the sun, each of these fish weighed just on the heavy side of nothing. But in Honolulu they could command prices of $15 to $20 per pound! And that was in the late '60s! Well worth the cost of mailing.

***

We've talked about gardening and fishing as pastimes among the people there on Roi. Now let's further our coverage with a few comments on their other agricultural activities, namely raising livestock. Mostly, but not exclusively, done by the

Hawaiians and Filipino employees, this activity had ulterior motives behind it. For example, there was Frank's Pig Farm.

Most of this has been covered in the commentary on animals. I may add that they experimented with many breeds and species that didn't work out particularly well.

Among those were rabbits, quail, partridges, and pheasants. Geese didn't take to island conditions. Ducks did, but only when confined so completely that native critters couldn't get in to plunder eggs and chicks.

Personal motor vehicles were never allowed on Kwaj. There the transportation was limited to official vehicles such as buses and work trucks and vans. Recreational use of these vehicles was not allowed.

Roi personnel were granted two exceptions to the above conditions. We were allowed small motor bikes and go carts.

The bikes were mostly Honda 50 cc size. Licenses for them were granted on Roi because of the nature of our work there. Public transportation was provided for mission support. But many of us were subject to call out on fifteen-minute notice day and night, in any kind of weather to get the radars up and running. New foreign launches were the usual reason for such call outs. There were a lot of them. Going from a sound sleep to a live console a mile and a half away was a real challenge on foot or by bike in the rain. The Honda population at Roi peaked at fifty-eight. These got used by their owners for recreational purposes during off hours.

Go carts were another matter. There were never more than a dozen of them at Roi and their tenure was short. But for the two or three years they were allowed, their owners had a ball with them. They were driven in the jungle and raced around the taxi strips and catchment basins at the airport when no planes were scheduled. Yes, they could do over twenty miles an hour. Had there been any children living on Roi, I'm sure go carts would never have been allowed.

There were and still are many clubs on the range. If you enjoy bridge, there's a club for you. One of the more permanent clubs runs the Micronesian Handicraft Shop, whose profits go toward Marshallese education. Elks, Moose, Masons, American Legion, VFW, and dozens of others have been represented at Kwaj. At one time or another there were two yacht clubs, two flying clubs, two gun clubs, two scuba clubs, two ham radio clubs, an actors' guild, a debating club, a public speaking club, a quilting club and a candle makers' club. Stamp collectors had a club at one time. There was a club for people who liked to cook, or bake. There was a macrame club. You name it. If there were enough interested persons to generate a club, someone usually did. And REC supported them all, in one degree or another. Some clubs were affiliated with religious denominations on island.

The existence and activities of these clubs varied with the ebb and flow of participating people on the range.

Masons, for example, have had a chapter there at varying times through the years. They require a quorum to conduct meetings. If the number of active Masons at any one time is high enough, and if among them are people with the requisite qualifications to constitute such a quorum, then the club may become active. When I went through the degrees there the club was very active. Once I moved to Roi, I couldn't make the meetings. There were Masons on Roi, to be sure. But never the numbers necessary to have our own active group.

Should you find yourself on the islands without anything to do, the only one to blame is yourself. With such a wealth of activities courtesy of the REC department, to be bored is to ignore the many choices available.

Tinker's Legacy

I was walking toward Sprint BQ one afternoon and I saw a beautiful Golden Shepherd sitting outside watching me. I had never seen her before. By that time (c.1985) there were no dogs left on Roi. I was entranced.

Walking over to her, I held out my hand to let her sniff, then patted her head and scratched her ears a bit.

"What a beautiful dog you are," I said. She wagged her tail.

"Get away from that dog!"

"Excuse me," I said. "Is this your dog? She's beautiful."

He too was a stranger to me. I took almost an immediate dislike to him. But he obviously had taken good care of the dog. She looked well fed and her coat had a healthy shine.

"She's a working dog," he said. "She doesn't like to be disturbed."

"Pardon me."

I walked into the building. When the door had closed behind me, a head poked out of a room at the far end of the hall. It was my friend Tusi.

"Hey man, you carrying?"

"Carrying?"

"Yeah, man. You know—like, stuff?"

"Stuff?"

"Pot, man! Maryjane!"

"Hell no! What makes you ask a question like that?"

"Well, that dog was taking an awful liking to you. I thought maybe you was carrying."

Then it hit me. She was a drug dog, trained to seek out illegal drugs.

Times sure do change.

It wasn't always like that. When I first got to Kwaj in the mid-'60s, there were probably a couple of dozen dogs on Kwaj.

Maybe more. I think all of them were family pets. But the only time we could count on seeing them was when the dining halls were open. Especially on Wednesdays and Saturdays, which were steak nights in those days.

The island dogs could be counted on to show up at the chow halls whenever there was meat to be had—and there was always meat to be had. Diners would bring out scraps and toss them to the dogs. The dogs never fought over the scraps; there was simply so much available that the dogs even got finicky over what they would eat. Of course, the remnants drew flies, so that practice was soon mandated away. But the dogs certainly ate well while it was permitted. However, no story about dogs on Kwaj would be complete without mentioning Tinker.

***

The operation was code named "Flintlock." The date was January 31st, 1944. The bombardment was horrible (and devastating). It lasted for thirty-six hours from 200 artillery pieces, 400 carrier planes, three battleships, seven cruisers, numerous destroyers and rocket launching craft, and anything else the Americans could cobble together to throw at the Japanese entrenched on Kwajalein.

You couldn't exactly call the sides evenly matched. 3,800 Japanese against 28,000 Americans; it wasn't meant to be. The Japanese had been cut off and isolated for months. Their supplies just weren't getting through. They lacked nearly everything but determination.

The 7th Infantry Division led the charge with support from the Navy. Even so, the fighting on Kwaj lasted four days. In the end there were twenty-seven Japanese left alive as prisoners, and all of them were wounded.

Then there was Tinker.

The Carrera marble monument reads: "Here lies Tinker, found on Kwajalein I February, 1944 Died August, 1963. Friend to all, she graced our lives."

Of indeterminate breed, Tinker was found during the battle for Kwajalein. As the story goes, she didn't even have her eyes open yet when a soldier of the Hourglass Division picked her out of a shell crater.

Tinker was born on Kwajalein and never left. She was adopted first by one group of soldiers, then by another, then by a line of Navy personnel when the island became a U.S. Navy Base. The civilian population explosion in the late '50s and early '60s insured her continued sponsorship.

Every person on Kwaj knew Tinker for nearly two decades.

She loved to ride in school buses and taxis—anything with wheels. All she had to do was stand expectantly beside the road and the first person who drove by would stop and pick her up. When she got where she wanted to go, she would walk to the doorway and wait until the driver stopped.

Tinker was born to the terror of exploding bombs and shellfire. She saw the hustle and bustle of an occupying army cleaning up the remains of war, then the humdrum of a decade when nothing much happened (except nearby atomic tests!).

Activity exploded there again in the mid-'50s. By that time the U.S. Navy had a major base at Kwajalein. An American community had sprung up and the infrastructure was installed to support even more growth.

By the time the '60s rolled around, Tinker had already had a full life. She had raised at least six litters of pups, some of which formed the basis for Roi-Namur's canine population. No one wished (or dared) to terminate her capacity to have babies, even though all other dogs on Kwaj had to be spayed.

Tinker lived sort of a charmed life on Kwajalein. The circumstances of her birth and battlefield survival and her many years lent her an authority, as it were, that even the Navy was reluctant to crush under the iron fist of conformity. She was blessed with good health all her life, and someone or another always sponsored her at the semi-annual vet's visit.

It was said that she died in her sleep one day in August 1963. It was also said that a lot of people on Kwaj cried when they heard the news.

I never met Tinker myself, but I did know three of her offspring. Their names were Blue, Supply Buster, and Beamus (from "Beam us up, Scottie"), and they lived on Roi.

Tinker touched many lives during her life, and her offspring comforted many more.

When she passed away a group of friends, brought together by their common acquaintance with Tinker, took up a collection and ordered the Carrera marble stone. It took nearly a year to get it appropriately engraved and shipped to Kwaj.

I was introduced to the Tinker "Tail" at the dedication of this monument. At the time I marveled that such an event could prompt over 2,000 men, women, and children (about one third of the island's population at the time) to congregate for the ceremony.

In retrospect of that experience at Kwaj, I gained a new perspective on people and their animals. I came to understand how important the relationship between humans and their pets is. Tinker gave love to every human she met. In most cases it was returned to her. She gave fully and without stint. And that love succored many of the people on Kwaj.

If you were there on bachelor status, she would be your friend. If you were lonely, she would give you company. If you were sad, a wag of her tail would bring a smile.

Race, color, creed, or economic condition meant nothing to Tinker. She refused to absorb any of the attitudes that separated groups on the atoll.

Marshallese, Filipino, Hawaiian, and Mainlander—they were all the same to her, all human. Simple, isn't it?

Tinker was the only dog I knew by name on Kwaj. On the other hand, I knew every one of the dogs on Roi by name. My own was Buster Bum. There were also Supply Buster, Blackie, Omar the Tent, Blue, Jason of the Golden Fleas, and half a dozen others.

The pedigrees of any of the Roi dogs could never be verified by any method we knew of. They were all mongrels.

The elder statesman of the dogs was Blackie. He was an aged cocker spaniel who could usually be found around the power plant. Rheumatism and deafness were his lot. When he moved at all it was with obvious difficulty and pain. Stair climbing was, in the years I knew him, beyond his ability.

Consequently, Blackie stayed at ground level at the power plant. It's hard to say whether his deafness was caused by the ambient noise or whether it was what made it possible for him to reside where he did.

Other dogs didn't like all the noise at the power plant. But, for some reason, they all liked Blackie.

Oh, I forgot to mention that Blackie was mostly toothless.

Power plant personnel saw to Blackie's feeding, comfort, and medical care. But it was the other dogs that brought him treats.

If there were a leader among the dogs, it would have had to have been Blue. Blue was a short-haired mongrel, not the largest dog on Roi. But he had charisma, of a doggie sort. He drew around himself a coterie of half a dozen dogs who mostly hung out together. They each had their own individual human feeders and caretakers, but they constituted the only "dog pack" on the island.

And together, they loved to fish!

Between Roi and Namur there is a small land spit the Marshallese call Akadrik, "the quiet place." This is mostly surrounded by flat reef between the islands. There is no living coral on it, but, when the tide is out, the water is just inches deep. There are narrow channels where the water is a bit deeper. There are also a couple of fair sized pools carved by the Japanese during their time here for swimming. (The pools illustrated in the Roi-Namur phone book as Japanese pools aren't Japanese at all. They were excavated from the flat reef for armoring rocks to be "rip-rapped" along the island's shores to prevent erosion. Those pools were created during the 1990s.)

The real "Japanese pools" are on the west side of Akadrik, north of the causeway, almost across from the command post on Roi.

The pools, channels, and reef between them were the hunting (fishing) grounds for the "Blue team."

With the incoming tide, shoals of reef fish feed on the flats. Some predators do too, including eels and small sharks. When the tides recede, these fish are sometimes temporarily trapped on the reef. They congregate in the channels and pools to await the next tide.

This was the "Blue team's" time. They formed a skirmish line near the reef's edge and drove fish into the extreme shallows, trying—and sometimes succeeding—to grab one of the fish. It was amazing to watch Blue "stotting" (jumping straight up and down) in water that sometimes came half way up his body.

All of this seemed to be a game with the dogs. They seldom ate the fish they caught, but they did an amazing thing with it.

Whenever an expedition was successful, one or another of the "Blue team" took a fish (preferably a small shark) to Blackie at the power plant. He always accepted it and might spend several hours gumming it!

Buster Bum and Supply Buster really didn't like each other. Fortunately, they had different territories and seldom came face to face. When they did, there was always a fight. No permanent damage was done, but they both had a number of scars as mementos of their encounters.

We thought Omar the Tent and Jason of the Golden Fleas were related. They were both longhaired, about the same size, and both had an extraordinarily thick ruff around their necks. The salient difference was their color. Jason was truly golden while Omar was brown and black.

Let me tell you about Jason of the Golden Fleas first.

The tale is not long: Jason couldn't stay away from the ladies.

As it happened, most of the female dogs in the neighborhood in those years lived on Ennibur, the third island southeast of Namur.

When the wind was right, almost every dog on Roi would go to the lagoon shore and look with undisguised longing toward Ennibur, three miles south. Most of them stayed on Roi. If the workboats were plying between Roi and Ennibur, one or two of the dogs would hop aboard and ride south for an hour or so of frolicking there, then jump back on the boats and back to Roi.

Jason walked. He walked the reef and spent two or three days in dalliance with all of the ladies he could find in heat.

He had to watch the tides though. Jason, like Omar, was about two feet tall at the shoulder.

Any tide high enough to wet his belly was dangerous.

We knew when he left Roi. But no one was particularly worried. A few days later he would always return, but one trip he didn't.

Inquiry established that Jason had made it to Ennibur. And he was reported to have been seen starting his reef walk back toward Roi early on an evening a few days later. Speculation was that some shark probably had an unexpected nighttime snack.

Who's to say Jason was foolish? On one hand, he didn't acquire the years that his brother did. On the other, there were large numbers of golden-haired puppies on Ennibur for a couple of years.

Omar didn't like the boats. Nor did he take to the reef. Once or twice, one of the Marshallese brought a bitch in heat to

Roi, specifically for Omar to service. So he, too, had offspring, but never as many as Jason of the Golden Fleas.

Omar the Tent's "territory" was the old Jakaroo club. Dogs congregated in the evenings to cadge eats from the human patrons. Many of them developed a taste for hot chili con carne and even beer—when they could get it. Occasionally two of them would get into a scrap over scraps, but such fights were usually short and not too serious.

But like I said, Omar's "territory" was the club. He didn't really like all the competition on his "turf." He assiduously patrolled the club each evening. If two dogs got into a dispute, Omar would sneak up on one of them and take a sharp nip of its haunch. That usually broke up the fight. If it didn't, a minute later he would sneak up behind the other combatant and bite his haunch as well!

Omar didn't exactly go looking for confrontations, nor did he back off when one loomed. He had a very unusual tactic. He would invite his opponent to go for his throat—a target they couldn't resist. Due to his extremely thick ruff, these bites never broke his skin. And they wouldn't let go.

Omar would simply walk to the nearest vertical object and literally scrub the other dog off, then go on his way. If that object happened to be a thorn bush, his enemy of the moment seldom came away unscathed.

Thus Omar the Tent became, and for years remained, "top dog" at the Jakaroo club.

What can I say about "my" dog, Buster Bum?

Buster was on Roi when I moved up there in 1968. He was already mature and no one could say for sure how old he was.

I adopted him (or did he adopt me? I've never been certain about that). Buster Bum had one endearing trait above all else: he paid attention! When we hung out together, which was often, my interests became his interests. When I walked on the reef, he splashed along beside me. When I was scrounging around the WWII dump, he was interested in all things about WWII dumps. When I wanted quiet to read, he would lie quietly nearby and think doggy thoughts. But he was always alert for any sound I might make and would sit up and wag his tail.

Needless to say, I fed him, groomed him, and saw to his vet visits. In return he gave me friendship, companionship, and a loyalty that always astounded me.

I seldom got really mad at anyone here. I didn't have to, because Buster Bum did it for me. He would give a low, throaty growl at whoever caused my pique. Buster Bum never made a move to attack anyone (except when he saw Supply Buster). But the threat was always implicit. Buster Bum was the best looking dog on Roi, if I do say so myself. He, somehow, never had fleas or any of the other parasites most of the other dogs took as their lot.

When I went to Canton Island at the end of 1973, I had to leave Buster Bum on Roi. I felt as though I was breaking up a team. It hurt.

By the time I returned to Roi in 1976, Buster Bum was gone.

All the dogs were gone.

The story was that one of the visiting dependents from Kwaj was taking a stick to all the dogs on Roi. One of them had the effrontery to nip him. His mother complained to the Army. The Army took this as an opportunity to mandate that all the dogs on Roi must be kept chained at all times. That had been the rule on Kwaj from the day the Army took over. But we had always maintained that because there were no children on Roi, such restrictions were unnecessary.

The Army was adamant about the regulation. A couple of PCS'ing (Permanent Change of Station) men took their dogs back to the States with them.

All the rest on Roi were "put to sleep."

Roi has been the poorer for it ever since.

Animals on Roi

Dogs weren't the only kind of animal to have been "imported" to Roi. In fact, there have undoubtedly been more species of animals raised on Roi-Namur over the years than on any other island in the atoll—perhaps more than anywhere else in the Marshall Islands.

Wild birds, fish, and insects are there to be sure, but I will speak of the more domestic kind.

I'm talking about dogs, cats, pigs, chickens, pheasants, quail, ducks, geese, rabbits, guinea fowl, and others, even peacocks. One man had a pet coconut crab. He used to walk it evenings on a leash!

"Ghost" crab. Beach gleaner par excellance.

Most of the farm animals were raised by some of the people with agricultural backgrounds, just to see if they would work out here. Most were raised for food so that their owners could eat dishes that reminded them of home.

Chickens still wander about Namur, living mostly off the land. Some of their ancestors were bred for fighting.

Cock fighting was a big element of the "entertainment" for many Philippine and Hawaiian workers here in the '60s and '70s. For several, the supplying and breeding of fighting birds was almost a second livelihood.

Then there was the knife man. His specialty was making artificial spurs for the cocks. A set of his spurs (8) cost as much as $1,000 then. These are steel knives specially shaped for use on the cock's legs. With fighting cocks their natural spurs (that talon up the leg of the bird) are removed and replaced with these razor sharp blades. The higher up the leg, the smaller an arc the bird can slash, and the further down the leg, the greater the arc.

Blades can be placed anywhere on the leg from the heel to the knee. They are strapped in place with a carefully wound silk ribbon. This wrapping is done by another specialist. All of this constitutes a system called "ri." This is intended to equalize the chances of each of the contestants in a fight. A small but feisty bird may have its spurs placed low, while a larger bird will have its spurs bound high.

This placement is done to promote gambling on the outcome of these fights. Raising or lowering the blades is called "giving or taking" ri. Eventually all bettors reach consensus that their favorite bird is equipped to win. Ri sets the odds of the betting.

Cock-fighting has always been illegal on Roi, so the contests were held secretly. The aim was not for one bird to kill the other, but to draw first blood. As soon as that happened, the fight was stopped. Fights could last for two or three minutes; or they could be over in less than a second. The amount of money that changed hands over a single contest was phenomenal. And there were a dozen or more matches in a typical afternoon. I once witnessed $7,000 won and lost in less than two seconds!

Watching the people at such an event was as fascinating to me as the fight itself. Fifty or more men would critically watch every step of the preparation. Then they would stand around a circle of specified diameter and watch. As the pre-fight tension mounted, almost all of the spectators would clasp their hands behind their backs. Then they would raise one leg and place the raised foot behind the knee of the other leg. By the time the fight started, it was like looking at a group of cranes, all balancing on one leg!

I never learned all of the complexities of the game.

Usually both birds survived to fight again, or at least to breed. Genealogies of the birds were scrupulously kept and made known at every opportunity.

If a bird was killed, it was given to the owner of the winner—usually to make a celebratory dinner!

Frank's Pig Farm

Dogs were relatively easy to keep on Roi. Pigs are another story. Raising and caring for pigs is labor and resource intensive and feeding them would be beyond the economic resource of all but the most fanatic porcine enthusiast. That took organization and planning. And Frank S. supplied it.

Frank was the outer island's manager for the logistics contractor here for most of the years when the technical and logistics support contracts were completely separate.

Frank took the long view of things and that included a concern for the health of all the Marshallese in this part of the Marshall Islands. He perceived a need for better nutrition and a wider choice of food resources.

His answer was a pig farm. You might say it was the first and possibly most successful recycling effort ever conducted on Roi-Namur.

Frank presented the Army with a request and a plan. He wished to build a pig farm on Roi.

He would build it at no cost to the government and operate it in like manner. (Frank's previous career was with the

Army Corps of Engineers. Suffice it to say that he had the Army's ear.)

There was tons of scrap steel lying around all over the island from WWII. Frank had all usable iron consolidated to a huge cache near the Speedball launch site. With the rest, he began the process of increasing the size of the island with numerous landfills along the beaches.

Concrete was a problem. There was always construction of one sort or another going on in those years. And construction always meant leftover building materials.

Frank headed a group of volunteers to erect the pens. After he did the survey work, he laid out the plan for an expandable set of pens. His volunteers dug footer trenches and constructed forms from scrap lumber for the footers and floors.

He used pierced steel planking (PSP) for reinforcement and fencing. The PSP came from the old WWII runways originally built by the Japanese. There were three runways then, all just dirt. The Seabees plated them with PSP after the occupation. Two of these runways were abandoned after the war and Frank had the PSP collected as part of the major island cleanup.

As for the concrete, Frank arranged with the construction contractors here in the '60s and '70s to empty their concrete trucks of any excess into the waiting forms.

The pens were built thus, one at a time, as material became available.

Clarence P., a welder, then welded up the PSP and angle iron into the walls and roof support framework for the pens.

As some of the older buildings on the island were removed to make way for newer ones, Frank collected the metal roofing and roofed the pens.

Then Frank went to Majuro.

At the time the U.S. Agriculture Department had an agricultural experimental station there. It may still be there.

They had brought in a starter stock of purebred Poland China and Duroc pigs.

That's where our starter pigs came from.

They were an instant hit. Numbers of the Filipino workers here adopted the farm and its resident herd.

Until the pig farm was started, all the garbage from the mess hall was hauled to the dump and buried every day.

Frank had the mess hall cleaners begin to separate the edible and inedible garbage.

The inedible still went to the dump, but the edible went to the pig farm. The herd prospered.

Frank had a couple of the more enthusiastic "farmers" keep detailed breeding records. Soon, there were pigs galore. I remember making a count one day; there were over 200! This included breeding and non-breeding adults and lots of babies.

Anyone who wanted a pig or two for a luau had only to ask. As I recall there was a nominal fee ($5) per pig. This went for vitamin supplements and vet fees for the semi-annual visit to check the herd.

Sometimes there were problems. We had to keep the boars separated from the sows. That's where the PSP came in handy. Regular fencing wasn't going to keep a lusty six or seven hundred pound boar away from any sow in heat. Even so, we had to dispatch one or two of our finest breeders because they had got hung up trying to cross from one pen into another. They broke legs or did other non-repairable damage to themselves. And it's just plain dangerous to try to help a several hundred pound boar who is in pain.

After the herd was well established, Frank went to step two of his plan. He started delivering gravid sows to other islands in the atoll. The intention was to upgrade the pig population on islands that already had pigs and to introduce them wherever they were requested. Pigs usually do fairly well on uninhabited islands. They live off the land. On the whole, the plan worked well. Occasionally we came across a cropper.

I remember well my only visit to Ebadon.

The Army had supplied a helicopter to transport a gravid sow to the people there. The plan was to have the folks allow the sow to birth her litter and mother them to weaning.

Before we were out of sight on our way back to Roi and Kwaj the sow had been slaughtered! Apparently the islanders were hungrier than we had suspected.

More than a few of the pigs from the Roi pig farm wound up as entrées at parties on Kwaj.

The pig farm itself was an occasional problem.

One day the Corps of Engineers came to Frank and said, "Frank, we've got a problem. We need to build an FM tracking station for Speedball. It has to be a certain azimuth and distance from the launch rails. And that's right in the middle of your pig farm!"

So Frank built a new pig farm.

Then they came to him again and said, "Frank, we're sorry. We made a mistake in our calculations. The real necessary location is right in your new pig farm!"

So Frank built another new pig farm.

Again they came and said, "Gee, Frank. We're really embarrassed. We miscalculated again. You'll have to move the farm again!"

"The hell I will!" said Frank. "Let me see those figures!" He looked them over and pointed out their mistakes.

Then the project sort of died. Rumor has it that so much money was spent on planning that there wasn't enough left to do the construction.

The newest pig farm was still here and in operation when I left in 1987. By the time I returned in 1997, it was gone.

While it was here, the pig farm was always a tourist attraction on Roi. The generals and the congressmen all wanted to see it. Families visiting from Kwaj, especially the kids, wanted to know where the pig farm was.

The last time I walked over to the pig farm site, there was nothing left but the smell and the memories.

Chapter 28

The Trust Territory: A Lesson in Faith

Sailing in Trust Territory

Most of my commentary about the relationship of the United States and the Marshall Islands makes it sound as though the U.S. invaded the Marshalls early in 1944, evicted the Japanese, and settled there as the new resident overseers. No hassles, no disputes, no jurisdictional issues.

That simply wasn't the fact of the matter.

There were a number of other players in the game, not all of them with the same goals and desires as ours.

For a number of geopolitical reasons the U.S. found itself, more or less willingly, engaged in a rather more complex situation.

Enter the United States Trust Territory of the Pacific.

The United States helped establish the United Nations at the end of WWII. Our politicians and diplomats deemed such an organization useful as an instrument of international relations, so long as it didn't interfere, too notably, with our activities and interests on the world scene or at home. It was a good sounding board for nations, large and small, to let off steam and to let the rest of the world know what was happening in their particular corner of the world.

I have no intention to go into the details of the United Nations' organization or activities, except to mention the UN Trusteeship Council.

It was the UN Trusteeship Council that established the Trust Territory of the Pacific and ceded its governance to the United States while maintaining a claim of oversight authority to assure the world community that we were behaving ourselves there.

One of the primary conditions of the trusteeship award was that the grantee (us) did not introduce or maintain offensive military capability or presence within the area covered. Another condition was that the trustee permit the UN Trusteeship Council to establish and operate regional offices within the territory for the administration of UN programs for the territory's indigenous populations.

It was this set of conditions that made the Kabua family (traditional leaders in the Marshall Islands) split its attention between the American presence at Kwajalein Atoll and the activities of the Trust Territory government throughout the trusteeship area.

The programs that the United States conduct (and its mere presence) at Kwajalein are the largest economic factor in the Marshall Islands, possibly in the entire area of what was the Trust Territory. Within what is now the Republic of the Marshall Islands (RMI) the activity at Kwajalein Atoll provides more income, employs more Marshallese, and is the source of more revenue for the RMI government than any other asset or activity in the area.

This being the case, it behooved Marshallese leaders to stay on America's good side even while they played international politics with the world organization. Use of certain islands at Kwajalein Atoll and other islands in the Marshalls was something the U.S. wanted and was willing to negotiate for.

Besides, the Americans were already there in numbers larger than the entire Marshallese population at the end of WWII. And their presence had been legitimized by the United Nations. Being a super power, it was unlikely that they could ever be forced to depart until they themselves chose to do so.

Thus it was that the Kabuas took council amongst themselves and decided to install Lejelan as "King." My sources tell me that it was felt that he could handle Americans better than either of the others.

He styled himself "King of the Marshalls," and claimed everything in sight, and out of sight for that matter. For example, he claimed as his property everything on the bottom of Kwajalein lagoon.

Many of the Marshallese commoners did not accept his claim to their islands as part of his jurisdiction. For example, those who lived on Bikini and Eniwetok had their own traditional "king." But who was to gainsay him? They all understood that insofar as dealing with the Americans, they needed to speak with one voice.

As for the Americans on Kwaj and elsewhere, they couldn't afford to ignore the Marshallese and their king anymore than they could ignore the United Nations. There was a sort of checks and balances system in place.

Everything that happened in the early days had to be filtered through that screen of varying interests.

One of the things we had to do was cater to the king. Marshallese couldn't shop on Kwaj. The king could, as well as his wife.

Marshallese who were not employed at Kwaj could not ordinarily avail themselves of medical services at the Kwaj hospital. The king could, same for his wife. Therein lies a small story.

The king's wife was extremely heavy. She would occasionally check into the Kwaj hospital for treatment of her obesity. The doctors there would put her on a thousand calorie (or less) a day diet.

While in hospital, she was constantly attended by members of her family and her friends from Ebeye who were allowed to come to Kwaj because she was there. They made a game of trying to sneak rich foods to her. Seldom did she not gain even more weight on that diet. Wonder why?

The King had first refusal rights on anything that was being disposed of on the range. For some time I was in charge of the furniture warehouse at Kwaj. As we got new mattresses in, we turned in old and soiled ones for disposal. The King had first claim on them.

We would load a couple of hundred old mattresses on a low boy truck, put the truck on a boat to Ebeye, and park the truck right on the pier there. The King would sell them for $10 each right off the truck.

Every Wednesday the King would impose a dollar per person landing fee at Ebeye. No one was exempt. If you didn't pay, you didn't get onto the island. That brought him an income of $600 to $800 per week.

He needed the money. He had heavy responsibilities around the Marshalls. For example, he had a boat. It was a two-masted sail boat with a diesel engine, named the *Waikiki Downtown*.

Lejelan had a full time crew for his boat, paid out of his own pocket. I think he got occasional help from the Trust Territory in meeting this expense.

In any event, he didn't use the boat every day, but he kept its crew busy cleaning and doing minor repairs on it. Major repairs were always done at the Kwajalein Marine Department. Because of that, the Marine Department always kept a stock of spare parts available for the *Waikiki Downtown*.

Therein lies another tale.

When the King didn't have immediate need of his boat or to give the crew training, he made it available to organized groups on Ebeye.

A choral group from one of the churches might want to go to another atoll to give a concert. Lejelan would make the *Waikiki Downtown* available to them.

A ball team might wish to challenge the team on some other island to a softball tournament.

The king would let them travel there and back on the *Waikiki Downtown*. This was a great adventure for the kids on Ebeye! Getting there was at least half the fun!

One Saturday morning one such team left Ebeye for Majuro, 250 miles away.

This was the first time some of these kids had ever been off Ebeye!

Moms all over Ebeye loaded their kids down with enough food to feed an army and sent them off with presents for their numerous relatives on Majuro and the intervening islands. This was to be a week-long excursion.

I was working in the main GSK (General Supply Kwajalein (602)) at the time.

Here's the scene: It's Saturday, just after noon. Four more hours and the work week is over. I have nothing in particular planned for the rest of the weekend.

My boss comes out of the office.

"Ted, we just got a call from the Marine Department. Take a regular pallet and the banding machine over to marine supply. They're breaking out a compressor head and a tool kit for the *Waikiki Downtown*. Pick them up and go to the Tarlang and pick up about a dozen life jackets."

The Tarlang was the large landing craft (LCM) used to ferry the Marshallese work force and maids from Ebeye to Kwaj and back each day. 600 contract employees and 100 or so maids packed it from stem to stern for the daily commute and the law required that we provide a life jacket for each one. Fortunately Kwaj and Ebeye were only about twenty-five minutes apart by LCM.

"Take the whole load to the airfield and stand by. Better take some plastic wrap with you, just in case."

Off I went.

The compressor head wasn't bulky, but it was heavy. The pallet, tool kit, head, and life jackets totaled something just over 500 pounds!

"What do you want me to do with this stuff?" I was talking to one of the supervisors at the airport.

"Nothing just yet. They're arguing. Just stand by."

"Who's arguing?"

"The Army, Global and the Trust Territory!"

"What are they arguing about?"

"About how to do this stunt. Or if we should even try to do it! It's a zoo!"

"Do what?"

"Air drop this stuff to the *Waikiki Downtown*!"

"Air drop it? That's crazy! What happened?"

"Well, nobody's sure for starters. That's one of the things they're hashing out now. It'll be a while. We might as well do our waiting inside. And I'll tell you what I heard so far."

We went into his office. He poured us two cups of coffee.

"You need a little background," he said.

"You probably heard that the Ebeye kids' softball team is going to Majuro for a tournament. Right?"

"Yeah. I heard something about that. The kids are really excited."

"Yeah. Well, the King let them use his boat for the trip. They left this morning and got as far as Namu Atoll, just south of here. They stopped there for a scratch game and to drop off a couple of visitors. When they tried to start the engine again something went bang and the compressor head on their diesel broke."

"Was anyone hurt?"

"No. Not that I heard of. All the kids were still on Namu having a ball."

"Anyway, the radio operator on the *Downtown* called the Trust Territory Office here and reported their problem."

"That's when the head Marshallese at the TT office decided to take matters into his own hands. He didn't bother to inform the Army. He just started calling out Global flight crews and mechanics to prep a C-54 to fly over Namu and drop the stuff you just delivered. Official TT business, he claimed."

I should tell you that Namu is only thirty-five miles south of Kwaj, and at that time there was no airfield there. That's close enough so that at night the people on Namu can see the beacon on the field at Kwaj.

"Be that as it may," said my supervisor friend. "The shit's really hit the fan on this one."

Once the Army found out, the situation got heated fast.

"This is an Army Base!" says the Army.

"No it isn't," says the TT. "It's an asset of the Marshallese people, leased to the U.S. government for the purpose of research and development. It's our job to see that the Marshallese have at least emergency access to it. This is an emergency."

"Global works for the Army. They don't want to get involved in this dispute. But they are concerned about how to do the job, if they have to do it."

"What do you want me to do?"

"If we have to do it, we'll wrap each piece completely with the life jackets and band them on. That way, if they hit the water in the lagoon, they'll float—probably."

"Trouble is, we'll have to put them in the passenger cabin. And I don't know if we can even fly with that door open, or if we can kick them out quick enough for an accurate drop!" So we waited.

Time passed. And the question of enough daylight remaining entered the equation. The Army wouldn't allow the planes to fly over open ocean after dark, especially for such a chancey thing as was being proposed.

Eventually dusk approached and the possibility of an air delivery was made moot.

My friend answered the phone. "That's that," he said. "The plane is out. Take the stuff back to the Marine Department. The powers that be have decided to use the *AVR-19*."

The *AVR-19* was one of two crash/rescue boats in use at Kwaj at the time. It was seaworthy and fully adequate to do the job at hand.

I took the pallet back to Echo pier and it was duly loaded onto the *AVR-19*. Life jackets were returned to the Tarlang.

With my part of the job over I took the forklift back to supply and clocked out. My weekend had begun.

Hoping for something different to do, I walked right back to the Marine office. A night ride on the *AVR-19* would do!

What I am about to tell you is not very complimentary. Therefore I will neither name nor title the "star" of what follows. Suffice it to say that he was a civilian, a Navy veteran, and adequately licensed for the position he held. And he was a decision maker who could grant my request. So we shall refer to him simply as DM (for Decision Maker).

He was busy chortling when I got to his office. So I kept my peace. At first he barely noticed me.

"I knew it!" he fairly shouted at his subordinate. "The flyboys couldn't do the job! I knew they'd have to come to me! And they did!"

"Yessir."

"We'll show them what the Navy can do! Piece o' cake!"

"It's night, sir, and cloudy."

"So what? The *19*'s got radar."

"But sir, the *19*'s radar has been out for the last two weeks."

"What? How come you didn't tell me? I'll have your job for that!"

"But, sir, I put the report on your desk two weeks ago."

"I never saw it!"

He began rummaging around on his desk and, there, under a pile of *Playboy* magazines, was the report in question.

"Never mind. Namu's only about thirty miles south. What can go wrong?"

"Yessir."

"Excuse me?"

"Who're you?"

"My name's Ted B."

"What do you want?"

"I've been working with your cargo all day. I wonder if I could go along for the ride."

"Hell, no! Get out of here!"

"Sorry, sir."

"Just get out. I'm in charge of this operation!"

"Yessir."

I left.

Now it happened that Lee W. was working the marine control tower that evening. And something interesting was in progress. So I went up to the tower to jaw with him.

The *19* left, with the DM in charge. They crossed the lagoon and eased out of SAR pass, then turned south. The time was just after eight.

Lee figured it would take about three hours for the *19* to get to Namu.

Lee called the radioman on the *Waikiki Downtown* and told him of the *19*'s departure and expected arrival time.

All was well at Namu. The kids were all ashore and hosted by friends and relatives. The *Waikiki Downtown* was safe in Namu lagoon, and the *19* was speeding to the rescue.

Now I must tell you that radio communication was not as sophisticated then as it is today. It happened that on that particular day, the marine control tower at Kwaj had two-way contact with both the *19* and the *Waikiki Downtown*. The *Downtown* could hear the *19*'s transmissions, but the *19* couldn't hear the *Downtown*'s. This, however, was not a serious problem because the control tower could relay to both boats.

So the stage was set for the climax of our little drama. There were three principals:

The *Waikiki Downtown* Radio Operator (WD)
The Kwaj Marine Tower Operator (MT)
The *AVR-19* (DM)

We waited.

9:00 came and went. 10:00 came and went. 11:00 came.

MT: *19*. You should be close by now. Do you see anything?
DM: Where the blankety-blank is that blankety-blank atoll?
MT: *Downtown*, do you see anything?
WD: No.
DM: This chart's all f-ed up!
MT: Gentlemen, you both have spotlights. I suggest that you turn them on and sweep around the compass. *Downtown*, if you see the *19*'s light, read off the bearing so he can home on you. *19*, if you see the *Downtown*'s light, head for it.
WD: Okay.
DM: Good idea. It came to me just before you mentioned it. Glad I thought of it!

They swept.

WD: Tower, I have the *19*'s light at 270 degrees.
MT: *19*. The *Downtown* has your light on a bearing of 270.
DM: 270. Got it. We'll be there in no time!

11:30 came and went. Midnight came.

WD: Tower, it's late. We're closing down to get some sleep. Busy day tomorrow.

MT: *19*. The *Downtown*'s wrapping it up for the night.
DM: We're on our way. Blankety charts!

The next morning the *Downtown*'s crew put up their sails, boarded their passengers and sailed back to Kwaj.

The *19* showed up about ten minutes after the *Downtown* pulled in.

The best we could figure was that instead of running the reciprocal (180 degrees off the cited bearing), the DM had only taken 100 degrees off. By the time the error was recognized they were well on their way to Majuro!

The whole business was pretty well hushed up. Embarrassment enough for everyone. The issues of jurisdiction, authority, and responsibility went all the way to the United Nations, the State Department, and the Department of Defense.

Eventually, they were resolved in the manner of all precedent setting negotiation. By the way, the DM left shortly after that incident. He was not missed.

Kinging Has Its Moments

The King wasn't directly involved with that last incident, but he showed his leadership often enough. Occasionally, he'd pull off something extraordinary.

There's something impressive about being "top dog," no matter what they say. It's a symbolic position, but frankly, most people wouldn't touch the job with a ten foot pole. For one thing, you're always on display.

Privacy is a concept understood only in the abstract by Kings, Presidents, Emperors, CEOs, Generals and other top dogs.

Another thing is that, as king of the mountain, you automatically become a target for snipers of all ilks. There's always someone out there who would like to displace you.

There's always someone who wants to take your place. You must always be on the defensive, watching every move you make, every word you utter. Sure as heck anything you do or say is going to yank somebody's chain.

It takes certain personality characteristics to be effective as king of the mountain. For one thing you've got to have a carload of confidence in yourself. It also helps if you are ambitious. And a dollop of controlled aggressiveness doesn't hurt the mix either. There are a lot of people who don't like these traits in leaders.

For another thing you've got to know the rules of whichever game you're playing; how to use them, which ones you can bend or break, and which ones you can ignore. Once at the top you may be able to change the rules of the game. But to get there usually means you have to follow the rules. And to do that implies that you have to be both familiar and comfortable with them. Communications skills are an asset, as are coalition building abilities. The good leader understands the art and necessity of compromise.

Most of all a leader has to produce, usually at the level of strategy and usually in the form of guidance.

Some of these things can be taught; many cannot. Where is the school people go to to study how to be President?

In one respect all leaders are equal, whether they lead a team or a nation. They are the embodiment of the group they lead. They give their group identity, and are its spokespersons. Their efforts would be well spent if they focused always on benefitting the group they represent. I'll give you an example of how this works.

Here is a man named Lyndon. He's President of a country of 3 million square miles with a population pushing 200 million citizens. His authority is immense.

He can start wars, or stop them. He can set his nation on this course or that. Through taxation and legislation and executive orders he can effect the financial, social and physical welfare of every citizen and resident of the land. With a spoken word or the flourish of a pen he can create or eliminate thousands of jobs. As Commander-in-Chief of the nation's military, he can impact the lives of people around the world. He is sworn to uphold and defend the constitution of his nation.

What he can't do is set his own schedule, drive his own car, prepare his own meals, go to just any party that strikes his fancy, travel freely in public, see to his own health, buy his own clothes, and a host of other things which his countrymen take for granted.

He sits at the tip of an immense pyramid of functionaries, bureaucrats and specialists whose job it is to protect and inform him, to advise him, and, in every way, to insulate him from the minutae of everyday life so that he can do the job of being President.

His minions largely determine where he will go, and when; who he will see, and for how long; and what he will say, in public and in private.

There is even an office of the Presidential Press Secretary. His job is to deal with the press from all over the world. He speaks for the President. His real job is to be a buffer—a lightning rod if you will—between the President and the press. He fields the tough and/or embarrassing questions and gives the President some breathing room.

The President is not an easy man to see.

Here's another man. His name is Lejelan. He's a King. He got the job because his brothers didn't want it. His realm has fewer square miles of land than is contained within the beltway surrounding our nation's capital. Lejelan's subjects (at the time of this tale) numbered no more than 25,000 (men, women, children and infants).

Yet, in the General Assembly of the United Nations, each of these countries had one vote.

And the U.S. wanted it that way! Under the law they were equal!

So, where is all of this leading? I'll tell you. It's leading to a trip.

It happened, at the time, that the U.S. was negotiating with the Marshallese to modify lease arrangements arrived at earlier. The U.S. wanted more room. The Marshallese wanted more lease money and the resolution of some labor related grievances.

Negotiations weren't going well. On the U.S. side they were being handled by low level functionaries who came in from elsewhere, didn't know local conditions, and didn't particularly care. Moreover, they were not authorized to make commitments on behalf of our government. All of that stuff would come at some indefinite time later.

On the other hand, to the Marshallese it was a big deal.

How to break the stalemate?

Lejelan decided to take a trip. He had been to Hawaii before, but never to the mainland. Buddy Y. went along as translator and guide. Just the two of them.

They went to Washington (D.C. that is).

They went into the White House on a guided tour!

You should know that Lejelan could speak passable English. Buddy was along for appearance's sake as much as anything.

Part way through the tour Lejelan said to the tour guide, "Tell the President I want to see him."

"Sorry, guy!" said the guide. "Lots of people want to see the President. But he's a very busy man. And besides, if anyone does want to see him, this isn't the way to do it."

"Tell him the King of the Marshalls is here!"

Panic!

The Protocol Office broke into a paroxysm of snit!

There was an immense amount of very hurried to-ing and fro-ing.

Eventually things were worked out. Exceptions were made. And Lejelan met with Lyndon.

After that meeting, orders were given. Negotiations were lit up and rapidly concluded.

How do I know this?

Lejelan told me the details after he returned from the trip.

And he had proof. He showed me a picture of himself, in the Oval Office, shaking hands with the President!

For decades another copy of that picture hung on the wall in the Trust Territory office on Kwaj.

"Look at his smile," Lejelan told me. "Then look at mine. My smile was for my people."

I did.

The picture was remarkable. The mouths tell a story.

Lyndon's says "You son of a gun. You rocked the boat!"

Lejelan's says "You son of a gun. I did, didn't I?"

Then I looked at their eyes. They both told another story. There were the faintest suggestions of smile lines at the corners of their eyes. They understood each other perfectly!

I guess Kinging does have its moments.

Chapter 29

Marshallese Friends

Nerai and The Big Mail Order University

Lejelan might have been "royalty," but the gutsyness of his move in the White House wasn't specific to his character. That kind of honesty in dealings was common among the Marshallese, especially with those that wanted to better their situation.

I spent four years at Kwaj, shifting jobs as promotion offered. I won't bore you with the details of these jobs. But I do want to tell you about some of the things that happened and some of the people I met.

Education never comes easy. And when you're 5,000 miles west of California, it's even harder to get one of those pieces of paper that says you've accomplished something in the academic arena that can help your career.

The easiest way is by mail.

Nerai was a Marshallese constable in the security force at Kwajalein Missile Range. His English wasn't very good, but that was all right. His job was to deal mostly with the Marshallese laborers who worked on Kwaj each day.

In those days he, like all the Marshallese, was earning a little over 50¢ an hour and trying to support a large family on it.

"Not much chance for promotion," said his American friend, the investigator. "But there is one thing you can do. Take a mail order course in Criminal Law. I'll help you."

So Nerai signed up for a course. He was paying for each lesson as he turned it in.

The first five or six lessons were tough for him, but with his friend's help, he got through them. Then they turned from hard to impossible. Stuff like "habeas corpus" showed up in the lessons and sailed right over his head.

Finally and reluctantly, he decided to throw in the towel.

He wrote a letter to the Big MOU (Mail Order University) that said something like this. "Look, I'm not getting anything out of your course. I don't understand the new words. So I want to quit. Thank you."

The Big MOU wrote back saying, "That's fine, but you signed a contract. You'll have to pay anyway. Send us $450."

This scared Nerai. So he went to his friend, and together they wrote a series of letters to the Big MOU. (I have copies of most of them.)

Nerai:	I can't afford to pay for something I'm not getting.
The Big MOU:	Pay up or else!
N:	Or else what?
MOU:	Or else we'll turn your account over to a collection agency!
N:	The nearest collection agency is in Honolulu, 2,500 miles away!
MOU:	Pay up!
N:	Okay. The medium of exchange here is coconuts and fish. I just put the first payment in the mail. (He mailed two fish to the Big MOU, parcel post, in a trash bag!)
MOU:	We were not amused with last week's mail. Pay up, or else!
N:	I've had it with you people! I tried to be polite. All I get are threats! Now I'm

> warning you! If you don't stop bothering me, I'll have my witch doctor put a curse on you and your typewriter!

Nerai never heard from the Big MOU again.

Don't Knock Nok

I guess most folks in this world are more comfortable working for someone else. They may bitch and gripe about whatever job they have, but they stay for the regular paycheck and any other benefits that may come with their position.

There is one breed, however, that doesn't do things this way. They are the entrepreneurs. They are the ones who live by their wits and abilities. They're the ones who make it big, or go bust trying. Athletes and business owners, some doctors and lawyers, some inventors and (dare I say it) writers—all of these are entrepreneurs.

There is something of the wheeler-dealer in all of them and just a tad more moxie than most of us have. For instance, Aralon Nok was one such person. I met him in the Marshall Islands years ago. He styled himself a business man, though no one could say exactly what his business was. Mostly he wandered around the Marshall Islands looking for opportunities to connect people with goods or services they wanted. Or at least to separate them from their money to keep himself going.

I won't call him a crook or a shyster. In fact I had one or two successful "partnerships" with him over the years. But you had to be careful. Agreements were by handshake and handing over enough money up front to let him get rolling on behalf of both of you. If things worked right, he was scrupulous in meeting his end of a deal. If not, he sometimes considered your "investment" simply as his payment for the effort he made.

For example, we both made money one time on some seashells. There was one shell listed in the books as rare. "Heck," said Aralon, "I know where there's lots of them!" He was right. That shell is no longer on the rare list.

Nok came and went on his own schedule. When he came to Kwaj it was always by one or another of the few small tramp freighters that plied the islands. He'd stop at Kwaj and wait for the evening boat to Ebeye. Since he wasn't allowed free run of the island, he did his waiting at the pier. Over the years most of the Security people on Kwaj got to know him. And he had dealings of the sort mentioned with a few of them.

One such was an arrangement he made with one of the security guards at the pier. The kid gave Nok $600. Nok took off.

Time passed. A month. Then two. The kid was getting nervous. Another month and nervousness began turning to anger.

By the sixth month, the guard was beside himself at how he'd been taken by Nok. He vowed retribution.

Now it happened that the next time Nok landed at Kwaj, his "partner" was on duty at the pier.

I should tell you that Nok was not exactly hard to spot. Mainly because he was bigger around than he was tall. And his feet were so wide that his shoes (when he wore shoes) were almost square.

The guard spotted Nok.

"Nok!"

Nok kept on walking.

"Nok! Where the hell have you been? Where's my money? Nok, you SOB! You come over here and talk to me or so help me I'll waste you!"

With that, the guard pulled his sidearm!

Nok looked at him, and then walked over to him.

"I'm not Nok. I'm Nok's twin brother."

And Nok turned around and kept on walking.

Sam's Career Choice

Though the notion of promotion and financial advancement was on the minds of many, I remember one friend whose primary concern wasn't money. I worked with him in the furniture warehouse, as a lead man. Our job was to set houses up for new arrivals and to strip them of furnishings when a family left so that work crews could get in and repaint and repair the quarters for the next tenants. We had to deliver "hospitality kits." These "kits" were the bare bones assortment of pots, pans, tableware, bedding, etc. that each family needed until its surface shipment arrived.

Not exactly rocket science, but it did require some planning and coordination with other departments to make things go smoothly. We were kept busy.

I had two teams, all Marshallese. They worked well, when they showed up.

"Sam," I'd say, "How come you don't come to work every day? You've got a lot of people depending on your income."

"Oh, I got plenty money."

"How come you got plenty money?"

"This my weito!" He swept his arm around.

It was true. Everything from the retail store south to the air terminal, all the way across the island, sat on land his family owned. And DOD was paying rent for the use of it.

Most of the islands in the Marshalls are long and narrow. On one side is the ocean, on the other, the lagoon. A weito is usually a strip running from the edge of the oceanside reef across the island across the island into the lagoon to "a man's height deep." The Iroij owned the land, but granted weitos to families who were loyal to his family. Everything that grew on the land, or on the reef, or in the lagoon within the boundaries of the weito was for the use of the family that lived there.

Now the Republic of the Marshall Islands owns the land, but the weito system still applies. And ownership passes down the generations on the women's side of the family.

"Well, if you got so much money, how come you come to work at all?"

"All my friends work here!"

Peace Corps

When I was working at Kwajalein Missile Range in the Marshall Islands, Peace Corps was invited to that country.

Somehow, the word got around to the new arrivals that I had previously been in Peace Corps. I guess I must have seemed something like a father figure to them. I was frequently visited by one or another of them who came with questions and problems.

One of the younger volunteers particularly sticks in my memory.

"Ted." he said, "I can't get any help from the old geezers on Ebeye. They all hate me!"

"Why should that be?"

"They don't like what I say to the kids."

"What are you saying to the kids that would make the 'old geezers' angry?"

"Well, I'm telling the kids that they are the future for the Marshall Islands."

"Nothing wrong with that. They are the country's future. I don't see what makes the adults mad about that. They recognize the fact, too. What else are you telling the children?"

"I'm telling them that their parents had their chance, and to look at what a mess Ebeye is! That should motivate them to clean up Ebeye."

"What else?"

"That if they work on Kwaj, they should get the same pay as Americans there!"

"Even if the government of the Marshall Islands has contracted with the U.S. government to have Marshallese work on a lower wage scale?"

"That's not fair!"

"Not fair? Not fair to whom? Don't you understand the reason for that decision on the part of the Marshallese government?"

"It's just not fair! That's why I tell them not to listen to their government. Everybody in the Marshall Islands should be making what us Americans make!"

"Wait a minute! What do you know about the government and the economy of the Marshall Islands?

"Everything."

"Really?"

"Well, enough, anyway."

"You sure couldn't prove it by me!"

"What do you mean?"

"Here you are telling the children not to listen to their parents or their government. Then you wonder why the adults don't like you or cooperate with you."

"When you put it that way..."

"I put it that way."

"But it's not fair!"

"Fair, shmair! Who said life was fair? What these people are trying to do is keep a roof over their heads and food in the bellies of their families. To do that they have to tap into the economy of the area any way they can. That's the prime directive in any society. The way they come to grips with that necessity is what shapes the whole society."

"Sure. But..."

"I'm not done. What's the single largest driver of the economy in the Marshall Islands?"

"Fishing?"

"Hell, *no*! It's the Kwajalein Missile Range! Tell me, how many Marshallese are there?

"On Ebeye?"

"No. Altogether."

"Around 60,000."

"That's right. How many of them live on Ebeye?"

"About 12,000."

"Right again! Figure it out. That's about a fifth of the total population of Marshallese. Why would so many of them jam into Ebeye?"

"To get jobs?"

"Yeah. Where are the jobs those people are trying to get?"

"Kwajalein Missile Range?"

"Right you are! Maybe you do know something about the economy here. How many Marshallese work on Kwajalein Missile Range?"

"Today? About twelve hundred, I think."

"Right on, if you include the maids who are privately employed. Run the numbers. 12,000 people on Ebeye. 1,200 of them work on Kwajalein Missile Range. What's that come to?"

"Ten percent?"

"Bingo!"

"Where's all this leading?"

"Bear with me. You'll see. Remember the number 1,200."

"1,200."

"Right. Now, let me ask you, how many kids (under working age) are there on Ebeye, compared to adults?"

"Geez, the kids have to outnumber the adults two to one at least."

"Okay, I can live with that ratio. Two kids for every adult. That's probably not out of line all across the Marshall Islands. Let's go with it and see where it leaves us. In a total population of 60,000 there are probably 20,000 adults and 40,000 children in the mix."

"Yeah, I guess around that. There are a lot of kids."

"Okay. Now, how many of the adults are too old to work? I mean like retired grandparents."

"Not so many. But there are some."

"How about one in twenty? That's five percent."

"Not that many."

"One in fifty? That's two percent."

"Maybe."

"Maybe's all right. I don't know for sure myself. But it seems reasonable. Especially if you count people who are too sick to work too. A lot of Marshallese have a real problem with diabetes."

"Yeah, they sure like candy!"

"Okay, let's go with two percent. Two percent knocks off another 400 from that 20,000. That leaves 19,600 workers, all adults.

"The latest census I've seen indicates that about half of the entire Marshallese population lives on just three atolls: Kwajalein, Majuro and Jaluit. The other half are spread out over the rest of the atolls, mostly on Likiep, Ailinglaplap, Mili, and Arno. Half of the atolls in the Marshalls have no permanent communities. All the land is claimed by one family or another, but it is visited only sporadically by its claimants. Two of the atolls are still too radioactive from the U.S. atomic tests of the 1940s and '50s to support human communities. Folks don't even go there to collect copra. The coconuts are radioactive.

"The populations of those two atolls had to be relocated to other atolls and islands that were themselves only marginally suitable for habitation.

"This is what the government of the Marshall Islands has to contend with. And the only leverage they have for negotiations with the U.S. is Kwajalein Missile Range."

"Oh."

"Quite aside from negotiating stance vis-à-vis the U.S. Government, the question of wage scales for Marshallese workers has huge impacts all across the Marshall Islands. Did you ever hear of Patsy Mink?"

"Patsy Mink?"

"Yes. She was a representative in congress for the State of Hawaii."

"No."

"Let me tell you what she did years ago and the effect it had on the Whole Trust Territory of the Marshall Islands. Patsy Mink got caught up in a rather impractical political scheme called the Pan Pacific Movement. I believe she harbored dreams of making herself a major player in the movement to consolidate all the minor communities in the U.S. Trust Territory of the Pacific into one nation. In pursuit of that objective she pushed a bill through congress to require that all indigenous people, anywhere in the world who worked on U.S. government funded contracts be paid at least U.S. minimum wage. The economic impact of that bill was huge. And the social disruption it caused was even worse!"

"What do you mean?"

"I can't speak for the rest of the world, but I can tell you what happened here in the Marshalls. First, you should understand that, under terms of the Trust Territory constitution, any TT citizen was free to travel anywhere he or she wished throughout the Trust Territory, and to work wherever they could find a job."

"So?"

"As soon as the bill became law, thousands of people from all over the TT rushed to Ebeye and Enniburr hoping to get jobs with the contractors working at Kwajalein Missile Range! They had no families there. There was no housing for them nor space to build more houses. There was not enough food to feed them all nor medical services to care for them. They had no land use rights whatsoever. It was a nightmare for the people of Ebeye and Enniburr! In a matter of a couple of months, the population of Ebeye jumped from around seven thousand to over thirteen thousand! Prices for everything skyrocketed! To top it off, there were no more jobs to be had at Kwaj anyway! The crime rate on the island went up over a thousand percent!"

"Why would they rush to Ebeye?"

"Think about it! You live on Guam. You're making at most fifty cents an hour. Suddenly, there's a place you can go to where, if you can get a job, you will earn five times that much! Wouldn't you try it?"

"Yeah."

"What I'm telling you is that what you want to see happen has already been tried. It didn't work! And the folks who lived on Ebeye had to live through that mess."

"Before it was over, the citizens of Ebeye and the Trust Territory office had to cancel the clause in the TT constitution that allowed for free travel throughout the TT!

"Now do you begin to understand why the adults don't like you or anyone flapping their jaws about a break between the generations, and about making demands for parity between U.S. and Marshallese wage structures?"

"I think so."

"The whole thing is a very delicate balancing act, especially now that the United Nations Trusteeship Council is out of the picture.

"Now the government of the Republic of the Marshall Islands has to keep the same sort of lid on the situation. If they don't, Marshallese from all over the country will flock to Ebeye again for the same reason. In some ways the job will be even harder. All of the Marshallese have relatives on Ebeye. There might be some sort of family obligations to take in new arrivals. And the government will lose the services of whoever goes to Ebeye from wherever they were doing productive work before."

"I still think it's unfair."

"Look, you asked for advice, and I gave you some. Now it's your ball. Run with it."

He did.

Shortly after our conversation, he was asked to leave the Marshalls.

And not too much later the Peace Corps was asked to leave as well.

It's hard to disabuse idealism in youth.

***

The Peace Corps was not the only group of American volunteers active in the Marshalls during those years. Several Christian churches had missionary presence there as well.

The Catholic Church was represented by a number of priests shepherding congregations on the various atolls.

Baptists were there as well, along with Wesleyan Methodists, Congregationalists, Unitarians, Seventh Day Adventists, and Bahai. There may have also been others of which I was unaware.

Eldon and Alice Buck were examples of the more notable missionaries. He ran his church. She wrote the first Marshallese dictionary and grammar book. It was Alice who first translated the King James Version of the Bible into Marshallese.

I recall an incident on a trip from Kwaj to Honolulu. The routing was Kwaj - Majuro - Johnson Island - Honolulu. I was on my way home on annual vacation.

101 Marshallese got on the plane at Kwaj, headed for Majuro. They were a church group going to Majuro for a vocal concert. All the ladies were wearing dresses of the same colorful pattern. All the men had matching shirts of the same pattern. They deplaned at Majuro.

As soon as they were off the plane, fifty-seven young Americans boarded for the trip to Honolulu. Most of them were in their late teens to early twenties, about evenly split in gender. The group was the Seventh Day Adventist doing missionary work in the Marshalls. They were going to Honolulu for convocation and some rest and recreation from their labors in the field.

Two of them sat next to me for the trip.

"What's the first thing you're going to do when you get to Hono?"

"I'm going to get myself a Big Mac and a chocolate milkshake!"

"Me too. What then?"

"Then I'm going to a store to buy four gross double A cells for my video recorder!"

I have not reported this conversation to belittle in any way the work those folks were doing in the Marshalls.

True, their agenda was oriented differently from that of Peace Corps. But they, too, were learning by doing and taking their experiences back to their home congregations wherever they might be.

Other Marshallese Stories

In a closet in the retail office I found a pair of exquisitely crafted outrigger canoe models. Each was about four feet long. The detail was astounding. Each was a different design, but each had exactly the same number of parts as its full-sized counterpart. Lashings were done with single fibers stripped from coconut fronds or pandanus leaves. One had a deckhouse on the sponsons between the main hull and its outrigger. The sails were woven so tightly that water would not pass through, and there were minute cryptic markings all over each model.

No one in the office knew whom the models belonged to, so I claimed them.

When I asked my coworker Bobo Keju what the markings were, he told me that the canoes were teaching canoes and that the markings were a form of instruction for a teacher to use in teaching students how to build the real things. He said his grandfather had told him about such models, but that these were the first he had ever seen, he said he figured they had to be at least 100 years old. They had not a bit of metal anywhere, and, he said, the Marshallese had begun using metal as soon as they could get it in trade.

They really were museum quality.

I wish I could have kept them but they were too big to pack and send home through the mail. And I didn't have room by my bunk to keep them.

Then Dad died, and I had to sell them to get money to help with his funeral.

***

Bobo Keju was an interesting person. He was one of the first Marshallese I met. He and I worked together in the retail office. He made 50¢ an hour doing the same work I was getting $2.40 an hour for.

But he had aspirations. He came to me one day and asked how credit unions worked. I didn't know. But I found out, and explained it to him. The next thing I knew, he had quit Global and started a credit union on Ebeye.

Now, the Ebeye Credit Union is the largest financial enterprise on Ebeye. The last I heard, Bobo was retired and living in a fine house on the southern coast of Oregon. He put six of his children through stateside colleges through his business.

***

We worked a lot of overtime stevedoring. Every time a boat came in, and it seemed they were always coming in, the call went out for stevedores. We had to get perishable foodstuff into the reefer plant (short for refrigeration plant) as soon as possible.

I actually enjoyed the work. I was in the habit of wearing

a white short sleeve shirt, Bermuda shorts, and knee socks. It was sort of a uniform. I found that if I kept working I could be comfortable dressed that way in the chill boxes. This astounded the local men and Hawaiians who were bundled up in the heaviest winter clothes the Army could provide. To them, I must've appeared quite insensible, to say the least.

***

I want to tell you about a Marshallese who coped.

Picture this in your mind. You are Marshallese. You have one of the very best jobs available on Kwaj, so you think. You're a cab driver. You drive freely all around the island, taking passengers here and there. When you're not busy, you can give housemaids a ride. They love to ride, just for the sake of riding.

There are a couple of hundred Marshallese ladies working as maids for families in the housing area. They are not contractor employees. They make private arrangements with housewives there to wash clothes, look after kids, do the dishes, clean up the yard, and whatever else needs to be done. One maid may have more than one client. She works a few hours a week for this one, a few for that one. Pay is not very good, but the benefits are considerable.

Clients' kids outgrow their clothes before they wear them out. Client gives maid clothes. Client makes more for supper last night than her family eats. Client gives maid the leftovers. Maids can't go into the stores on Kwaj. Clients can.

You get the picture.

Anyway, you're the cab driver. One of these maids happens to be your wife, or your girlfriend.

You get the picture?

Akna was a cabdriver. He didn't want to lose his job.

But he loved to fish!

About every third month the urge to fish overcame his urge to work.

Problem? No!

What would you do in his shoes?

He'd take his cab to the long stretch of road by the runway and drive it back and forth as fast as it would go until Security stopped him. They'd slap him with a two-week suspension for speeding.

And he'd go fishing.

By the time his suspension was over, he was ready to go back to his cab.

Chapter 30

Hearts of Glass

Jodie R., A Lesson in Ingenuity

The Marshallese weren't the only ones on the atoll who coped. This is the story of a lovely lady I met for only a day. That was while she was in the throes of grief over the recent loss of her husband and the father of their several young children. Jodie's husband Bob was Fire Chief at Kwaj during the Global years. Because of his position in the organization, Bob had authorized family housing.

Bob and Jodie were active in the social life of the island and enthusiastic supporters of the many sports programs there.

Then Bob died. One of the athletic fields on Kwaj is named in his memory.

Picture this. You're 5,000 miles away from the rest of your family. Suddenly your husband and the family breadwinner is gone. You have several very young children, one still a babe in arms. You sold your house when you left the States because you had no idea how long you would be gone.

Getting some family member from the States out there to help you was very difficult in those days, especially on short notice. Things were going on there at the time which were so sensitive that the Army closed the airport to all commercial traffic.

The future that was once so comfortable and assured is suddenly painful, clouded, uncertain, perhaps even terrifying. To top it off you're (it seems to you) being kicked out of your home!

In the midst of this crisis, Jodie maintained the presence of mind to make a remarkable decision and the courage to act on it.

She spent several thousand dollars buying Macy's West's entire inventory of glass balls. Let me tell you about glass balls.

I suspect that there are hundreds of thousands of them still floating around the Pacific, perhaps millions. After all, fishermen have been using and losing them for at least 200 years. Today the glass has been replaced by plastic. But in those days glass was the material of choice. In use, they each had a tightly woven rope net around them for attachment to whatever they were supporting.

Glass balls come in a variety of sizes. Most of them were from about ten to twenty inches in diameter, but I have seen them as small as two inches across and as large as eight feet! The Coast Guard Loran station at the south end of Ebeye had an eight footer hanging from an I-beam frame in its pavilion for years. The glass in it was almost two inches thick. I know that when the Loran station closed, the glass ball was removed and carried away by the Coast Guard buoy tender *Mallow*. I have no idea what became of it. They also come in a variety of colors, mostly green, sometimes blue, sometimes clear.

Every maritime nation made them. Most of what we found were Japanese or Chinese. Now you may think that finding them would be easy. After all, glass glints and sparkles in the sunshine. Far from it.

Such nets are hundreds, sometimes even thousands, of feet long. They are fed off the rear of a fishing boat to surround whole schools of fish.

Even the ones with intact nets seldom made it to shore intact. Being thrown by waves onto rocky shorelines was usually fatal to the integrity of the glass. But it did happen that one made it now and again.

Even then they were not easy to spot. The rope nets were fine attachment points for barnacles, which proliferated during the ball's wanderings around the ocean's currents. Algae and small clams also attached themselves. These balls eventually became miniature ecosystems.

In the course of events, numbers of them came free from the nets they supported. A storm, abrasion or other rough usage left them free to circulate in the Pacific currents. The Kunihiro current carried them north along the Asian coast to Alaska and down the western coast of North America until they were swept westward again by the North Pacific counter current. The "grand tour" could take from seven to eleven years. Colonies of barnacles hitched a ride.

Glass balls make a good decoration for things with a nautical theme. At Kwaj and Roi, every quarters might have one or more on display. Of course the ideal method of getting them was to find them yourself. But most of them were bought through Macy's.

Macy's had a contract with my friend Aralon Nok. Nok wandered the Marshalls picking up anything he thought he could turn a profit on. Glass balls were one of his mainstays. So were giant clam shells (until the RMI forbade their removal). As a commercial commodity they were a source of income to people who had no other. So Nok had thousands of eyes seeking them out for him.

Macy's sold them for anything from $1.75 up.

Jodie knew this. She also knew she could sell them for rather higher prices if she could get them back to her home area on the west coast. It was the old truism in commerce about moving things from where they are to where they are needed.

I knew of this because two of my gangs from packing and crating did her packout. She told me she intended to use them as starter stock for a souvenir shop she was going to open.

Jim M. told me there were no weight limits on this particular job. I don't remember exact numbers, but I remember that we used more than 200 dish pack boxes on glass balls alone!

Jodie, I salute you. I hope you sold them for 100 bucks apiece!

Glass Ball Lew

Jodie and Nok weren't the only ones to take advantage of free-floating glass balls. Lew H. scouted them out so well that "Glass Ball Lew" became his nickname. He was in charge of General Supply on Roi when I came on the scene in 1968. He had a crew that varied in number from two to about six—most of them Marshallese.

Lew was retired Army, though I don't believe he ever accepted that fact in his own mind. He knew the standard government supply system inside and out. All of its forms and procedures were comfortable to him as old slippers. You could really light his fire by making requests outside of the Army system.

I had billeting and the aviation desk at the time and we worked very closely at times to assure that perishable foods were distributed to the chow hall or store as soon as they came off the planes or boats. Otherwise, such items had to be taken into cold or freezer storage instantly upon their arrival at Roi. Leaving perishables on the airport tarmac or on the ground at supply was not an option. Tropical heat would thaw frozen food within minutes and promote rotting in everything perishable that was allowed to warm up. Medicines had to be gotten to the Dispensary the instant they were taken off the planes. The same went for mail to the post office.

Planes had to be offloaded and back-loaded within ten minutes. So it goes without saying that we were busy at plane times. There were twenty-five planes landing at Roi every normal work day, and more on mission days.

Lew also had to check everything that came in on the weekly supply barges. His gang didn't take stuff off the barges; that was handled by the heavy equipment gang. But as soon as the stuff was physically on the island, Lew was responsible for it. All of the paperwork attendant to this flow of goods and material had to go through Lew's hands. Let's just say it was a very high pressure job.

The work week was six days long. And by the time Saturday afternoon was over, all Lew wanted to do was get away from everything and everyone.

And he did.

Lew had made an arrangement with one of the landowners on Sixth Island to set up a small camp there. Otherwise, the island was uninhabited. Lew used his camp on Saturday nights. To get there, Lew walked the reef nearly every time he went. As long as the tide was no more than two feet deep, he had no trouble making the trip down and back.

His camp was minimal. He kept a mattress of sorts there. Actually, it was a piece of foam rubber six feet by two feet from a packing crate. It was two inches thick. There was an inflatable plastic pillow. These were rolled tightly inside a thin sheet of black plastic wrap five feet by ten, along with a small box of waterproof matches and a candle. There was also a quart water bottle and a ball of twine. This package he hid under a pile of palm fronds during the week. In the nine years I was acquainted with Lew on Roi, no one ever raided his cache.

When Lew walked the reef to Sixth Island each weekend, his load was a fresh water bottle tied to his belt, a walking stick and a machete. He also carried two sandwiches he had made in the mess hall. They were in a zip-lock bag. Nothing else.

Each trip, each way, he'd stop and say a short prayer at the Marshallese cemetery on Fourth Island. That was but a five-minute detour.

Lots of folks there, including me, walked the reef in our spare time. Most of them were looking for seashells. My friend Domingo G. looked for dog tags. I looked for copper shrapnel. Lew looked for glass balls.

Over the years he found hundreds of them.

Lew could spot them from greater distances than anyone else I ever knew, in any and all of their states of colonization. And, to Lew, spotting them was tantamount to claiming them as his own.

I remember being on the reef ocean-side of second island one day, looking for copper shrapnel, when Lew was returning from Sixth Island. Just to see him walk in the water flowing over the reef was to learn a lesson in ergonomics. With every step he would lift his feet completely out of the water—even if it was knee high! Try it some time. No small feat. Most reef walkers (like me) just slogged along dragging our feet in the water. And we wondered why we could never keep up with Lew.

Anyway, balanced over his shoulder was a long bamboo pole festooned with seven glass fishing floats. He grinned at me. It had been a good trip.

I joined him and we continued our return to Roi walking near the ocean edge of the reef. As we cleared the visual blockage of TRADEX point on Namur, Lew spotted another glass ball just rolling landward over the edge of the reef behind the mess hall on Roi. A mile away? Probably. I couldn't see it even after he told me its exact location. He started toward it. Suddenly, to his dismay, someone else right behind the mess hall saw it too and walked out about fifty yards to pick it up.

Lew went ballistic!

"Stop!" he screamed. "You can't have that! It's mine! I saw it first!"

Of course the guy behind the mess hall couldn't hear Lew. And that's not how the game was played anyway. But it does illustrate Lew's mindset on the matter.

Lew called to me one day at the terminal as we were waiting for the cargo plane. "Ted! You gotta see this!" He pulled out of his pocket a sweat sogged envelope. It bore the logo of a seafood restaurant in Des Moines, Iowa. In it was a receipt for sixty glass fishing floats and a check for $2,300!

As time passed and new plastics became available, the production of glass floats tailed off. Plastic ones were much more rugged, and they had an attachment loop molded right into them. They didn't get as fouled as the glass ones because they had no need for a rope net woven around them.

Lew started picking up the plastic floats as well.

I was not on island when Lew finally left. But I got the story from others when I returned. Lew had several tri-walls of glass floats which became his authorized pack-out. All the plastic ones he dumped back into the lagoon!

When people told him that they wanted what he was throwing away, they said his response was, "I got these out of the water. If you want them, you can do the same!"

Chapter 31

The Jakaroo Club

Dressed to the Nines

When I was at Roi, the Jakaroo Club (named for a Marshallese drink) was where you went to relax. Of course, the definition of "relax" varies from person to person, and some strange things happened there during my stay.

***

This couldn't happen today. But in the late '60s it did.

There was lots of construction going on. Martin Zachary had a lot of contracts and a lot of people working on Roi then.

The building, housing most of the Roi contingent of MZ, was 8154 (called the MZ Barracks). It's not there anymore, but if you look at the new supply warehouse by the fuel pier, you'll see where it was.

Now walk westward along the lagoon beach, past the Parrothead Club to where you can see the large pink slab of cement. This was the site of the original Jakaroo Club. On the beach at this point used to be a small wooden pier. That sets the scene.

The Jakaroo Club opened daily at the close of the regular work day.

And some of the regular early customers were the MZ men just getting off work. Usually they came in, in their work clothes, for a quick cooler to relax from the day's labors. They often came in stripped to the waist.

This particular day Buddy R. was standing in for the bar keeper.

To this day I don't know whether he was serious or not. But he said to the first group of men who came in, "No way you guys, this is a classy joint. I don't want to see you in here like that. Get out of here and don't come back until you're presentable!"

The six men didn't say a word. As one, they walked out and went over to the MZ barracks.

Half an hour later they came back in dressed to the nines. One of them had on a tux jacket, long-sleeved shirt with diamond studs and tie. The rest were dressed in either sports jackets or suit jackets and ties.

From the waist down they were naked.

They ordered a round for the house, then filed out the back of the club to the pier where they carefully disrobed the rest of the way, leaving their clothes on the pier, dove into the lagoon, and swam back to their barracks. Buddy never made that mistake again.

There were other fun times at the Jakaroo. I remember this story of a fellow named Carl B.

Carl B's Bridge

Carl B. was a retired Marine, rather good at his job, and drunk most of the time. He stood (when he could stand) at least 6'4" and weighed in the neighborhood of 280 pounds.

Carl and I lived in the same barracks, though we had separate rooms. Fortunately, from his viewpoint the back door of our building was only about 100 feet from the back door of the

Jakaroo Club, the island watering hole. Carl got watered there every day.

He went directly from work each afternoon to the club and his "private" stool at the bar. There he drank until he slid off it, eyes closed. Once on the floor he got on his hands and knees and crawled across the club, out the back door, across the yard, and down the hall to his room. It was an amazing demonstration of blind navigation!

Standing up at that stage wasn't an option for Carl. He'd turn so that his back was against the door of his room, and over the course of ten minutes or so, push himself into a sitting position with his head next to the doorknob. Fumbling at his belt he would pull up his key ring and start stabbing keys at the door lock. He never opened his eyes, but eventually he would hit the key slot with the right key, the lock would turn, the door would open, and Carl would fall backwards into his room with a drunken grin on his face.

You didn't help Carl.

My first day on Roi someone pointed him out to me at a distance. Later, when I walked into my quarters, I saw two feet, toes up, sticking out of the door of Carl's room. It was Carl. I went over and said, "Mr. B., are you all right?"

His reaction astounded me. He very slowly raised his right hand, with the middle finger extended! "Hi."

We had a drainage problem along the road that ran through the club and billeting area. It was decided to build a runoff swale across the lawn from the roadside to the lagoon. The effort resulted in a very shallow ditch, maybe eight inches deep, but graded over a twenty foot width. So shallow that most people hardly noticed it.

But Carl noticed it! The morning after the swale was graded, Carl was in my office. "Jeesis Christ, Ted!" he said. "It's hard enough getting from the bar to my room! Why'd they have to build that canyon there?"

So we built a bridge for Carl. It was twenty-four feet long, twenty-four inches wide, and eight inches high! And it had hand rails three inches off the deck! It came to be known as B's Bridge.

View of the Jackaroo Club from west end of Ted's barracks.
B's Bridge is located on the front-left side of the Club.

Harold G: Cap'n Grumpy

Cap'n Grumpy spent more years in the Marshalls than he did at Kwaj. He spent his first years in the Marshalls at Eniwetok and Bikini working on the "Operation Crossroads" project. Even in those days he was a water craft operator. His usual assignment was a Landing Craft Utility (LCU). Cargo here, cargo there. Men here, men there. Harold liked a libation now and then among friends at the old Jakaroo Club. He was a long standing member of the A-Team (everyday, all-evening drinkers) at the bar. But his drink wasn't beer. It was Courvoisier VSOP! He claimed it was the only thing that could relax him from the day's work. He'd have a shot or two before the nightly movie at the Tradewinds theater next to the club. Just before show time he'd order a "tworple" (that's a triple triple!) and nurse it through the movie.

Then it was home to bed. I roomed with him for almost five years, and I can honestly say that I never saw him drunk.

What it was doing to him was a private matter between him and his liver. Obviously he eventually had a problem, though he never talked about it, because one day he stopped. Cold turkey. I remember the day because I was keeping records of the bar sales. Our sales of Courvoisier VSOP dropped from almost two cases a month to less than one bottle!

Now Harold loved to go fishing and he was also a very good cook. He took a lot of people fishing over the years and sometimes he got fish from grateful passengers. Harold made the world's best gutted, skinned, fileted, cubed, marinated, blown dry, hickory smoked Wahoo ever! The A-Team at the club always appreciated his efforts at the stove in the Club backroom. Harold was definitely the ultimate chili chef.

"Let's do chili!" he'd say.

"Yay chili!" they'd shout.

"I can eat hotter chili than any of you guys!" he'd say. "No way!" they replied.

They could make quite a show of it. Everybody at the bar gave the bartender their lighters and matches. These were serious chili—macho men! Each contestant was issued a clean bar towel to wipe his fevered brow.

Harold would step into his "kitchen." Out would come small bowls, no more than half a cup each. Beautiful to look at, the chili was rich and savory. A wonderful aroma filled the club.

Scattered throughout each serving were minced pieces of some particular chili. They only had to eat one mouthful of each serving. Macho ones ate it all. Out went the bowls. In they came again with a different chili as they worked their way through the heat rainbow that chilis come in, each offering hotter than the last. Fresh baked pumpernickel bread and a shot of beer cleansed their pallets between rounds. Sweat broke out. Tears followed. Tongues burned, lips burned, fingers burned, even their farts burned!

(This was the stated reason for turning over their lighters. They didn't want to take a chance of being blown off the barstool by a flatulence-fueled fire ball!)

Harold matched them serving for serving. He grinned. They returned a rictus of pain. By ones and twos they dropped out until only Harold was left. Champion!

He was unbeatable!

Harold took on all challengers.

Until...

One night someone walked in to the back room and caught Harold adding drops of food color yellow to the mild chili bits in his serving.

The rest of the A-Team was really pissed! They made him an offer and wouldn't let him refuse it. It was a very "special" bowl of chili.

All I can say is that Harold didn't sleep very much that night.

Chapter 32

Roi Rats and Kwaj Cats

Chuck M: One Tough Customer

Not all of us overseas Americans frequented the Jakaroo every night. Here are some stories about other people I encountered over my years there, and the scrapes that they got themselves into (and occasionally out of).

***

Chuck M. was working on his third career (at least) when I met him on Kwaj. He had a full-time job working in the base power plant with Burns & Roe and he worked eight hours a day for Global repairing radios and electric appliances.

Chuck had, it seemed to me, been everywhere and done everything. I can't say for certain where he was from. He was American by nationality. He had raised a family in the Philippines and been interned in a Japanese prison camp for most of WWII. The Japanese killed his first wife and five of their eight children during the course of the war.

His second wife and their two children were with him on Kwaj. Nadia, his wife, was from Beirut, Lebanon, the daughter of a high-ranking Lebanese family involved in international banking.

While he was still in the Philippines, he had met Harry Winston, a major jeweler in New York. Their acquaintance grew into friendship, the result being that when I knew Chuck on Kwaj, his wife's family was brokering the sale of "The Pearl of Allah" to a Mideastern potentate for donation to the Muslim Church.

The "Pearl of Allah" is in the *Guinness Book of World Records*. It was found by a Moro tribesman in the Philippines in the early years of this century. The finder gifted the pearl to the tribe's chief, who held it for a number of years.

Then the chief's son got sick. The medicine men of the tribe couldn't help him. But a medical missionary from the States cured the lad. In gratitude, the chief gave the missionary the pearl. Thus, the "Pearl of Allah" came to the States. When the missionary died, his family sold the pearl to Harry Winston.

Harry knew Chuck had family ties in Beirut banking circles. So he contacted Chuck and offered him 15% of the $4.5 million he was asking for the pearl.

I never heard how that deal worked out. Civil war broke out in Lebanon. Beirut was destroyed.

Chuck was, in some ways, an odd duck. His imprisonment at the hands of the Japanese marked him for life. They used him as a target for judo practice, and they weren't gentle. He was allowed, even encouraged, to defend himself. He learned from the beatings they gave him on the judo mats.

Eventually he became something of an expert in the martial arts himself. He gained a sort of grudging respect from his captors, which probably contributed to his survival as a POW.

After the war he wrote a book on the subject of Judo that became sort of a standard reference for the many Americans who took up the discipline.

Chuck ate two meals a day, at noon and at midnight. He had come to believe that the body extracted all the nutrition it could from food within two hours. Moreover, he decided that it was best to get rid of what he had eaten after that. So he got into the practice of purging himself two hours after each meal!

When I met him, I was working in the retail office. He came in and ordered two cases of Pepto Bismol! (By that time his "habit" required a quarter bottle a dose to be effective!)

This had a funny consequence. One time he went into the hospital at Kwaj for a barium x-ray check. The procedure called for a pre-treatment purge. The nurse who was to administer it didn't know Chuck. She came into his ward with a bottle of Pepto and a spoon.

"I know you won't like this," she said. "But it has to be done."

"Give me the bottle."

She did. He drank half of it. She lost her cookies!

Chuck was one of those people who could subsist on very little sleep. And he did. Four hours a night. He used to joke about it, saying he had to because of Nadia's spending habits and that he was trying to keep her in the style she had become accustomed as a daughter whose wealthy parents doted on her.

Four times during the years I knew Chuck, Nadia took the kids to see her parents and shop in Paris.

Chuck died at Kwaj after I had gone to Roi. He had lived at least three lifetimes and he's probably running the angels ragged.

The Mysterious Chavez

Chavez was a loner.

Doing shift work in the Fire Department at Roi, he stayed in a single room. He didn't talk much and kept mostly to himself. This is not to say that he shunned human contact.

On the contrary, many of us gravitated to him like iron filings to a magnet. We didn't come to talk; we just came to listen.

Chavez traveled light. When he came to Roi, he came with one small suitcase and an old Gibson classical twelve string guitar.

It was this guitar, or more specifically Chavez playing it, that enthralled us.

He never accepted requests for a specific song. But his repertoire was broad and deep. He played jazz, country and western, classical, and flamenco, according to his whim and mood.

Think of Chet Atkins. Think of Andres Segovia and Julian Bream. Think of Carlos Montoya and Luiz Bonfa. Think of Lorindo Almeda and Antonio Bribiesca. In their respective musical genres they were or are supreme.

Yet there are those of us who knew Chavez who would aver that he was on a par with any of them in their own fortes!

Chavez never used sheet music when he played for himself and the listeners who flocked quietly to hear. He had mastered hundreds of scores in the technical sense and what we heard were moods, interpretations, and applications of the music to different situations.

The one thing he forbade was anyone recording his performances.

We all wondered at his expertise, but one of the unwritten rules in the islands was that you didn't pry into the private lives or history of another. It was part of the accommodation we all made to the general lack of privacy there.

Now in those days we had the occasional USO show; ours was an Army base after all. Most of the performers in these shows were not yet "names." A tour with USO was a chance for these folks to practice, work on their routines, smoothe out their presentations and have, for awhile, that most prized of accomplishments for an artist—a steady job.

One of the acts on our circuit that year consisted of Nat King Cole's sister and her husband. They were developing an act in which she sang and he accompanied. They billed themselves as "The Two Black Coles."

Chavez normally avoided these shows. That wasn't hard because he worked long hours. But this one he apparently wanted to see.

The Jakaroo Club was where we staged the shows. It was roofed, but open to the yards facing the lagoon. These yards were lighted at night for safety.

Ms. Cole was in the middle of a song when Chavez walked through one of the lighted areas outside the club. He never entered the club, but Ms. Cole saw him.

She stopped in the middle of a phrase, stared, turned pale, and called him by another name!

"What are you doing here? We thought you were dead!"

The next day Chavez "pulled the pin" and disappeared!

Roi: Jerry W's Sanctuary

What is there to say about Jerry W.? By the time I met him on Roi he had an immense attitude. He didn't give a damn what anyone thought of him. Take him as he was or not, it was of no concern to him.

Jerry worked for Kentron/Lincoln Lab. His field was communications, and his hobbies were guns and EOD (Explosive Ordinance Disposal).

In those years there was a very active gun club on Roi. Jerry was one of the most active members of all. Not only did he buy guns in large numbers, calibers, and types, he also used them. Jerry played at war.

He liked nothing better than to take his Uzi, or his AR15, or his AK47 (he had more than seventy to choose from), tog out in his combat dress, and go sneaking through the "jungles" of Namur.

Jerry loved finding old, unexploded WWII ordinance so that he could report it to EOD and work with them to "neutralize" it. Especially if doing so resulted in him being allowed to play with plastique or primacord. He liked things that went BANG!

Walking into Jerry's room was like entering an arms warehouse. From the door to his bed was a path ten inches wide. From the bed to the sink and bathroom there was a path ten inches wide. Every other square inch of the room was stacked, piled, or otherwise crammed with guns of every size.

Once he offered to sell me the only 12 gauge shotgun I ever saw with a fifty round drum magazine and spare barrels in the stock. I should have bought it from him because I've never seen another since.

This is not to say that Jerry was an outlaw. On the contrary, he stayed scrupulously within the law. He just pushed it a little—*all the time*!

I enjoyed talking with Jerry. He had a perspective that was refreshingly direct and to the point. One time, I asked him why he spent so much on his gun collection. He replied, "Why not? I might as well spend it on something I enjoy. No sense to save it."

I asked him how long he planned to stay on Roi. He said, "Probably another two years. I like it here and people don't bug me like they do at home."

"What then?" I asked.

"Then," he said, "I'm going to retire."

"Where?"

"To a little island in the Bay of Bengal. I visited there last year and fell in love with it."

"Jerry, isn't twenty-eight a little young to be retiring?"

"What would you do if you were me?"

"If I were you," I said, "I'd probably keep on working."

"Well, you're you and I'm me! I want to have some fun and the girls there don't mind me."

And he did. Two years after that conversation, Jerry left, armory and all. And he went to his island and his girls. He had always maintained that he had enough money to last him.

And he did.

Jerry died eleven months after he left here. Mutual friends told me they found a letter in his wallet instructing them to pay off his debts, and to split the residual in his account with the three girls he had living with him. The letter was accompanied with a notarized general power of attorney. The girls got about $1,000 each.

How did Jerry die? Well, he died of severe neurological malfunction. Oh, didn't I mention it? Jerry was a hunchback.

Li'l Fuzz

Bill B. spent several years at Roi as a security officer, in spite of the fact that he barely broke five feet in height or 100 pounds in weight. His time there spanned the years when we were busiest, that is to say from the mid-'60s up to '73, just after the signing of the first Strategic Arms Limitation Treaty (SALT).

Bill garnered the nickname "Li'l Fuzz" for obvious reasons. But rather than be offended or embarrassed by it, he played to it. He even bought himself a child's tricycle, which he rode into the Jakaroo Club on occasion. It always drew a laugh. But it also pre-empted any move on the part of bullies or drunks from giving him a hard time. Everyone else was on his side.

Bill was Jewish. The Jewish community at Kwaj was not large, nor formally organized. Christians (Catholic and Protestant) outnumbered them fifty to one or more. There was no staff Rabbi on the island, nor a synagogue. Meetings were informal and held in the home of one or another of their members. Once or twice a year a military Rabbi would visit the range for a day or two. On these occasions a community read from the Torah and formal services were conducted.

Bill practiced his faith, though never in an obtrusive or intrusive manner. To him his faith was an intensely personal thing between himself and God.

I guess the same could be said for most of us.

Anyway, Bill found out that the community didn't have a container for their Torah. This was conventionally a cabinet with two doors on it.

Now it happened that a very fine and large log of rosewood had washed ashore on Roi. It had rested above the high tide line for a couple of years, slowly drying, before we realized what it was. When we did realize it, Bill had a thought that we might cut a piece from the log large enough to fabricate such a cabinet.

He got the dimensions of the scrolls and the log cross-section was large enough to hollow out such a container in one piece. It would make a unique and appropriate (given where we were) cabinet.

Using a large band saw in the carpenter shop we trued the base so that it stood flat and stable on the workbench. Then we cut a slab from one side of the log large enough to make the two doors.

Bill got the work on the doors. I got to work hollowing out the interior.

Bill had an absolute talent working with wood.

He started by shaping the slab in the form of the slabs of the Ten Commandments as held by Moses. Within these forms he carved in bas-relief two Lions of Judah facing each other. Then he took an electric burner that looked like an old fashioned soldering iron and carefully seared the surface of the carvings to bring out details of the lion carvings. It worked beautifully.

A carpenter friend helped with two pieces of brass piano hinge. He installed these in such a fashion that the doors would open wide without the hinges being exposed. His work was critical and perfectly executed. By the time he was done the outside of the doors melded almost seamlessly with the cabinet's exterior.

In the meantime I had been working with drills and chisels to shape the interior of the cabinet into the requisite form to hold the scrolls upright. The carpenter helped with this too.

Then he enlisted the aid of an upholsterer to line parts of the interior with gold colored velvet.

Then Bill and I spent a couple of months sanding, oiling and burnishing the cabinet to bring out the grain and color of the wood. My major contribution was lots of elbow grease.

The results were remarkable. I have to say that it was far and away the finest thing I have ever helped to fabricate.

We presented it to the community, and it was put in immediate service. I have no idea whether it's still there or not.

Bill left Roi before I did. We corresponded for several years. He had returned to New York City. He once asked me to go into business with him. He was opening a tuxedo rental store and needed financial assistance that I was not able to provide at the time. I am sure he got it somewhere.

Wherever you are Bill, whatever you're doing, thanks for being my friend. Shalom.

Domingo G's Dog Tags

If you asked any or all of the hundreds of folks who worked at KREMS over the decades to list people they knew there, one name that would be on everyone's list would be Domingo G. There may have been other Domingos on the range over the years, but there could be no mistaking this one. In my opinion, he was what every employer would consider the perfect employee.

He came early on in the range's existence. He was at Roi before I got to Kwaj in 1964. He may have been there before Transport Company of Texas came. I know he crossed over to Global Associates when they got the contract in February of '64.

In the early days Global had a tacit understanding with the Navy, then the Army, that a certain percentage of their employees would be drawn from the State of Hawaii. To this end Global opened a major office in Honolulu. As a matter of fact, that office was where I first signed on with Global. I had been with the company nearly ten years myself before I ever saw the inside of the main office in California.

My situation was a bit different from that of most of the people who hired on from Hawaii. I was there as a student at University of Hawaii doing graduate studies.

Most of the employees hired from Hawaii in those days were residents of the State and had families there. As such they had to agree to pay Hawaii income tax on their earnings from Kwajalein. So while they were exempt from Federal income tax, their packages were not as good as the mainlanders who worked on the range.

I'm sure that Domingo and the other Hawaii hires knew of this inequity. But I never knew Domingo to cry about it.

Domingo was a janitor, and he did his job well. In due course he became Leadman in his group at KREMS. Most of his team in the early years were Hawaiian Americans of various ethnic extractions. Many of them were legal residents of Hawaii while their families resided in the Philippines. These folks didn't think in terms of the U.S. economy at all. So they could multiply their comparatively low income by six or seven or whatever the exchange rate was between the U.S. dollar and the Philippine peso. In those terms they were very well paid.

Those of them who sent their incomes back home to buy property ended up very well off indeed.

Time and normal attrition reduced their numbers. New agreements with the government of the Marshall Islands slowly brought more and more Marshallese into these positions, but Domingo stayed.

Overtime was never a problem with him. He was allowed to work each week as long as he felt necessary. And overtime was abundant because much of the cleaning had to be done when technical people were not working.

He kept busy, but not always at his assigned job.

Domingo and I used to walk the island's shoreline together.

We were each looking for interesting artifacts of one sort or another. I was particularly interested in pieces of the copper rifling bands from the large shells that had bombarded the islands during the invasion of February, 1944. Domingo's particular interest was dog tags.

I should mention that Domingo has lost the use of one eye due to glaucoma. Even so, he had a knack for finding dog tags.

There were two types of tags, Japanese and American.

Japanese dog tags were made of bamboo. On each was the owner's name, his rank, and his operational speciality within the Imperial Navy. Each tag was about an inch wide and maybe an inch and a half long. The identification was burned onto the convex surface of the bamboo piece. Domingo found scores of them. I never found one.

His real pride was the collection he accumulated—nearly fifty U.S. dog tags.

One day an acquaintance of his who had been in the Marine Corps asked Domingo for a list of the American dog tags in his collection. He gave it to him. Then without asking permission and unbeknownst to Domingo, his acquaintance sent the list to Marine headquarters.

In due course the list was published.

Ex-Marines and their families began writing to Domingo pleading for the dog tags of their sons or comrades.

In no time at all the American portion of his collection evaporated.

Domingo finally called it quits on Roi about the same time I did.

I ran into Domingo in one of the stores in the Ala Moana Shopping Center in Honolulu on my way home. He was well.

Roi-Namur was diminished by his departure.

Poor John E.

John E. died at Roi-Namur in his sleep.

He was usually at the Security office before his shift began, so when he was late that morning, Pete LH went over to his room to check on him. He knocked on the door.

No answer.

Pete got the pass key and unlocked John's door. John appeared to be asleep in his bed. But he couldn't be roused. An autopsy showed that he had suffered an embolism in his brain.

John was a shift captain in Global's Security department and had been here on Roi for several years. He had completed a career in the Air Force before he came to work for Global. He was well liked by all of us.

John E. had been separated from his wife for a number of years, but they had never divorced. Standard procedure for an event such as a death was to seal the room until a witnessed inventory could be conducted. As billeting supervisor at Roi, I was a member of the inventory team. Our sad job was to itemize, evaluate, describe, and pack every item of personal property of the deceased.

Now, you should know that John had a passion. He was a fisherman. And I do mean a *fisherman*!

He lived and breathed fishing. His planned retirement was to go to British Columbia, where he would spend his days challenging the wily trout.

John wasn't interested in the fishing here, good as it was. His passion was fly-fishing. Off-duty hours were spent scouring the market for the very best equipment. He acquired a museum class library of books relating to fly fishing. And he was an expert at tying flies in his own right, that being his hobby.

John was a very organized person and kept meticulous records of every purchase. This made our inventory much easier.

When we entered his room, we saw the depth of his profound passion.

The numbers went something like this:

Library: 103 books	$7,700
Rods: 17 Custom-made	$5,950
Tied fly sets purchased: 28	$6,620
Tied fly sets homemade: 19	$3,800 (est.)
Reels: 12	$2,700
Accessories	$ 800
Tying equipment	$1,990
Total	$29,560

Of course, there was the usual assortment of clothes and incidental items.

The only reason I mentioned the figures above is because of what happened to the fishing gear. The law required that we ship all of John's personal effects to his next of kin. In this case the indicated recipient was his estranged (but not divorced) wife.

John had broken off all contact with his wife and he never talked about her. It soon became clear that she too had a passion: She detested everything and anything having to do with John.

Several of the guys here wanted various items of the fishing gear and they made written offers which accompanied the shipment. A couple of them even contacted her by phone.

Not interested!

What happened to the things we sent her?

I asked one of the guys who contacted her about the equipment:

"She had taken all of the boxes, unopened, piled them up and burned them!"

Poor John E.

Fred M's Strange Addiction

We had a fairly rapid succession of "secretaries" at Roi during the years I was there with Global. The position was actually part typist, part accountant, part cashier, part confidant to the manager, and, according to those whose hobby it was to bait the manager, part stool pigeon. This last arose from the propensity of Frank (the boss) to sound out his staff members for a "status of the troops" report.

Fred M. was in many ways typical and in some ways unique of the secretaries we've had. A good typist, expert stenographer, organized to the nth degree, Fred was one of those people who, like secretaries everywhere, were the real managers of the goings-on in the company. This left Frank largely free to do what he liked best as island manager, mingle with the workers.

Fred lasted one contract. I don't suppose he was really cut out for overseas work. He did his job well. But he was a social person and his position led many to believe that anything they said or did in his proximity would get back to Frank. A "zone of silence" moved with him. Conversations stopped or changed when he was present. Eyes averted and watched where he was. And he sensed it, and resented it.

Fred had two habits by which people remembered him. One of these was his addiction to Coca Cola.

He drank more than a case a day! He never came to work in the morning without his six pack and cooler of ice cubes. Like a chain smoker, he would refill his insulated mug as soon as he had taken the last swallow of the previous filling. At 10:00 each morning, Fred took a ten-minute break during which he went to his room and grabbed another six pack. This was gone by noon. He brought another back with him after lunch and husbanded this until quitting time. Then he settled down for some serious consumption! All of us were amazed that he didn't have ulcers.

His other habit was his daily call to his mother. He was on the phone with her exactly one hour, every day of the week.

In those days calls were free to the satellite terminal at Palos Verdes, California. His mother lived twenty miles from there. Yet his monthly phone bill exceeded $500!

Fred completed his contract to the day and left Roi. From that day on, no one, not even Frank, ever heard another word from or about Fred M.

Melville M's Marvelous Memory

Mel was one of the people who stayed.

Lucky for the Air Force and Army. Lucky for MIT and Global Associates. Lucky for me. Most people at the power plant where he worked on Roi called him "the old man." And, in terms of time on the job, he was.

Mel ran away from home when he was sixteen to join the Army in 1939. He was with the 7th (Hourglass) Division when they invaded Kwajalein in 1944.

He stayed in the Army after the war and was assigned to occupation duty in Japan. That's where he met and married his wife, Mitsuko. They had one child, a girl.

I was one of the few people out there he let get away with calling him Mel. He didn't particularly like his given name and accepted it from we few only because he was certain we weren't trying to embarrass him.

Mel moved his family to San Diego where they settled in while he completed his twenty-year stint in the Army. He was a sergeant when he retired in 1959.

Among other assignments, Mel spent the entire Korean War in Korea. I am guessing that that is where he got more or less used to being without his family. And they without him.

In any event he started looking for a civilian job as soon as he got out of the service. He heard from Navy neighbors in San Diego that something big was happening at Kwajalein. He remembered Kwaj from the war and developed an itch to see what it looked like fifteen years after the invasion.

So he hired on.

Roi-Namur was just building up when he arrived on the atoll, and he was assigned there as a laborer. He helped with the ground breaking for the precision power plant installation. It suited him.

And it gave him a chance to apply his greatest asset besides his intelligence. He was one of those rare individuals whose memory was both photographic and eidetic!

You're probably acquainted with the connotation of a photographic memory. It usually means that you can remember everything you've read. He could.

Eidetic refers to the capacity to clearly visualize everything you've ever seen. He could do that too!

This is an immensely powerful combination of abilities.

Picture this in your mind.

A young black man from the Mississippi of the '20s and '30s. Never finished high school. Enlisted in the then strictly segregated Army by lying about his age. Relegated to stereotyped job assignments in the service with no great possibilities for career advancement. Yet he made master sergeant during his enlistment!

Mel taught himself enough electronics to understand what he was involved in as a power plant-builder. He offered to set up a filing system for the power plant documentation, which was accepted. This gave him access to every piece of paper relating to the plant: the blueprints, the operating manuals, the correspondence, the numerous photos, the equipment inventories, everything.

He read, he looked, he studied, and he remembered it all!

People soon were coming to him with questions when problems arose. If the answer was in the documentation, he was able to instantly cite source and quote verbatim what the documentation said or showed. At first his superiors or questioners went to the files he had created and cited. But he wasn't mistaken. He became something of a legend on the island.

And he liked it. He basked in the almost awesome regard of the plant personnel and the engineers from the technical contractors.

Mel taught himself the operating procedures of the machinery in the plant and was promoted to operator. He taught himself the systems and procedures in the control room and was promoted to controller. And while keeping up the filing, he kept aware of every work order, every change, every new piece of equipment.

Mel soon became "the authority" in questions pertaining to the power plant. His manager knew it, the engineers knew it, and the Army knew it.

But he never aspired to management position. He was that most treasured of employees from the manager's perspective—a personnel asset who could have challenged for the manager's job, but didn't want it. His job did not merit family housing on Kwaj. It was offered and he declined.

Mel had asked Mitsuko if she wanted to come there and she said no. They reached a modus vivendi: he spent a month each year in San Diego with his family. She and her daughter made their own life there for the rest of the year. There was love between them, but it became almost platonic over the years.

His real home was where his work was: Roi-Namur.

Mel had a physical problem which made many people feel uncomfortable in his presence. He had a growth on his tongue which slightly impeded his speech. It had grown, then stopped. He was terrified of having surgery to remove it. Some of the doctors he saw had told him that such an operation might trigger a malignant regrowth which could endanger the entire tongue. So he learned to live with it.

What sort of a person was he?

"Well, I reckon I'm the best checkers player I ever met."

I couldn't let the implied challenge go by. But I never came close to beating him.

He saw an ad in a checkers magazine one time for a very sophisticated electronic checkers game. It had twelve levels of difficulty ranging from beginner to grand master. At a price of $150 he reckoned it might be interesting.

And the ad guaranteed satisfaction "or your money back."

He sent for it.

When it came in the mail he stopped at the store, bought two batteries for it and came to the mess hall.

"Ted. It's here. Why don't you try it and tell me how it is?"

I set it on level one and beat it, level two, and beat it, level three, and beat it. At level four I won two out of three. Level five was two out of four. Level six was one out of four. I had had enough.

Mel took it and set it at level nine, and beat it. A crowd had gathered. He set it at level twelve and beat it six games straight.

The next day it was in the mail back to the vendor with a note that said they should contact him again when they got a machine that was a real challenge. He got his money back.

"Mel. Do you ever play chess?"

"Not any more."

"What do you mean, not any more?"

"I used to. But it's too slow."

It reached the point where the only games Mel could get were from new arrivals on the island.

Part of Mel's daily routine was writing a letter to his wife and/or daughter. They, in turn, wrote him with equal regularity.

And there was real affection among them. But their lives did run on different tracks. Mel was reading one of these letters in the chow hall when I sat next to him one day.

"Oh, oh. This is going to hurt!"

"What's that?"

"That damn wife of mine is going to drive me to the poorhouse!"

"What now?"

"She's decided to build a tea house for her and the kid!"

"A big one?"

"Probably not. The yard ain't that big."

"So what's the problem?"

"The problem is you don't know my wife. She doesn't know anything about tea houses, only that she wants one!"

"So?"

"So she's hired a Japanese Teahouse architect! She says it has to be perfect. You know what that means!"

"Well, no."

"It means money! It means she'll have the yard landscaped into a Japanese garden so the setting will be proper! And that's only the beginning!"

"Why does she want a teahouse?"

"Because there's a bunch of Japanese biddies living in our neighborhood and she wants to one-up them all!"

"Can you afford it?"

"Probably not. But I guess I gotta try."

A little while later, I saw Mel again.

"Ted, I swear that woman's going to drive me to an early grave!"

"What now?"

"It's that damn teahouse! Look here."

He had a dozen photos that had come in the letter. They showed a beautiful little teahouse set in a perfectly scaled Japanese garden.

"Mel, that's beautiful!"

"Yeh, I guess so."

"You don't like it?"

"Oh, I like it fine. But, like I said, it's only the beginning."

"What now?"

"Now that crazy woman wants to take the girl and go to Japan to buy stuff for it."

"Like what?"

"Like antique tea service stuff. It'll cost me a fortune!"

"Can you afford it?"

"Well, she is my wife."

Mel went on his annual leave. And came back.

"Hey! Welcome back, Mel! How's the teahouse?"

"It looks nice. But I don't like the door."

"The door?"

"Yeah, the door. I forgot the damn door! They make it so small you have to get on your hands and knees to get in! Do you know how long it's been since I had to get on my hands and knees?"

"Did she get the stuff you mentioned?"

"Yeh, she did. It's all right, I guess. At least it's all certified antiques. I could probably sell it if I had to. But, like I said, it ain't over yet. Ted, that daft woman's driving me nuts!"

"What now?"

"Now she wants to take the daughter to Japan so's they can study under the most famous tea ceremony master in the country. He's one of the people they call 'a living national treasure!' It'll cost me a fortune!"

Time passed. About one year later Mel was leaving for his next annual vacation. He had left Roi for Kwaj on the earliest commuter flight in the morning. His plane was to leave from Kwaj at noon.

"Ted. Phone call, line three. It's Mel."

"Hi Mel. What's up?"

"Ted, I got a problem. Is anybody listening?"

I looked around. "No."

"Good. Look. I forgot something in my room. Would you run over there and pick it up for me? The mid-morning plane just left here for Roi. But it won't be on the ground long enough for me to go to the barracks myself."

"I'm on my way. What is it?"

"It's my paychecks." He told me where he had them hidden. "They're in a manilla envelope. Hand the envelope to Jerry C. He's stewarding the plane. I'll get them from him when he gets back here."

"Ok."

There were twenty-two paychecks in the envelope!

All of his growling and complaining about how much money his wife was costing him for her teahouse and he had nearly one year's paychecks uncashed!

It appeared that his wife had managed for years on his Army sergeant's retirement pay! Or at least closely enough so that he could accumulate nearly one year's back pay out there.

Mel kept up the pretense of his wife's extravagance, at least in public. But once I knew his secret, he mellowed out about her in our private conversations.

Dick J. the Viking

I guess I've grown jaded over the years.

I used to stand in awe of people who had advanced degrees in almost anything. In fact, the prospect of being associated with such people was, for me, one of the real enticements in going to Kwaj. As things worked out, our paths didn't cross as often as I could have wished.

I went there in a low-level position and, at various times, worked my way up to supervisory and mid-level management. Always on bachelor status.

Degreed people went to Kwaj on family status in mostly mid to top-level management positions, or at least highly technical job slots.

Such was my friend, the Viking.

Dick J. was quite loquacious and delighted in telling anyone who would listen about his extremely interesting background and life experiences. I was a willing listener.

Dick was one of the very few people I knew at Kwaj whose security clearance had reached levels beyond what I had needed over the years.

We had crossed paths, like ships in the night, at the National Security Agency, but I never knew of his presence at the time. Our fields of interest were too far separated by levels of technical focus and circumstance. I was there as an enlisted Air Force crypto-linguist, trying to analyze such things as order of battle and the like.

Dick was there as a civilian consultant whose job was focused on certain aspects of the Soviet Missile Force's capabilities and vulnerabilities. He knew rockets; I didn't. He knew radar; I didn't. On the other hand, I spoke and worked with certain applications of Mandarin Chinese.

Even in those years the NSA cast a very wide web.

Dick knew certain things about missile penetration aids and their neutralization.

This is what brought him to Roi.

During the several years I knew him at Roi he worked in both engineering and management slots. For a time he was sensor leader for the ALCOR and MMW radars.

Dick was out there on bachelor status. He had been married a couple of times and had a couple of grown children. His positions qualified him for family housing on Kwaj, but he opted to live on Roi. At a time when his peers lived mostly on Kwaj and commuted to work by air each day, his living on Roi cut into his socializing time rather severely. On the other hand he avoided the daily commute, which occurred whatever the weather. Not only did this give him more sleep time, it facilitated quick response time when one or the other of his radars developed a glitch.

Lincoln Labs was happy with the arrangement. The Army was happy with it. And Dick was happy with it.

Dick had a hobby. He played the acoustic guitar. And he had the financial resources to acquire the very finest, made to his order. He had at least two of them with him on Roi that were worth several thousand dollars apiece. He practiced a lot. I think his constant practice helped him fend off the effects on encroaching Parkinson's disease. Though he never spoke of it, the observant could detect the occasional trembling of his hands when he was not occupied with his instruments.

Our interactions with Dick were mostly at evening meal times. Several of us would gather round to hear his tales of ancestral deeds both daring and dastardly. We could listen as long as he was willing to regale us.

For my part I knew very little about the real history of northwestern Europe during Viking times. Courses in Western Civilization during college had little to say on the subject. That omission has since been corrected, but at the time Dick was a fountainhead of information on the subject, particularly where it concerned his ancestors.

And it seemed to concern them a lot.

There was once a part of England known as the Dane Geld. More than half of this land was conquered and held by Dick's lineal ancestors. Had they not made a mistake and chosen the wrong side during the Cromwellian episode of English history, they would still be there.

It seems you can't keep a good Dane down.

In any event, a number of Dick's antecedents migrated early to the northern reaches of Mexico and Texas to take up land grants there. His family still has extensive holdings on both sides of the border. And Dick is heir to all of them!

Jason's Piano

My friend Jason was a fireman.

Like most of the firemen there and most of the other personnel as well, his presence there was a means to an end.

He was there to pay for a piano.

And he made a deal.

Jason's home was in Honolulu. His aspiration was to become a concert pianist.

So he went to "The House of Music" across the street from the Honolulu International Center and there contracted to buy their very best full size Baldwin concert grand piano. His intention was to pay off the $30,000 as quickly as he could by working overseas (i.e. Kwajalein) and putting every cent he cleared there against the contract. Being unmarried, he figured he could accomplish this in three years, and he did.

Jason's needs at Roi were simple. He didn't drink or smoke. His room and board were part of his employment contract, as were medical and dental coverage. And he had access to the chapel piano there to continue practice.

This left him with one problem: what to do with his purchase while he paid for it. Storage of grand pianos is expensive. In the tropical humidity of Honolulu humidity had to be taken into account as well. Things left to themselves in the islands tend to go to pot; especially things made of wood like furniture and pianos.

So Jason asked the folks at "The House of Music" if they could store his piano in their facility while he paid it off. They quoted him a price (which he blanched at), then offered him a proposition:

"It so happens that we've just contracted with the Honolulu International Center to provide them with major musical instruments for their concerts. Your piano would be perfect as one of them. If you would agree to let us use it for that purpose, we'll keep it in new condition and store it for free!"

"That sounds wonderful. But who would be playing it?"

"We don't know exactly what the Center's schedule is, but we can assure you that anyone who plays your piano will be professional, and probably world class. Maybe even famous!"

Jason thought it over, then agreed—conditionally.

"That's great! But could I ask one thing further?"

"And that is?"

"Could you arrange to have the Center people ask each performer to autograph and date his or her performance somewhere inside the piano?"

"Of course!"

"We have a deal!"

I heard Jason telling the story at the Crossroads Club on the night he made the final payment. He was boasting that there were eighty-seven dated autographs in his piano. He completed his third contract some months later and left Kwaj.

I never heard anything more about him after he left. Perhaps he's playing professionally today. Or perhaps not.

The only thing I know for sure is that he had one hell of an autograph album!

Captain Holmberg's Fancy Furniture

Activity at the furniture warehouse called us into the housing area almost every day for official business. My teams were always out delivering things or picking up things. We were among the first people newcomers met on arrival at Kwaj. Fine tuning furniture inventory was a constant chore. People came to us for light bulbs and air conditioner filters.

Every house and trailer on the island (except the Commanding Officer's) was equipped with overstuffed rattan furniture left over from Navy days. So were the dormitories that housed technical contractors' bachelor staff.

There are bachelors and there are Bachelors. If you worked for a technical contractor, you had access to better housing, the Yukweyuk Club and theater, the commissary, and other amenities denied to the peon bachelors of the base support and construction contractors.

We serviced them all.

Since I mentioned it, I had better tell you what was different about the CO's house. Captain Holmberg, the last Navy CO, had furnished his quarters completely in Nara Wood. This was beautiful furniture! It was said that he had the set commissioned in Hong Kong out of his own pocket.

There were sofas that comfortably seated six people, armoires, breakfronts, desks, occasional tables (some of them exquisitely inlaid), and more. The dining table alone could seat at least thirty people in its extended configuration, with matching dining chairs padded seat and back with silk brocade. Chests of drawers ran from four to ten drawers each. There was an escritoire to die for.

Everything was hand crafted out of dovetailed solid Nara wood, no veneers.

I know these things because we were occasionally called upon to help him prepare for a large party.

Total number of pieces in the house? I have no idea. Cost? Ditto. I hope you noticed the number of plurals in the recounting.

There are few things I have coveted in my life. But I must tell you I coveted that furniture! Totally irrational, I know. But I did.

Captain Holmberg bequeathed the furniture to the house when he left Kwaj! A magnificent gift to the future generations of Commanding Officers since!

Harold G: Antics in the Ocean and at the Track

I mentioned Harold's antics at the Jakaroo, but there was more to him than Courvoisier and chili.

His crew consisted of an engineman, at least one deckhand, and himself as pilot. That was for the usual runs.

He was expected to be intimately familiar with waterways from his home base to whatever island he was heading for. Some had channels cleared to and from. Some of these were even marked with buoys and/or lights, but many weren't.

He was expected to know where all of the coral heads in the atoll were, and how deep their tops were at all tides. Some of these were buoyed, most weren't.

His assigned craft occasionally came equipped with radar, most didn't. He had to know how to use it if it was on board and working. In either event he was required to know the precise location of his craft while under way, in calm water or stormy, on clear days or pitch black nights.

On occasion, during "Operation Crossroads," such a run was not unusual.

Here's a story he related to me years after the event.

"We were taking a 'special cargo' from the assembly point to the test site. The 'special' was lashed to the bed of a lowboy, and the truck was gingerly backed into the well deck of my boat. The loading crew secured the truck and left. A couple dozen Marines came aboard led by a Captain. They were posted along the sides of the well deck with weapons drawn. Their assignment was to protect the 'special.'

"Only when they were in place were my crew and I allowed to board the boat, and then only in the pilothouse and engine compartment. I cast off.

"To do that, I told my deckhand to release fore and aft lines and dog down the ramp. He could do that from the sides of the boat, but he had to squeeze around armed Marines. The Captain objected. Guns came to the ready.

"'Captain, my job is to get this boat and its load to the test site. I can't do that unless you let me cast off.'

"'Well, okay. But no funny stuff!'

"We started across the lagoon. It was a little rough. There was about a twenty knot crosswind and some chop. The boat began a soft dip and rise. The truck started to move back and forth in the well deck.

"'Joey,' I shouted to my deck hand, 'Get down there and chock that damn thing!'

"'No,' said the Captain. 'Nobody goes onto the well deck!'

"'Captain. That truck has to be secured now! It's heavy enough to tear my boat apart!'

"By now we were dead in the water. The radio came on: 'What the hell's going on out there?'

"'The truck's rolling in the well deck.'

"'Well, get the damn thing chocked and get moving!'

"I turned to the Captain: 'My man knows how to set the chocks right. Do yours?'

"No answer.

"'Look, your job is to protect the "special," isn't it?'

"'Yes.'

"'So's mine. We're in this together. It's both our asses if anything happens. Would you let my man go down there with an escort?'

"'Yes.'

"'Let's do it.'

"The Captain assigned four Marines to closely escort my deckhand. In three minutes the job was done.

"The rest of the trip was uneventful.

"The 'special,' an atomic bomb, was delivered to its test site, installed, and in due course, detonated."

***

I don't know for sure when Harold transferred to Kwaj. He told me that he spent one year there and jumped at the chance when a boat operator's slot came open on Roi. He was on Roi when I met him. He found a home there.

Harold hailed from Massachusetts and detested the cold of winter. The tropical climes of Kwaj suited him right down to his chilled bones. Strange to say, he also didn't much like the sea. I remember him telling me one day "If the water's deeper than the soles of my shoes, it belongs to the fish."

Strange attitude for a person who made his living on water. But it might have been just that attitude that kept him alive and well all those years.

On his job at Roi he usually worked a split shift. Up at 4:30 during the week, he had to have his boat at Ennibur to pick up Marshallese workers and travelers and bring them back to Roi in time for them to get to work at seven. Then he had to take travelers to catch commuter planes to Kwaj so they could get to Ebeye for shopping.

Then he was off until noonish when he made a second trip. His final trip each day began at five in the afternoon when returning travelers and workers had to get back to Ennibur. In the intervening hours he was on call to move men and gear to remote islands in the northern part of the atoll for work details on technical installations sited there.

Some of these transportation tasks were taken over by helicopters when they became available after Nam.

Harold was one of the very few hourly employees at Roi whose claims for overtime were never limited or questioned.

I remember an event that well could have resulted in the death of many people but didn't because Harold was at the helm. It was a recreation department sponsored deep sea fishing trip. These were available two or three times a year and were popular among the fishing fraternity at Roi.

About fifteen people signed on for this all-day outing and the fishing was good. They went out to North Pass and ran east around the northeast corner of the atoll a half mile off shore.

They were returning to North Pass and had just rounded the sea side of Namur when they were caught in a rogue wave. Up an unexpected crest, and down into a deep trough, then up a second taller crest and down a deeper trough.

Everyone was hanging on for dear life when they topped the third crest and the ocean seemed to drop straight down before them.

The boat hit the bottom of that trough so hard that the ramp tie downs popped off. Then the ramp dropped so hard that its safety chains gave way! With that the ramp continued to drop until it was vertical beneath the boat.

By that time the rogue had passed and the sea calmed. Miraculously, everyone was still aboard the boat and it was still afloat. More miraculously, no one was even seriously hurt!

But the boat was dead in the water. The ramp hung beneath it like a giant anchor—and a plow!

Forward motion was impossible. The time was a little after four in the afternoon.

Harold managed to get the boat turned around by shifting the engines to reverse and pouring on the coal.

By 11:00 that night he had managed to back the boat the three and one half miles to North Pass. By 11:30 it was back in the lagoon!

He shut the engines down just before four in the morning at Yokohama Pier on Namur.

Not a soul in administration said a word when they saw Harold's time sheet with its claim for twenty-one hours of overtime for that Sunday!

Cap'n Grumpy, at the helm, and his boat

Cap'n Grumpy didn't like some of the Marshallese adults a whole lot, mainly because they wouldn't follow orders on his boat. But he did like the kids. And they liked him.

If I'm not mistaken, Harold was the original "Roi Rat." Look at the earliest Roi T-shirts created by Howie Y. at Security, a gifted cartoonist. He created the Roi Rat cartoon, the one with the rat leaning on a garbage can with a drink in his paw. Look at the bottom edge of the garbage can. It bears the initials "HC." That stood for "Harold's Club"—not the one in Reno.

Harold gambled as much as others in those days, but his real passion was the horses. The only thing I know he subscribed to was the *Racing News*.

You know how that's set up. It's divided into two sections: The first half is the morning line, with all the horses racing that day listed with their stats and racing history; The last half is the day's racing results. It's supposed to be an aid in placing bets.

It was Harold's bible. He'd look at the morning line, do a whole bunch of calculating. Then place imaginary bets, keeping voluminous records. Then he'd turn to the daily race results in the back half of the paper and see how his bets had fared.

He took great pleasure in showing me his paper results. While he was at Roi his horses finished in the money almost 70% of the time.

Then he went on vacation.

"Harold. Welcome back! How was your vacation?"

"Rotten!"

"Gee, that's too bad. I thought you were looking forward to it."

"I was."

"How did the racing go?"

"Lousy! That's what made it rotten."

"What do you mean?"

"I made a mistake."

"I don't understand."

"You know the system I had worked out with the *Racing News*?"

"Yeah. Sort of. I know you got good results with your method here."

"Well, I started it the same way back there. I took the morning line and did all my calculations and decided how I wanted to bet. Then I screwed up."

"How so?"

"I went to the tracks. Never shoulda done it!"

"Why?"

"Because I started watching the horses. That's why. I'd see this long shot going off at 72 to 1. I never would have touched him using the system. But he was the only horse in that race who was up on his toes! He can't lose—I thought. So I forgot all my figures and laid a bet on him that would make me a bundle! He didn't even show!"

"Not much you could do about that," I opined.

"Sure there was. I should've placed my bets off track! Then I wouldn't have been screwed up by seeing the horses in person. TV just isn't the same thing as being there!"

"I see what you mean. How much did you drop?"

"Eight grand!"

"That's slightly lousy!"

"That's all right. I'll get 'em next time!" No, he wouldn't.

Mr. Pencils

Irv V. was an iconoclastic "old geezer." His acquaintances unanimously shunned him, only partially because of his smell. I suppose he changed his clothes at least twice a month. But the only showers anyone could be sure he took were the ones he took on the eve of his annual departure on vacation.

Irv didn't much like people. The people he didn't much like the most were those "pissy-assed" young engineers who tried to tell him how to do his job!

They could come to him with a problem involving sheet metal (anything less than a quarter inch thick and thicker than aluminum foil). Titanium, stainless steel, Monel, brass, aluminum, silver or gold—he worked them all at one time or another, and knew them well.

Irv always had at least one general helper assigned to him. When he was ready to start production, PRESS Work Center would increase his staff with additional help as needed. He would insist that he do all the measurements himself, though he might let an experienced helper do straight cuts, simple bends and folds. He told me one time that he worked to a standard of 1/64th inch!

Air conditioning was absolutely essential in most parts of the sensor buildings. And that required lots of ducting. That was Irv's specialty.

Once he had milked the requester of all the information he needed, his general instruction was for the guy to get out of his way and never again interrupt him until the job was done. Then he'd retire to a worktable in the corner of his shop, set up his defenses, and start figuring.

His main defense, aside from his acerbic nature, was garlic. Irv bought it by the pound. When he was figuring, he always had a clove in his mouth, and could go through a bulb in a morning. Did I say he had an air about him?

Irv always worked with pencils. He was never without them. He used only number 4s, and always had at least two dozen of them, sharpened to almost needle points, in an oversized pocket in his work shirt. To accommodate them, he cut off the standard pocket on his work shirts and sewed on an extra large one. Hence the moniker "Mr. Pencils."

Irv was not what anyone would call a widely educated man. But within his specialty, he was widely admitted to be "the expert."

Now I am likely to be the least handy man around. I am not dexterous, and my ability to conceptualize does not extend into the area of solid geometry. But I was fascinated by his talent and admitted it to him. Moreover, I have a sensory lack that made it possible to tolerate his presence. My sniffer signed off about forty years ago. We got along well.

I have somewhere in my bric-a-brac a sixty-sided "Bucky Ball" Irv fabricated out of a four inch square scrap of thin Monel. He closed it with less than an inch of silver solder wire!

Irv is gone now. But I expect he's making halos somewhere and telling those "pissy-assed" angels not to bother him until he's done.

Chapter 33

Kwajalein's Capabilities

ALTAIR

Mr. Pencils sure was difficult to work with, but it was people like him that made the technological marvels at Kwaj possible. Things like the Spartan and Sprint missiles, TRADEX, and ALTAIR were all due to individuals with the skill to bring such complex ideas to fruition, which brings us to one of those ideas, ALTAIR Radar, the largest sensor at Kwajalein Missile Range.

The **A**dvanced Research Projects Agency / **L**incoln Laboratory **T**racking **A**nd **I**nstrumentation **R**adar (ALTAIR) on Roi weighs something in the range of 465 tons with a reflector 165 feet in diameter. On its driving and support mounting, it stands 212 feet in the air. It has no dome around it. It rests on a circular track that looks, in cross section, like a railroad track on steroids. The feed horn at its center is about the size of a freight car. At the outer end of the feed horn is a sub-reflector, larger than the reflectors on most of the other radars at the range.

In the world of radio and radar, the size of everything depends on the wavelength of the broadcast signal. That is tied exactly to the frequency of the transmission, which is to say, how many times per second that transmission pulse is repeated. It is said that the wavelength is inversely proportional to the frequency. This means that the lower the frequency, the longer the wavelength. Range is determined by wavelength and power.

The more oomph you can pack into a signal, the farther it will go with sufficient energy that any target intercepted will reflect enough of that energy back to the transmitter to be detectable. That's good in radar.

ALTAIR with its new feed horn and longer braces. These reduced structural strength safety redundancy from 123% to about 7%.
Photo by Pam R.

But there's a trade-off to be made and that trade-off is in detail.

ALTAIR broadcasts and receives at frequencies in the VHF and UHF bands. VHF stands for Very High Frequency and UHF stands for Ultra High Frequency. This may sound impressive, but these frequencies are at the very bottom end of radar technology. While it can reach out a very great distance and detect an object, it can't supply much information about that object beyond distance, speed, and direction of travel. However, that is by itself enough to be extremely valuable to certain "customers." ALTAIR builds files of what are called "orbital parameters." These specify precisely where in space an object is and how fast it's going to wherever it's going.

These files can be passed off to other radars to tell them where to find any object they are looking for. In the case of Roi-Namur, a suite of radars has been developed to take these files, find the object in question, and observe it in ever finer detail using frequencies in the L, S, C, and X bands of the radar spectrum. Each of these bands is of a higher frequency (and shorter range) than the one before it. At 95 gigahertz, MMW (MilliMetric Wave) has the highest frequencies of the radar sensors on the island. Its files are passed off to the Super RADOT, an optical tracking assemblage that rounds out the detection sensor suite on the island.

With current technology, these sensors can work together to produce very remarkable data sets on anything being tracked.

The quantity and quality of the information gathered so far is impressive. It allows interested parties to discern the various components of a re-entry vehicle sufficiently to disregard non-threatening objects and to guide the intercept and destruction of the dangerous ones.

It is not my desire, nor within my ability, to go into the technical details of how this is done. Had I that knowledge, I undoubtedly would have had a much higher income over the years.

ALTAIR came into existence partly to answer some serious questions the Air Force had concerning the ballistic missile defense system the Soviets had placed around Moscow.

Under terms of the first ABM treaty, each signatory was allowed to develop and install one system. The U.S. chose to place its one permitted system where it could (hopefully) protect the fields of ICBM silos in the American Midwest from a first strike by the Russians.

The Soviets on the other hand, had opted to site their one-permitted ICBM defense installation in the immediate environs of their capital, Moscow, for some reasons we were aware of, and some we didn't understand at the time. The time I'm referring to is the early to mid-'60s.

For starters, Moscow had almost always been the cultural, intellectual, financial, and spiritual heart of Russia to be defended at all costs. It was the hub of Russian communications, transportation networks and the likes, as well as being the bureaucratic center of government. Napoleon had squandered an army trying to take Moscow in the Nineteenth Century. Hitler did the same during WWII. The Communists did take it in 1917 to end centuries of rule by the Czars. It was reasonable, in the Russians' view, to continue to focus their defensive efforts there.

Part of the complex of sensors they built was an extremely long-range radar, the better to detect incoming missiles from the greatest possible distance. It was this long-range radar that had our military concerned. How good was it? What could the Russians detect with it and in what detail? How could it be used to integrate the defensive system as a whole?

If you think you may someday have to penetrate that system, as our Air Force thought, then you had better have the answers to those questions. Thus ALTAIR.

Essentially ALTAIR was a copy of that long-range sensor in the Russian defense system.

Once built at Roi-Namur, it served to fill an important gap in our own radar shield. That was in addition to allowing us to answer many of the questions we had about the Russian capabilities.

As soon as ALTAIR was up and running, NORAD (North American Air Defense Command) out at Cheyenne Mountain began integrating tracking data from it into what the Distant Early Warning, Mid Canada, and Pine Tree lines were already providing. The effort to assess the reliability of the Russian system evolved into the Pacific Barrier (PACBAR) Demonstration.

GTE Sylvania had the helm at ALTAIR in the first years of its operation and development. Well, that's not exactly accurate. MIT Lincoln Lab was the prime contractor and in charge overall at the Kiernan Re-entry Measurements Site (KREMS). GTE was subordinate to MIT, as was RCA. The Logistics Support was on a separate line of accountability with a contract directly tied to the DOD.

I don't know whether Transport Company of Texas (said to be owned by Ladybird J.) was the first logistic contractor there or not. But an upstart company called Global Associates replaced it in February of 1964.

It was said that TCT's behavior at the time of turnover was so abominable that DOD forbade it from ever bidding on another government project.

I know that when I joined Global there in May of 1964 we were still cleaning up the mess. According to reports and the evidence of my own eyes, TCT went through the supply department and removed all bin tags from the parts bins. After the last meal they served in the dining halls and clubs at Kwaj, they had taken all the dinnerware and thrown it into the shark pit. TCT claimed that all open requisitions were proprietary to their company and ordered their supply personnel to destroy them all. It was done on Kwaj.

On Roi Frank S. was working in supply. Being retired from the Army, he refused to follow those instructions, and made copies of all relevant documents, which he hid until TCT was gone from the scene. It was in gratitude for this action that Global management assigned him as Manager, Outer Islands—a position he held for the next seventeen years.

The above story will help to explain what we were faced with in the early years of my work on the range. It was more than one year before we finally stopped getting unexpected orders and got a handle on the supply situation there.

It also contributed, I am sure, to the decision of the technical contractors to establish their own supply systems for materials unique to their own needs and activities on site. Thus, even today, there are two parallel but not contiguous supply systems in operation at Roi-Namur. ALTAIR fulfilled its tracking duties so well that it soon became an integral asset to NORAD. In the course of doing so it was discovered that the radar could detect objects at great distances and provide tracking data for the ever-increasing flood of satellites and detritus in the Earth's near environs. This ability, over the years, evolved into what today is Space Track.

Except for programmed shutdowns, ALTAIR is expected to be available for tracking assignments at virtually any time, day or night, on fifteen minutes notice. Do you have any idea what this means in terms of accomplishing necessary maintenance?

In the warm salt spray environment of a tropical atoll, corrosion is simply a fact of life. Unprotected, all metals corrode. Typically, bikes last one year.

460-ton antennas corrode too. ALTAIR is a three dimensional structure with a surface area exceeding an acre in size. Every square inch of it must be inspected, scraped, chipped, and painted on a continuing basis to prevent even the least bit of bare metal from being exposed to the salt air. It's a job for whole teams of painters. And it cannot be worked on when it's raining, or when the wind is too high, or when it is engaged in mission work. In spite of this, the job got done.

The last time I heard the figures, ALTAIR had performed at 100% of response to more than 40,000 tracking assignments per year for two consecutive years. That's one for the *Guinness Book of Records*!

Like TRADEX, ALTAIR was designed and built for a life expectancy of seven years. As a consequence it was deemed unnecessary to enclose it with a dome. The advantages of no dome are considerable. No dome means no distortion of the radar beam and no attenuation of its strength. This translates to greater range and sensitivity. No dome means a release from certain dimensional constraints when one wants to modify the antenna equipment. For example, when longer struts are needed to support a longer feed horn or larger sub reflector. No dome means no necessity to maintain that dome—no small task in itself. Lastly, not having a dome allows for freer wind flow through the space occupied by the structure of the antenna. A dome large enough to enclose an antenna the size of ALTAIR, (i.e. about 220 feet in diameter) would present an area to the wind—no matter its direction—of more than an acre. Try hoisting that on your sailboat.

So much for discussing both the good and bad things about having a dome around a radar. With the long duration of the Space Track activity at ALTAIR, it became the only sensor on the range that actually earned money for the range.

I should point out that although the name of the radar remains the same as when it was first designed in the late '50s and early '60s, internal systems development has made it a much more capable instrument than was even conceived possible for the original ALTAIR. Electronic technology and programming technology have evolved over the years. And every few years, things came to a near standstill while modifications were incorporated into the system. Today's ALTAIR, like all the other radars and sensors on site, is of a more capable and flexible magnitude than its predecessors ever were.

What does the future hold for ALTAIR, and for that matter, for the entire site at Kwajalein?

That's hard to say. The integrated system of sensors at the site is approaching the point where it can fulfill the original, tacit mandate of the United States. That was to build a system which can detect, analyze, track and allow us to counter threats from other nations in the near space above our country, and even from the outer reaches of our solar system.

The Cold War may be over, but nuclear weapons and delivery systems are still around in plenty. And a new, perhaps infinitely more perilous threat to the whole planet has in recent years come to be recognized. That is the threat of an asteroid impact anywhere on Earth.

Between Mars and the outer planets is a band of debris from the planet's building activity known as the Kuiper belt. It consists of billions of pieces of matter, which may themselves be the remnants of a primordial planet blown apart by impact.

These range in size from grains of sand to mountains larger than Everest. They are locked into the gravitational field of our sun. Gravitational mechanics hold them in place, mostly, but they occasionally jostle one anther. And, like billiard balls, one may carom into a closer orbit to the sun.

If that orbit should happen to intersect the Earth's orbit, disaster is in the making.

Astronomers and physicists accept that such an impact on the early Earth blasted out the material that re-consolidated into our Moon.

About 250 million years ago such an asteroid impact on Earth is said to have wiped out 90% of all the species of plants and animals on Earth. 65 million years ago, another asteroid impact killed off the dinosaurs, fortuitously allowing our own distant ancestors to evolve.

In the last decade or so astronomers have begun a search for asteroids tracking on an Earth crossing orbit. To date they have identified nearly 2,000 bits of debris that fit that bill. And they admit that they have found less than 10% of the ones that probably do.

So it's not a question of whether Earth will be hit again, only when. Many of you watched, as I did, enthralled at the coverage of the comet Shoemaker/Levi as its parts impacted Jupiter. Some of the impact zones were larger than the Earth itself.

Plans and schemes are even now being debated on how to defend ourselves against such a threat. If such an object is headed toward the Earth, we will need the most sophisticated tracking devices available to help avert the threat.

Wouldn't it be ironic if the complex of sensors at Kwajalein Missile Range was remembered, not for the work done during the Cold War, but for the crucial part it played in the defense against the incursion of a wandering asteroid? ALTAIR and KREMS would be the centerpiece of the range's activity in that direction. And it is already in place and operating!

Even more ironic would be the political decision to diminish the installation "because it's too expensive!"

Too expensive?

This "little blue marble" is the only home we've got gang, all of us!

KARP

Not all projects such as ALTAIR see the light of day. The Kwajalein Atmospheric Research Project (KARP) was a concept of the National Oceanic and Atmospheric Administration (NOAA) in the late '60s and early '70s that never became a reality.

Its intent was to establish, on Kwajalein, a long-term research facility for the study of the air/sea interface.

There were many proposed elements of its activity on Kwaj. They included launching constant altitude balloons every six hours, firing meteorological rockets every hour around the clock, operating a fleet of twelve weather research aircraft around the clock, and operating and maintaining the research vessel FLIP.

I don't recall what the acronym FLIP stands for. I think it's something like Floating Linear Immersible Platform. It's a ship, almost 400 feet long. It floats horizontally in the water as all ships do, but it is designed to rotate so that its long axis is vertical and partially sunk.

In research mode about two thirds of the ship is under water and one third above. The various compartments within the hull are on gimbals and can swivel ninety degrees to stay horizontal to the water's surface while the hull itself is vertical in the water. Sophisticated sensors penetrate the hull to study in detail the mechanisms of the sea's surface and the atmosphere directly above it. This program would have been the most extensive and intensive study of the world's weather makers ever undertaken.

Why at Kwajalein?

First of all there is location. Kwajalein sits at the northern edge of the inter-tropical convergence zone (ITCZ). This zone circles the Earth at the equator. It is where the Earth's northern and southern atmospheric hemispheres intermix, as do its northern and southern oceanic hemispheres.

This intermixing generates some curious phenomena. For example, I know of nowhere else on Earth where weather systems converge on a single point from all directions simultaneously. I've seen it happen at Kwaj numerous times over the years. If you've been at Kwajalein and watched the weather channel with any regularity, I'm sure you've seen the same thing. This probably happens elsewhere around the borders of the ITCZ but I'm not aware of it. The equator, at the center of the ITCZ, is the part of the Earth that receives most of the sun's radiated energy, which causes various meteorological events. The ITCZ is a weather maker.

Secondly, Kwajalein has a collection of resources relevant to KARP unsurpassed in the world, with weather, launch and tracking radars; rocket, balloon and aircraft launch facilities; marine department facilities; satellite up and down links; complete logistics support for a sizeable community; and communications links to the rest of the world.

Moreover, KARP planners saw Kwajalein as an ideal spot to study the genesis of typhoons that do so much damage in the western Pacific.

Kwajalein is not often subject to those storms. But many of them first begin to get organized as tropical depressions in that area and strengthen as they move westward toward Asia. Sounds like an ideal program looking for and finding an ideal place, doesn't it?

Well, not exactly.

The problem was time, or rather timing.

At the time KARP was first proposed there was neither time on the schedule nor room at the inn.

The Cold War was in full boom.

ICBMs were still under development and not as accurate or reliable as the warlords wanted. But progress was being made.

As for interceptors, they were still awaiting advances in technology that were decades in the future. Computers weren't big or fast enough. Interceptor rockets couldn't stand the acceleration of launch or maneuver. Sensors were not up to discriminating between decoys and the real McCoy.

In fact there was not even 100% certainty that rockets as interceptors were the way to go at all.

New technologies came on-line and were tested. Lasers were attempted, rail guns were tried, and proton-beam weapons were tested. The list goes on, right out of *Buck Rogers* and *Star Trek.*

Each new program brought in dozens, scores, or hundreds of scientists and technicians. Some on temporary duty (TDY), many for the duration of their particular program, filled every nook and cranny. Low-level employees were sometimes living as many as eight to a cubicle.

Land was added to Kwajalein at the north end and at the west end. I was there when a single shipment of 200 Angeles house trailers were delivered as deck cargo on an aircraft carrier.

And we were busy. I saw weeks when we had more test activity than we did all of the previous year. The permanent population of Americans at Kwajalein Atoll was spooling up towards a peak of about 7,800, which it reached in 1972.

It was into this splitting at the seams situation that the KARP planners projected a requirement to support another 2,000 people.

As I said, there was no time on the schedule, and no room at the inn.

That was then. This is now. Things have changed.

The U.S. population at Kwaj is one third what it peaked at in '72. The Army is looking for paying customers.

Satellites have taken over some of the tasks (but not all) that the KARP planners wanted to study. Knowledge of immense value could still be derived from an updated KARP effort at Kwaj.

Whether the political and budgetary will can be revitalized is an unanswered question.

Chapter 34

The Future of Kwajalein Missile Range

Remoting Roi: The Logistical Impact

The following is an analysis of the information presented to the ALTAIR staff by MIT personnel and RSE (Range System Engineering) management as it relates to logistics activities here in the coming months and years.

We have been wondering what the real impact of the KMAR (Kwajalein Modernization and Remoting, or "Remoting Roi") program will be. While not addressed specifically, the plans presented for the upgrading of the sensors on Roi-Namur provide clues from which we can deduce some of the future activities in the logistics arena.

The overall objective of this modernization is to develop the capacity to operate the sensors at Roi-Namur from Kwajalein. All programming will be done from Kwajalein. If this works, it is likely that eventually all programming will be done from the U.S. mainland. This per se will have little impact on logistics.

All research and development will be done in the U.S., as will all prototyping and testing.

Once tested, new equipment will be installed as needed on the respective sensors. This will reduce the need for the highest levels of scientist, engineer, and technician at USAKA.

Sensor control equipment will be upgraded so that each sensor, previously designed to operate with a customized set of management protocols, will be equipped with a custom-built interface/translator to permit a single command protocol system to speak to and manage all of the sensors simultaneously. It is this new equipment that will have a major impact on our logistic operation.

This impact will have two sides, which I'll address shortly.

First a word about the architecture of the new equipment. I call it new, although the concept is tried and proven. It is based on the LRU (Line Replaceable Unit). The Air Force pioneered the LRU in the form of its "little black boxes," which could be pulled and replaced rapidly in field conditions. A defective LBB (little black box) would be sent to a centralized repair point where the special diagnostic and repair facilities were concentrated. Once repaired, the LBB would be returned to the user to be held for future needs. The system worked and conferred the benefit of getting a piece of equipment back into service quickly and of doing it with personnel less extensively trained than the previous electronic engineers.

The Navy picked up on the idea at least as early as the beginning of the AEGIS ship-building program. This is where I had my first encounter with the system.

It's simple. When a ship is in port for overhaul and modernizing, the new equipment is installed and provided with a complete set of spare PCBs (printed circuit boards). These boards are stored in proximity to the equipment in question. Once the ship is at sea, the electronics cabinets holding the equipment are closed and not touched unless something goes wrong. If something does, a relatively basic field-level diagnostic program identifies the PCB with the problem and, in effect, says, "The problem is on this specific board. Replace it," which the maintenance technician does. The defective board is then put into the repair pipeline.

How will this effect logistics? In many ways.

In the first place, consider the thousands of line items we carry in stock. What do most of them consist of? Resistors, capacitors, single printed circuit chips, and the like. Ask yourself, when was the last time you had to know how to read the color code banding on a resistor to verify its value? When was the last time you issued one?

What we have here is a veritable museum of antiquated parts (many of which may have deteriorated beyond use simply due to the ravages of forty years of storage!).

As the old equipment is replaced, we will find that thousands of these parts will no longer be used. Excising will become an even more important activity for logistics.

In their place we will be receiving hundreds, perhaps thousands of LRU's. These may be kept in the stock room, though they may also be kept near the equipment they pertain to. Nevertheless we will have responsibility for the logistics control of them. For example, the additional information in our database *must* in the future include mention of the equipment they relate to. This is so that we can assure that repaired LRU's are returned to the proper equipment ready reserve.

To summarize, we are at the beginning of a transition from research and development to operation and maintenance. No matter what happens on the scientific side, the sensors must be serviced and maintained. The logistics role in this will change in some ways, but the necessity will still remain. The emphasis of day-to-day activity may shift, but the experience we have gained in our role will stand us in good stead. We will continue to be needed.

On the Other Hand

While those in Logistics are looking on the bright side of things, here are some recent developments on Roi with the KMAR project as it affects day-to-day life:

The colonel came up to Roi to announce the Army's decision to eliminate the twenty-four hour a day presence of a trained nurse on Roi. This, he said, would save the Army $40,000 per year. At the same time he said that $50,000 per year would be retained in the budget for the one-hour fireworks display each year at Kwaj on the Fourth of July! They planned to leave the medical care on Roi to the EMTs at the fire department. That scheme has been abandoned for the moment, but the seed of the idea has been planted, and it will probably be tried again sometime in the next year or two.

Now, if we have to see a doctor, it means an all-day trip to Kwaj costing a day of PTO (Personal Time Off), equal to a day's wages.

The labor contract is being re-bid with the stated end of replacing as many workers here as possible with Marshallese who are to be given OJT (on-the-job training) by the people they are replacing.

It has been over three weeks since we have received any mail and prospects are dim for any coming in for at least another week. This seems to be an emerging pattern.

We've had KEAMS (Kwajalein Enterprise Asset Management System) for one year now and it still doesn't work.

"KEAMS" was proposed and implemented starting on the 1st of January, 2001, with the introduction of "CITRIX" and "MIMS," which replaced "AMC," "NOVEL," "GOLD+," and parts of eleven other computer databases.

In the estimation of users all over the atoll, MIMS still doesn't work and CITRIX is overloaded and crashes an average of sixteen times a day. The reboot time averages ten minutes per cycle at Roi. I have had to reboot as many as twenty-seven times in one day!

When the system crashes or locks up here, we're supposed to call IT (Information Technology) and they'll correct it on the spot. If they cannot fix it immediately, they'll give you a case number and promise to get back to you as soon as possible.

Case numbers started at 1. My first assignment was number 124. This case number assignment didn't start until February 1st of 2001. By the end of the year the number had climbed to nearly 39,000! There's a message there. Only IT doesn't see it—or admit there's a problem.

Chapter 35

Change is Coming

Kwajalein Modernization and Remoting is not a pipe dream. It's a long-range plan, parts of which have already been achieved. The modernization is expensive, but it will keep the installations there on the cutting edge of radar and the space sciences.

There is a new radar there called GBR (Ground Based Radar). It is being tested as the detection and control core of Strategic Defense, the program which may result in our real ability to defend the skies and space above our country from incursion by ICBMs or other objects that threaten us from both near and far.

The modernization is proceeding apace.

Whether Remoting the operation and control of the range's sensors all the way back to the mainland is possible remains to be seen. At the very least, it's a much tougher nut to crack.

The reason for this is that we are running up against one of the truly formidable barriers in the nature of the universe: the speed of light.

Physics books inform us that the speed of light in a vacuum is 186,000 miles per second. Radio and radar pulses propagate at the same speed.

When the astronauts of Apollo 11 landed on the moon, the first thing they set out was a flag. The second thing was a reflector mirror instrument that reflects light (read: laser) beams back to their source where associated instruments detect it.

The moon is roughly 240,000 miles from Earth. That means that the round trip to the moon and back covers 480,000 miles.

At the speed of light that trip takes roughly 2.58 seconds.

In like manner light from the Sun (93,000,000 miles from Earth) takes just over eight minutes to reach us.

Let's look at something closer to Earth.

Here's a geo-stationary satellite. That's a satellite that is placed far enough away from the Earth that its orbital speed exactly matches the rotation speed of the Earth. It appears to hover over the same spot on Earth all the time. Its altitude above Earth is approximately 22,000 miles. If such a satellite were ideally positioned straight above our transmitter, it would take nearly one twelfth of a second for a transmitted signal just to reach the satellite.

From its high vantage point the satellite is in line of sight from both the transmitter and a receiving station, say in Huntsville, Alabama. Good. Now we have three points of a right triangle, two on Earth and one in space.

Let's play with the mathematics of right triangles for a bit. We have to do this to determine how far the satellite has to relay our signal to the ground station in the States.

The Greek mathematician Pythagoras demonstrated that right triangles have some peculiar characteristics such that there is a calculable relation between its sides. He called the sides A, B, and C. A is the line that is the base of our triangle. B is the line that is the height of our triangle. C, which he called the hypotenuse, is the side we want to know about.

In geometry there is a definition that says that a straight line is the shortest distance between two points. These points have to be identified. Let's call them (a), (b), and (c).

Let's call point (a) Huntsville, Alabama; point (b) our transmitter at Kwajalein; and point (c) the satellite.

(a)-(c) is the base of the triangle and side A.

(b)-(c) is the height of the triangle and side B.

(c)-(a) is the hypotenuse of the triangle and side C.

Side A is 8,000 miles.

Side B is 22,000 miles.

Pythagoras's theorem says that A squared plus B squared equals C squared.

To get the square of a number, you multiply it by itself.

A squared is 64,000,000.

B squared is 484,000,000.

Therefore C squared is 548,000,000.

Take the square root of that and Side C is 23,400 miles.

At light speed that's another one twelfth of a second.

Suppose that it takes the computer at Huntsville one twelfth of a second to integrate the received data and assemble and transmit a controlling command back to our radar. The return route is the same as the inbound route. That's another two twelfths of a second. Further suppose that it takes the radar one twelfth of a second to begin to respond to the received control instruction.

So the total elapsed time thus far is half a second. Doesn't sound like much, does it?

But what's been happening to the target in the meantime?

It takes an ICBM about twenty-seven minutes to travel from its launch site at Vandenberg Air Force Base in California to splash down in the lagoon at Kwaj. That distance is about 5,000 miles. That means the average speed is roughly 11,000 miles an hour or about three miles a second!

Now that half-second looms large indeed. If you're sending an interceptor missile up to impact the incoming target following commands that are a half-second old, you'll miss the target by more than a mile!

All of the above figures are approximations. But they do serve to illustrate the problems relating to remote command and control over very long distances.

Are there ways to resolve this problem? Yes, to a degree.

Fiber optic cables could significantly shorten the message transit time both ways. One-way distances for data transmission can be reduced from about 45,000 miles to something in the neighborhood of 8,000.

As a matter of fact there is already such a cable in place running from Guam to the West Coast of the States. Part of the long range plan for Remoting Kwajalein involves running a tie-in cable from Kwaj some 600 miles north to the neighborhood of Wake Island and tying it in to the Trans-Pacific cable there. Satellites would be out of the picture as relay instruments.

Interceptor rockets could be made more maneuverable and sophisticated to home in on their targets independent of ground control. Development in this direction is ongoing and projects relating to that goal are slowly coming to fruition.

However, perhaps rocket interceptors are not the way to go. Chemical powered satellite or airborne lasers may prove to be effective. The Air Force is currently more involved with airborne laser intercept studies than is the Army. I don't know who might be involved in the development of satellite based laser interceptors, but I am aware that they are in development.

Perhaps the answer will be found in the development of rocket based laser platforms. That too is under consideration.

The military development of ICBM intercept capability may not be the answer at all.

***

Perhaps the best approach is through international diplomacy. After all, the real answer is the removal of the threat of nuclear weapons and the ICBMs that carry them.

This may seem to be the most improbable approach of all. But ironically it has to date been the most effective approach yet tried.

The SALT treaties have resulted in the reduction of thousands of nuclear warheads and their delivery systems on all sides.

Protagonists on the world stage have invested trillions of dollars in the production and maintenance of such weapons systems, and the defense against them.

Such expenditures were no small part of the financial ruin that brought down the Soviet Union.

The United States was crippled in its ability to engage in conflict as a result of having only the nuclear arrow in its quiver when crisis arose. Its options were two. Do nothing. Or exercise the nuclear option. Not a good position to find oneself in when one is conducting international relations.

***

It may seem that the above comments are irrelevant to questions about the future of Kwajalein. Not so.

It is true that Kwajalein was developed as a research and development asset to produce a defense against the threat of nuclear weapons. The threat still remains.

When we couldn't defend against weapons delivery, the protagonists settled upon a posture of Mutually Assured Destruction (MAD).

It has been said that man is not a rational being, but a rationalizing one.

Here's how the rationalizing went.

If my enemy is going to hit me, he'll try to wipe me out before I can hit back. That way he survives, and I don't.

What will he have to destroy to wipe me out? This gave rise to the Target Lists.

Target List (Fictitious)

What	How Many	How Many Bombs
Major cities	100	200
Military bases	100	200
Seaports and shipyards	75	150
Major power plants	100	200
Major bridges	100	100
Refineries	75	75
Dams	60	75
Steel mills	50	50
Rail centers	100	100
Airports	300	300
Major industrial plants	300	300
Misc	50	50
Total	1410	1800

This list is totally fictitious, but it illustrates the thought processes involved. Numbers would change for each target country and for special circumstances.

And it's the sort of list a bureaucrat loves. The list gets played with all the time. Priorities change. Bomb numbers change. Bomb sizes change. There are endless permutations possible.

I've met a couple of people who have spent their entire careers making and adjusting such lists.

To continue with the MAD rationalization, the Target List says I need 1,800 bombs. What if my enemy hits them all in a first strike? I'd better have more ready and hidden where he can't find them. We'll put some on subs, some on airplanes, and some in underground silos, or on rail cars so we can move them around all the time. We'll put our control center someplace deep underground, like Cheyenne Mountain, where no bomb can knock it out. If we can ever make a defense system that works, we'll place a system near each of the places on the enemy's target list.

That was why Kwaj got started. That's why Kwaj is still needed.

What made MAD a credible deterrent was the fact that the enemy *knew* we could still kill him no matter what he did to us first. After all, wouldn't he do the same thing? Pogo the possum summed it up well in an old-time comic strip years ago: "*We have met the enemy, and he is us*!"

Scientists who studied the question concluded that the nuclear powers at the time of their study had amassed an aggregate of nearly 100,000 warheads! Most of them were in the hands of either the U.S. or the USSR.

So we've demonstrably reduced those stockpiles by 50%. So what? That still leaves enough atomic weapons out there to do the job ten times over!

That's why Kwaj and the work that's being done there is still critical to our nation.

Negotiations only recently concluded have extended our lease arrangements under the Compact of Free Association through at least 2016.

We can be reasonably sure of an American presence there until at least that time.

***

I suppose the logical way to end this narration is to try to guess what might be going on at Kwaj during the next dozen or so years.

Let's step back and take an overall look at what we have at Kwajalein.

Kwajalein was built up in the first place because the United States was faced with the threat of annihilation by inconceivable violence; indeed, the whole world was.

Civilization as we know it could certainly be ended by the application of an increased understanding of nature and its "laws." Perhaps it could be defended in the same way.

You might say technology lay at the root of the problem. Many people over the last couple of thousand years have said so.

Some have responded by backing away from technology. Look at the Luddites. Look at the Amish. Look at the ultra conservative Muslims who would like nothing better than to see the world returned to the state it was in 500 years ago. Margaret Meade, in one of her last works titled something like "The Protagonists of Change" tried to point out that there are elements of every culture that resist change. This is worth further consideration, but not here.

***

Thomas Malthus did a study of population growth. His conclusion was that the human race was headed for catastrophe because it was bound to reach a level at which it could no longer feed itself. Wars, he said, were fought to assure access to satisfy an insatiable demand for finite resources. Detractors said technology and scientific discoveries would save the day. No, he said. They would only postpone it. Who's right? Look at the mess in the Middle East today. This, too, is worth further consideration, but not here.

We came to the conclusion that if technology could threaten us, so could it save us.

So we built up Kwajalein. We have spent fifty years developing the means of defense from just one category of threat. We're not quite there yet. Maybe this year. Maybe next. Maybe never.

So what do we have at Kwaj? Not a lot. Just one of the largest agglomerations of scientific equipment ever assembled in one place. There is so much electronic equipment there that it became necessary to build one of the world's most sophisticated calibration labs just to tune it all up and keep it working.

Machines that detect, observe, record, sample, analyze, synthesize, and even extrapolate and predict are there in profusion. So are the people who know how to use them to answer questions never posed before. Tools are there with the people who can use them to fabricate new machines as needed.

Kwajalein is ideally situated for the study of the air/sea interface and the benthic depths of the ocean.

It is in the genesis zone of much of the weather that affects nearly half of the world's population.

People from the temperate lands of the world would describe the weather there as perpetual summer. The air there is so clear that productive astronomical studies have been conducted there despite the fact that the observatories are at sea level! Nor does light pollution at night constitute a problem.

The water in and around the lagoon is so clear that a person on the surface can often see the bottom at depths of 120 feet or more.

Proximity to the equator (nine degrees north latitude) makes it a very good site for space launches. And several launch facilities are already in place.

History is there too, for the observant, from the Stone Age to the Space Age.

Best of all, it is not some scientist's or academician's fondest dream. It is there. It is up and running. It is available.

Kwajalein is a scientific asset of unparalleled value to the U.S. Our country has poured billions of dollars into making Kwajalein what it is today.

What will it be tomorrow? The near future is fairly predictable. Beyond that, only time and the will of our government can say. The scientific community can have an influence on Kwaj's future. So can the tourist industry. But they must make their voices heard.

Perhaps we will walk away from it as the Air Force did on Canton in the Phoenix Islands. I hope not.

Conclusion

Kwaj — Where Do All the Range Rats Go?

The average length of a tour at Kwaj was three years. This was built into the recruitment offerings in the early days. First year: 15% bonus. Second year: 10% bonus. Third year: 5% bonus. All subsequent years: no bonus. Unless you leave. Then you can come back at some later time and start the progression again.

What was the use of this? For the professional scientist, mathematician, or engineer, it reduced the incentive to stay. Their employers judged that if they stayed more than three years, they stood the risk of falling behind the state of the art back stateside. Catching up was difficult to do.

New technologies arose while you weren't looking.

The first "r" in radar stands for radio. When TRADEX and ALTAIR were first conceived, radio tubes were in—Big Ones! The power tubes for ALTAIR were glass monstrosities eight feet in diameter and over twenty feet long. (Incidentally, they were built in the Westinghouse plant in Horseheads, New York.) If you took all thirty passenger seats out of a DeHaviland C-7 cargo plane and put the plane crew in the cockpit first, you could just squeeze one crate holding such a tube into the cargo compartment. The tube had to be off-loaded before the plane crew could exit the plane.

Tubes became more powerful and smaller over the years.

Circuit cards in the earliest designs were hand built by soldering together miniature tubes with old fashioned resistors, capacitors and the like onto phenolic boards stacked into three dimensional cubes that would be hardwired into circuits.

All of this stuff put out huge amounts of heat, thereby affecting the amount of air conditioning needed to keep the glass cool enough not to melt.

Transistors made the scene and heat output shrank by several orders of magnitude.

Micro-processors (the little black chips so ubiquitous in more recent electronic equipment) were next in line.

Switching mechanisms shrank and got faster.

Lasers and fiber optics sped signal transmission even more, while again reducing heat output.

And so it has gone.

Each of these developments represents the application of new technologies that the original staffs there were not necessarily comfortable with.

This is why the employers said "three years and out!"

There is an adage amongst engineers to the effect that the "half life" of an engineering education is seven years. This means that what you have learned in college engineering courses is only about half relevant after seven years. After fourteen years, only a quarter of what you learned in school is still useful. Et Cetera.

Al G. said to me one time, "I know that I can't hold a job in the States anymore. I don't understand any of this new fangled stuff! But I know TRADEX transmitter! I was here to build it, and my experience here, on this job, gives me a feel for what's happening. If anything goes wrong, I can find and fix the problem faster than anyone else!" Al was transmitter leader at TRADEX. He never left. Al died there two weeks before he was to leave on mandatory retirement!

Young engineers come to site with new technologies and procedures. They don't like learning the old ways that relate to earlier design elements still in use in parts of the sensors they work on. But that's part of their job. They have to learn how to meld their new with the pre-existing knowledge and make the whole shebang continue to function. That's engineering!

For the mid level technicians, the story's a little different. They follow orders and have the experience to actualize some engineer's concept.

I understand that Dan N. has finally left. He spent more time on Roi than I did. He's a machinist—a very good one. He ran the machine shop on Roi for more years than I can remember—all the time using WWII vintage machine tools. Drill presses, lathes, milling machines, you name it he, could make it sing.

Dan could use the old, worn out clunkers and produce shapes in steel and aluminum to within a quarter thousandth of specification. The new numerical control machines and computer run ones that finally began to filter into the machine shop made him antsy.

Where did he go when he left Roi? I understand that he has taken a series of jobs as a production consultant in places where the only tools available are the old clunkers he had mastered. There are still a lot of them around.

Many of the companies that originally made the machines are no longer in business. Those that are often no longer support the oldies with spare parts. That's where Dan comes in. He's good enough to build the spare parts as needed.

He told me one time, "Ted, give me a lathe, an old milling machine, and a set of Johansson Blocks (very accurately machined pieces of steel used as measurement standards), and I can build any machine in this machine shop!" And he could, too!

Pam R. and her husband, John, are no longer at site. She is a registered nurse specializing in operating room and intensive care procedures. He flew helicopters at site.

She and John returned stateside, bought a fifth wheel pickup and a trailer to call home, and went traveling. She has taken short-term contracts as a temporary fill in at hospitals that have temporary staff shortages (to cover for vacations and the like). They are presently back in the northwest, her original stomping grounds.

Jim G. is a plumber. There is nothing about plumbing he can't handle. He came to Roi from the ice (Antarctica). I used to enjoy chatting with him of an evening, sitting on the patio of our dorm, watching the sunsets there at Roi. Don't know where he's gone. I think he's in Europe or Russia helping with the rebuilding of American embassies and consulates. The Soviets of old Cold War days who built the originals incorporated so many eavesdropping bugs in them that it has been deemed cheaper to send our own work crews in to tear down the old and replace them with new ones that are really spy proof. Good luck, Jim.

Herb H., who spent years there on Roi as transmitter operator at ALCOR, is retired now and living in Florida. He still gets calls from his buddies there asking about how to fix problems with it. I chat with him from time to time yet.

Mike V. had his own industrial heating and air conditioning business for eighteen years right in Horseheads. He arrived at Roi shortly before I left. He could fix old units no one else there remembered how to fix. His wife is from the Philippines, though he met her on Guam.

When I departed Roi, he was looking for a job in the Middle East. For the money. Halliburton was looking at him. I tried to talk him out of it. Too dangerous, no matter what the pay. (Look at what happened to the civilian employees there recently.)

He finally talked the incumbent into promoting him to head of all the HVAC shops on site. That gave him housing and his wife and children are out there with him now. His wife's happy. The kids are happy. I think he's happy too. He only makes half what he could in Halliburton land, but he's safe. And his wife has a number of Philippine ladies to interact with there at Kwaj. Besides, she's much closer to her own home. Good luck to the both of you, Mike.

Bob A. is in retirement near Coco Beach in Florida. He comes to Roi to run the ALTAIR transmitter whenever Fred F.

and his wife are on vacation. His contracts as consultant are door to door (from Coco Beach to Coco Beach), usually about a month long, and pay very good money.

So it goes. I think that over the years, there have been more than 40,000 Americans who have lived and worked at Kwaj and thousands more who have spent short periods there on specific programs or missions.

Range rats all. Roi Rats, some.

We have all ridden a wave of the Space Age.

Marriages on Roi do happen. Herb H. (left) and author Ted B. escort the bride to her chapel—a sandbar on Namur. The groom walked out of the lagoon to join her. Photo by Pam R.

Christmas time at Kwaj. How about a sandman snowman? Photo by Bill Cleland, from the 2003 calendar.

Roi Marina sign. Anchors replaced Japanese 37mm pack howitzers.
Plumerias in background were planted by Peteh and author.
Photos by Pam R.

Pistol Packin' POL. Whimsical sculpture guarding POL (Petroleum, Oil, and Lubricants farm on Kwaj).

Echo Pier on Kwaj. Perspective shows pier to be almost as long as Kwaj is wide. It is. The ship is the *Worthy*, a relatively new tracking ship. Photos by Pam R.

Sunset on Roi with TRADEX in the distance.